Judith Butler in Conversation

This is a unique text that takes us into a sophisticated discussion between Judith Butler and some of the scholars who use her analytics for applied work. With Bronwyn Davies as facilitator you are in the best hands when entering this exceptionally interesting conversation with one of the most influential feminist philosophers of our time

—Dorte Maria Søndergaard,
Institut for Pædagogisk Psykologi

This book brings to life a series of compelling conversations with Judith Butler by academics using her work to explore the subjective grounds for an ethics of everyday life, an ethics that is based on a relationality that binds us to the Other. The result is a truly inter-disciplinary and scholarly work. It provides readers with a lively interchange of ideas at the interface between philosophy and other social science and humanities. Butler challenges academics to understand how acknowledging the limits of self-knowledge can serve as an ethics of responsibility. I thoroughly recommend this book for all academics and students who are interested in the operation of agency and the question of how individuals struggle to account for themselves.

—Johanna Wyn,
University of Melbourne

This terrifically exciting collection is a textual representation of a two-day symposium in which several scholars met with Judith Butler, one of our pre-eminent feminist philosophers, to talk about how they have taken up her work. Organized as papers, written responses to those papers, Butler's oral responses to both, and then general conversation by all present, the book reflects what must have been a very exciting event in which I, for one, wish I had been included. Many of us avidly read Butler's published work, but we seldom read transcripts of her talk. In her responses, for example, she troubles that lauded feminist concept, embodiment, and reflects on the policing of academic disciplines and those whose work is out-of-category. The unusual format of the book makes it compelling and a page-turner. It's a fine addition to our collection of work by and about Judith Butler.

—Elizabeth A. St.Pierre, Professor,
University of Georgia

Judith Butler in Conversation

Analyzing the Texts and Talk of Everyday Life

Edited by

Bronwyn Davies

New York   London

Routledge
Taylor & Francis Group
270 Madison Avenue
New York, NY 10016

Routledge
Taylor & Francis Group
2 Park Square
Milton Park, Abingdon
Oxon OX14 4RN

© 2008 by Taylor & Francis Group, LLC
Routledge is an imprint of Taylor & Francis Group, an Informa business

Printed in the United States of America on acid-free paper
10 9 8 7 6 5 4 3 2

International Standard Book Number-13: 978-0-415-95654-3 (Softcover) 978-0-415-95653-6 (Hardcover)

Library of Congress Cataloging-in-Publication Data

Judith Butler in conversation : analyzing the texts and talk of everyday life / edited by
    Bronwyn Davies.
        p. cm.
    ISBN-13: 978-0-415-95653-6 (hardback : alk. paper)
    ISBN-13: 978-0-415-95654-3 (pbk. : alk. paper)
        1. Philosophy, Modern--20th century. 2. Civilization, Modern--20th century. 3.
    Butler, Judith, 1956- 4. Self (Philosophy) I. Butler, Judith, 1956- II. Davies, Bronwyn,
    1945-

    B804.J85 2007
    305.3092--dc22   2006032347

Visit the Taylor & Francis Web site at
http://www.taylorandfrancis.com

and the Routledge Web site at
http://www.routledge.com

Contents

Acknowledgments

This kind of book would not be possible without the generosity extended by Judith Butler to both the authors and to the participants from the symposium: 'A lived history of the thought of Judith Butler' presented by the Narrative, Discourse and Pedagogy research concentration at the University of Western Sydney, Australia in June 2005. Thank you to the participants at the symposium for contributing to lively conversation: Peter Bansel, Kellie Burns, Vicki Crowley, Katrina Jaworski, Robert Payne, Mary Louise Rasmussen, Kerry Robinson, Margaret Somerville, and Jane Ussher. The attentiveness Judith Butler offers suggests much about the ethics of listening, and of response. Engaging with Butler's oeuvre, the authors in this volume present innovative scholarship that is particularly resonant for the humanities and social sciences.

I am grateful to Wayne McKenna, the executive dean of the College of Arts at the University of Western Sydney, for his support of the forum that generated the conversations reflected in this collection. A thank you to Professor Michael Atherton, the associate dean of research, for his support. Also, thank you to David McBride and Brendan O'Neill, who started this project at Routledge, and to Steve Rutter, Anne Horowitz, and Marsha Hecht, who saw this book through to its completion. Special thanks are due to Michael Gottsche for all his efforts in compiling the manuscript and references, and particularly to Cristyn Davies for her editorial contribution, her tireless negotiation with authors and publisher, and for her work in driving this project.

Judith Butler's essay is an adapted and shortened version of her chapter by the same title in *Giving an Account of Oneself*, New York: Fordham University Press, 2005.

vii

Contributors

Jonathan Bollen researched the choreography of the dance floor at Sydney's Mardi Gras Party and Sleaze Ball for his doctorate. His more recent research is on masculinities in Australian theatre since the mid-1950s. He has taught theatre, dance, and performance studies at the University of New England, Monash University, and the University of Western Sydney. He has also worked with David McInnes on research into gay men's sexual cultures and on collaborative projects with the AIDS Council of New South Wales and the Australian Federation of AIDS Organisations. He now lives in Adelaide and lectures in drama at Flinders University.

Judith Butler is Maxine Elliot Professor in the Departments of Rhetoric and Comparative Literature at the University of California, Berkeley. She received her Ph.D. in Philosophy from Yale University in 1984. She is the author of *Subjects of Desire: Hegelian Reflections in Twentieth-Century France* (Columbia University Press, 1987), *Gender Trouble: Feminism and the Subversion of Identity* (Routledge, 1990), *Bodies That Matter: On the Discursive Limits of "Sex"* (Routledge, 1993), *The Psychic Life of Power: Theories of Subjection* (Stanford University Press, 1997), *Excitable Speech: A Politics of the Performative* (Routledge, 1997), *Antigone's Claim: Kinship Between Life and Death* (Columbia University Press, 2000), and *Contingency, Hegemony, Universality: Contemporary Dialogues on the Left*, with Ernesto Laclau and Slavoj Zizek (Verso Press, 2000). In 2004, she published a collection of writings on war's impact on language and thought entitled *Precarious Life: The Powers of Mourning and Violence* with Verso Press. That same year, *The Judith Butler Reader* appeared, edited by Sara Salih, with Blackwell Publishers. A collection of her essays on gender and sexuality, *Undoing Gender*, appeared with Routledge in 2004 as well. Her most recent book, *Giving an Account of Oneself*, appeared with Fordham University Press (2005) and considers the partial opacity of the subject and the relation between critique and ethical reflection. She is currently working on essays pertaining to Jewish philosophy, focusing on pre-Zionist criticisms of state violence. She continues to write on cultural and literary theory, philosophy, psychoanalysis, feminism, and sexual politics.

Bronwyn Davies is a professor of education at the University of Western Sydney. She is best known for her international bestselling book *Frogs and Snails and Feminist Tales: Preschool Children and Gender*, and for her work on positioning theory. Her theoretical writing has been published as the collection of essays: *A Body of Writing*. Her interest in writing, in poststructuralist theory and in embodiment led to her book *(In)scribing Body/Landscape Relations*. She has published ten books and more than 100 research papers and chapters.

Cristyn Davies is completing her doctorate "Chilling Tales: NEA vs Finley, Or, Performing America in an Era of Moral Panic" at the University of Western Sydney, Australia. She is currently involved in a number of research and writing projects including guest co-editing a special edition of *Sexualities*. Her research interests and publications focus on: the culture wars; performance art; gender, sexuality and citizenship; homophobic violence; writing and affect; and constructions of masculinity. A particular interest is exploring the collaborative work relationships between academics and artists discussed in the forthcoming publication: *Artistic Bedfellows: History & Discourse in Collaborative Art Practices*, UPA/Roman and Littlefield.

Susanne Gannon explored poststructural and transgressive writing practices in academia in her doctoral research. She has recently co-authored, with Bronwyn Davies, the chapter on "Feminism/Poststructuralism" in *Research Methods in the Social Sciences* (Sage, 2005), the chapter on "Postmodern, poststructural and critical theories" in the *Handbook of Feminist Research: Theory and Praxis* (Sage, 2006), and the book, *Doing Collective Biography* (Open University Press/ McGraw Hill, 2006). She is currently engaged in research in writing practices and ethics. She is a senior lecturer in the School of Education at the University of Western Sydney.

Fiona Jenkins is senior lecturer in philosophy at the Australian National University and has a long-standing interest in Judith Butler's work. She has published essays on contemporary issues and events from a philosophical perspective often informed by Butler's thought in journals including *borderlands, Angelaki, Contretemps,* and *Constellations.* Her current research project is organized around the theme of "ungrievable lives."

Sheridan Linnell is an art therapy educator and practitioner. She works in independent practice and as a lecturer in art therapy and the expressive therapies in the School of Social Sciences at the University of Western Sydney. Before involvement in the politics of women's health led her to become a community worker and counsellor, Sheridan studied and tutored English Literature at the University of Sydney. She has a particular interest in narrative and poststructural approaches to therapy and is currently extending the theoretical dimensions of this work through doctoral research. Sheridan is a practicing poet whose first collection was published in 2001.

David McInnes is a senior lecturer in the School of Humanities and Languages at the University of Western Sydney. His research interests include the experience of gender nonconformity for men and boys, specifically melancholy and the dynamics of recognition. David has published several papers and book chapters, including a paper with fellow sissy and colleague Murray Couch titled "Quiet Please," about the power of epistemophilia as an ir/resolution to sissy boy shame. David has also, with his colleague Jonathan Bollen, undertaken and published research on gay men's sexual experience and sexual cultures. Their joint publications focus on interaffectivity and bodily negotiation in adventurous sex.

Eva Bendix Petersen is senior lecturer in sociology at the School of Humanities, Communications and Social Sciences at Monash University. Her research interests lie in the intersection of academic culture, processes of subjectification, and postfoundational research methodologies. She holds a Ph.D. in sociology from the University of Copenhagen, granted on the basis of the dissertation "Academic Boundary work: The discursive constitution of 'scientificity' amongst researchers within the social sciences and humanities."

Sue Saltmarsh is a senior lecturer in the School of Teacher Education at Charles Sturt University, Australia. Her research concerns the discursive production of subjectivities and social relations, with particular reference to issues of consumption, institutional violence, and social justice. Her current work utilizes poststructuralist theory to consider how neoliberal governance and its permeation of public discourse is constitutive of gendered and racialized economic subjectivities and functions to reproduce social inequality and violence across a range of institutional sites.

Linnell Secomb teaches in the Department of Philosophy and the Department of Gender Studies at the University of Sydney. Her research focuses on social philosophy, philosophy of the emotions, and on politics and ethics within poststructural frameworks. She is the author of *Philosophy and Love: From Plato to Popular Culture.*

Affrica Taylor has worked inside and outside academe in Indigenous Australian education and feminist and queer politics. She has a Ph.D. in cultural geography and is currently a lecturer in School of Education and Community Studies at University of Canberra. She researches and writes at the intersections of spatial, postcolonial, and queer theory and ethnographies of place and identity. She has authored and coauthored publications about queer and postcolonial geography; queer and postcolonial early childhood; and the cultural politics of national belonging. Taking up on Butler's ethics of self/other, she is cultivating a pedagogy of difference and engagement in her teaching practice.

Introduction

BRONWYN DAVIES

University of Western Sydney

In this book, you will find dialogues with Judith Butler and with her work in which Butler responds to a group of scholars from the social sciences and the humanities who set out to examine the ways her philosophical writing has informed their own thinking and writing. They include people working in cultural geography, education, gender and feminist studies, narrative therapies and art psychotherapy, philosophy, psychology, rhetoric and cultural studies, sociology, and theater and dance. This dynamic exchange thus works at the interface between philosophy and a range of other modes of studying human existence.

We undertook this project in order to trace the ways that Butler's thinking opens up a certain freedom, and a space in which the repetition of old thought is no longer necessary or inevitable. Our working definition of *thought* was, following Michel Foucault, "[the] freedom in relation to what one does, the motion by which one detaches oneself from it, establishes it as an object, and reflects on it as a problem" (Foucault 1994, 117). This book thus contains not only those considered reflections on the impact of Butler's work on the thought of others, but also her reflections on the thinking that each of the scholars engaged in as they took up and worked with various aspects of her work.

This began as a symposium at the University of Western Sydney. There were five essays written, and each of these essays was followed by an essay that responds to it. The essays and responses were then followed by Butler's spoken response, and by open discussion among all those who were present. The dynamic exchange was produced when the participants sat for two days around a table, presenting their papers and responses, and engaging with Butler in her critique of them. As convener of the event I opened up the discussion with questions about the work we were engaged in as we crossed these disciplinary boundaries. The questions I asked, and Butler's replies, along with some others' comments and questions, are included as section 1, "Conversation with Judith Butler I."

Following this opening discussion, Butler then presented chapter 1, "An Account of Oneself." In this essay she argues that the "I" who gives that account "does not stand apart from the prevailing matrix of ethical norms and conflicting moral frameworks" that preexist the subject and provide the conditions under which it is possible to become a subject. Her essay explores the implications for ethics of the notion that subjects are both conditioned by and dependent on the prevailing norms, and at the same time, each singular subject must "find her way with morality." She discusses Friedrich Wilhelm Nietzsche's view of the origin of ethics as arising from a primal scene of violence in which the other threatens punishment for the subject's deeds, and finally puts this aside in favor of Foucault's ethics in which "the subject forms itself in relation to a set of codes, prescriptions or norms, and does so in ways that not only (1) reveal self-constitution as a kind of poiesis, but (2) establish self-making as part of a broader operation of critique." She is careful to point out, however, that there is no self-making without subjection, no self-making "outside of the norms that orchestrate the possible forms that a subject may take." Agency lies in the practice of critique that Foucault elaborates as central to self-making: the practice of critique exposing "the limits of the historical scheme of things, the epistemological and ontological horizon within which subjects come to be at all." Butler's point in this essay is to show how a theory of subject formation that acknowledges the limits of self-knowledge, limits that are necessitated by the mode of our making out of materials we did not ourselves make or necessarily choose, "can work in the service of a conception of ethics and, indeed, of responsibility." In order to complete her argument, Butler shifts Foucault's ethical question, "What can I become?" to Adriana Cavarero's question, "Who are you [that I address]?" As Butler notes, Cavarero argues that we are necessarily "exposed to one another in our vulnerability and singularity." "If I have no 'you' to address," Butler observes, then I have lost 'myself.'" Butler then draws in Foucault's point, that the terms on which one narrates oneself to "you," and is exposed to "you," are not solely one's own terms: "The norms by which I seek to make myself recognizable are not precisely mine. They are not born with me; the temporality of their emergence does not coincide with the temporality of my own life." Butler draws these threads of Cavarero and Foucault together to argue for relationality as an indispensable resource for ethics.

In her response to Butler's essay, Fiona Jenkins examines the notion of the gift (in giving an account of oneself) and also what is implied in Butler's dependence on the notion of forgiveness in her account of ethics and the failure that the need for forgiveness implies. This failure may be the conventional failure to become "the subject of a freedom connoting self-origination, mastery, and causal power, and threatened by deterministic or external forces as well as by its own internal weakness." Jenkins suggests, rather, that Butler deconstructs the image of sovereignty and isolation characteristic of the traditional subject of responsibility in favor of acknowledging the productive inscription of a certain necessary failure in our constitutive dependency upon and relationality with others. Jenkins argues that the stakes for an ethical life as it emerges in Butler's writing might be "(1) how to give an account of the relation to the other that is not inherently hostile; (2) how to locate responsibility in its temporal and material inscription and thus beyond the figure of ideal self-identity and stability; and (3) how to think ethics beyond a guilt that 'deadens' life."

Following her deeply insightful analysis of how it is that Butler addresses these questions, Jenkins concludes her response to Butler's essay with three further questions that—because of the inescapable binds we find ourselves in—we must accept practically and responsibly as our own questions: "How can the primary vulnerability of our constitution in relations that always precede and exceed ourselves come to be seen not as the constant stumbling block of morality but as the binding place of ethical life? How, in the exposure to violence that we risk here, might we avert immediate recourse to that further and inflationary violence of subjecting all our relations to the force of law? How might reaction pause, and take on the burden of opening up a space of forgiving?"

The space of forgiveness, I would like to add here, could be said to require a prior moment of compassion; a compassion that recognizes our own and each other's vulnerability to the other, and to the norms that precede and exceed us, through which we each seek to make ourselves and each other recognizable. Those norms do not coincide with us, temporally or spatially. They are, as Butler notes, careless of our existence, even though it is through our (collective) existence, through our becoming recognizable in their terms, that those norms have any existence. As the essays that follow graphically argue, the terms of recognition offered within the domain of one or another normative order may stifle us or may lend us agency, but one way or another we become (and come to be through being) dependent on and vulnerable to the other's willingness and ability to recognize us within those terms. In the shifting relations of power in which we are each caught up, we are each always at risk of negating the other in the task of managing our own vulnerabilities—to each other, and to the normative discourses and practices through which we are made, in any particular moment and place, to make sense. In comprehending this vulnerability of oneself and of the other, one can extend compassion to the other as that other engages in the struggle for existence, seizes moments of power that are made available, and seeks pleasure in the possibilities of existence. To forgive that trespass on one's own struggle seems to me to require at least the insight that such compassion might bring.

The first of the essays that takes up Butler's work in a different disciplinary context comes from Eva Bendix Petersen, who asks, quoting Gustave de Beaumont and Alexis de Tocqueville, "What breach of order is it possible to commit in solitude?" In order to address this question Petersen also asks, "How do discursive constructions take hold—take hold of the body, take hold of desire? And how are certain discursive constructions appropriated while others are discarded, relegated as irrelevant or even life-threatening?" Her essay takes us into the solitude and the sweaty heartbeat of a young academic sitting at her computer writing, moving her finger to the backspace key. Using Butler's concept of performativity, Petersen explores how the academic comes to desire as her own the knowledge that takes her finger to the backspace key in order to render herself "not that"—not the writer of that which, for the moment, has emerged onto the screen. The academic subject thus accomplishes for herself an appropriation of herself and her knowledge as legitimate, as one who has been successfully subjected and who willingly goes on subjecting herself, at the same time as she appropriates for herself the position of one who questions the very order in terms of which she was and is subjected.

Petersen thus brings Butler's analyses of subjection, power, and performance to bear not on the process of gendering but on the process of engendering academic subjectivity, positioning oneself as an academic subject in a way that will serve to signal "This is who I am." The process whereby subjects are made is thus fleshed out in a new context, lending new insights to the philosophical analyses provided by Butler and Foucault and bringing fresh perspectives to the particular context of academe.

Sheridan Linnell's response to Petersen adopts a poetic, reflexive mode of writing. Linnell takes up the problem of address, and questions who it is she might be addressing in her reply, and how and in what ways Petersen has addressed her. She asks who Eva is, who Eva's imagined subject is, and who she, or we, might be in response. "How does Eva's subject become 'our' subject?" Linnell asks. "How is the quickening pulse, the beating heart, the tapping foot intertwined with our bodies? How does what she, the imaginary subject, feels course through our blood, raise our temperatures, wrench our hearts, lift our spirits? Is this only because we, too, are subjects of academicity? How are we, who are constituted over and again as autonomous, doomed to fail so miserably at this independence?"

Taking up Butler's idea of the unknowability of the self, Linnell writes, "My effectiveness as subject of whatever order is always somewhat mysterious to me, displaced from intention, played out in layers of histories, memories, relations, and bodies. Having attempted to dethrone the self-identified agency of a phenomenological subject, I cannot rely on the intervention of a critical theory to pull the wool from my eyes. Sovereign theory is as problematic as any other sovereignty. The effect of this realization, as Butler points out, need not be nihilism, paralysis, unbounded relativism, amorality, or despair. Humility, connectedness, and open-endedness might rather be the implications of such radical uncertainty."

In the lively conversation that followed, included here as "Conversation with Judith Butler II," Butler, Petersen, and Linnell discuss this experimental writing and the enigmatic condition of academicity in which the necessity of compliance works with and against the ideal of innovation and creativity.

The next essay, by David McInnes, asks how Butler's work on melancholia and gender, ethics and humanity can help us to think through the constitution of "masculinities" and the constitution of boys in school contexts. McInnes provides a critique of the work of R. W. Connell and Wayne Martino, in which he argues that the insistence on plural masculinities as a means to make space for boys who might otherwise be seen as marginal to hegemonic masculinity does not accomplish what it hopes for. Instead, it accomplishes an essentializing of the relation between bodies and gender in a way that *fixes* difference rather than loosens it. Hegemonic boys, in the educational programs developed on the basis of the idea of multiple masculinities, are invited to understand the vulnerability of the nonhegemonic boy. This invitation reiterates the authenticity and naturalness of the hegemonic boys' masculinity and so perpetrates a form of ethical violence.

Drawing on the German concept of *re-cognition* (*Erkenntnis*), in which the act of recognition has constitutive force, and combining this with Butler's discussion of the vulnerability we each have to the other in any ethical relation, McInnes offers an alternative approach. He asks us to imagine an educational ethics in which all students reflexively engage with their own precariousness, their own incoherence in order to "make an ethical demand on all within circuits of recognition." He asks, "What if, instead of attention being paid to the proliferation of types of men and boys, attention was paid to circuits of recognition in their iterative unfolding and to the tensions experienced by and investments made by those involved?"

In her response to McInnes's essay, Cristyn Davies examines the process of naming and how it is that naming freezes meaning and forecloses the fluidity that the act of naming was intended to halt: "The process of 'fixing' or 'freezing' suggests a prior fluidity," she notes, "and would seem to promise an intelligible social future, one in which the subject is made recognizable through normative discursive regimes." Davies works with two vivid examples of naming, one in which she as lesbian is named as faggot, and one in which a thirteen-year-old boy is *re-cognized* as homosexual, apparently independent of desire or sexual activity. The focus of her analysis is on the work that the person so named in each case does to re-cognize themselves as that which they are named. In this way she commences the work that McInnes suggests we should undertake if we are to act responsibly as social theorists. In her conclusion, Davies emphasizes that McInnes's call for a pedagogy of incoherence is not a call to celebrate incoherence, but to attend "to the liveliness of language, the subtle workings of power through the circulation of discourse, and the regulating effects of normative practices."

In the discussion that follows, "Conversation with Judith Butler III," Butler talks about the relations between her work and those working in the social sciences. She expresses puzzlement at the critique that Connell levels at her work for not addressing "work and families" and talks about the productive relations that can exist between philosophical work and the more applied disciplines. She depends on that applied work, she says, to extend her understanding and to push her theoretical claims, a relation she sees as more productive than an accusation that she has not done the applied work herself. The discussion then moves to typologies and to the implications of the work done in both McInnes's and Davies's essays for thinking about the processes of naming, of melancholia, and of the turn toward or away from the name.

Linnell Secomb's essay, which follows, is situated "within the context of a concern about varying conceptions of the human and non-human. It approaches this question by investigating recent debates about asylum seekers, analyzing the Australian government's linguistic constructions and pronouncements, as well as the resistant words of refugees." The essay "attempts to 'trouble' the predominant discourses about refugees by utilizing aspects of Butler's and [Maurice] Blanchot's theories of language, each of which are themselves, perhaps, rearticulated through their juxtaposition."

Secomb posits that insufficient attention has been paid to Butler's extension of the concept of *linguistic performativity* to *somatic performativity*. Butler's somatic performativity, she argues, "shifts our understanding beginning to illuminate the complex relations among body, action, and language." "Against a deterministic account," Secomb points out, "Butler focuses on the radical indeterminacy of the speech act. As a result of iteration and citation the signifying effects of words are open to transformations proliferating the effects of utterances." Alongside this, Secomb proposes Blanchot's analysis of the ways in which "language negates the world, replacing it with the concept, though through the materiality of words language also gestures toward the ineffable being of the world." Holding these two ideas together, Secomb explores the way asylum seekers are turned, through the words of the Australian government, into illegal immigrants who are without rights to freedom or to refuge. She concludes with the proliferation of words that refuse this turning, and with the particular anonymous words of a refugee who "reverses the Australian government's constructions of humane and inhuman through a constative account that also performatively constructs new images of the human."

The response to Secomb's essay is written by Susanne Gannon and Sue Saltmarsh, who write both in cultural studies and literary modes, the latter mode turning the essay toward a performance of an encounter between citizens and refugees. They take up the substantive topic that Secomb has offered, the constitutive work done by the Australian government to deny human status and rights to refugees, and the refugees' turn to language to constitute themselves differently. In doing so, Gannon and Saltmarsh turn in particular to Butler's writing in *Precarious Life*, combining it with concepts drawn from Sarah Ahmed and Michel de Certeau to look at the way "language figures in establishing—and troubling—the limits of human intelligibility and viability within social and civic life." Then, also through the writing of refugees, Gannon and Saltmarsh work to "dislodge us each from our sedimented subject positions" and invite a recognition of "the other" that "entails recognition of our mutual particularity and vulnerability, recognition that the other is enfolded within us and we are enfolded within them." In this writing about performance, which is itself a performative writing, the authors set out to accomplish the conditions of a sustainable language in which "[l]oss, mourning, and love all become possible in its embrace."

In the discussion that follows, "Conversation with Judith Butler IV," Butler discusses her relation with the writing of Blanchot, and how it is that his theorizing prompts a correction to the tendency in her own writing toward constructivism, in which she uses "the language as this active, productive, constituting kind of medium and resource." In the complex discussion that ensues, the focus turns to intentionality, and the question is asked whether in analyzing the discourses of government we inadvertently shift our attention from discourse to intention, and thence to the "evils" of particular rulers and government officials. The conversation turns on what sense we are to make at the site of a struggle for nomenclature and its politicization, and to a discussion of the generation of new possibilities through a generative play with language on the part of the refugees—and others—who have suffered atrocities. In relation to this point, Butler analyzes the dilemma of the refugees in terms of a confrontation between international law and nationalism.

The essay that then follows, by Affrica Taylor, removes us in one sense to the spatial scene of the kindergarten. But Taylor argues this is not a space separate from the kinds of struggles we have been discussing. The kindergarten is far from being an innocent space unshaped by global politics. Taylor examines the ways in which "childhood belongings are 'nested' within the uneven and contested power relations of the nation" and then goes on to reimagine what a postnational identity might look like if it were inspired by children's fantasy play. She draws on Butler's notion of fantasy as a "challenge to knowing beyond the limits of reality. In sympathy with [Butler's] interpretation, 'Fantasy is what allows us to imagine ourselves and others otherwise; it establishes the possible in excess of the real; it points elsewhere, and when it is embodied, it brings the elsewhere home.'" Some of the fantasies in the essay are gendered adulthood in which male privilege is insisted on and accomplished in relation to subordinated female others; or in which whiteness and speaking "like us" are established as the criteria for acceptability in dominant boys' play. Others, however, involve transgressions across gender boundaries and across human/animal boundaries in play that repeatedly offers pleasure to the children as they play out the possibilities of male princesses and transformations of princesses into wild and magical horses who sometimes agree to be contained in the royal stable. In relation to this last scenario, Taylor observes, "Taking a glimpse into a childhood world like the royal stable ... brings us the possibility of creating new kinds of community based on sociality and an ethics of open belonging," offering us an "insight into the kind of embodied enactments, both queer and postnational, that might enable us to 'bring the elsewhere home.'"

In his response to Taylor's essay, Jonathan Bollen provides an implicit critique of the links between fantasy play and identity that are generally made in preschool studies. Bollen presents stories in which that play can be seen as repeated pleasurable possibilities entered into as who one *might be*, and yet which are not finally taken up as the signifiers of who one *is*. Bollen traces his own engagement with the concept of performativity and on some of its loose confusions with performance. Much of what happens in theater is dismissed as "only performance" that makes little difference to the real world. Nevertheless, Bollen wants to ask "how occasions of queer performance might exercise a performative force on those who participate or attend, or how the theatricality of queer performance might figure in quite mundane ways in our ongoing engagements with the performative banality of everyday life." Following a discussion of his own (now abandoned) drag performances, and the dressing-up performance of a young man Michael, Bollen proposes dressing up for children and young people as good for growing up, suggesting that "improvisational practices of dressing up in innovative ways are useful for growing up into a future that is thereby different from the now."

These last two essays were welcomed by the symposium participants for their optimism, their playfulness, and their open engagement with fantasy. The gorgeous images of Bollen and his friends in drag, and the delightful images of the children at play, seemed to provide a resting place—a place of fluidity and of pleasure, at least in the worlds of fantasy. In the lively discussion that followed, "Conversation with Judith Butler V," however, Butler suggests that both Taylor and Bollen might be overly optimistic about the possibilities of play for opening up new futures. Questions are raised in response to the optimism of the essays, about the negative aspects of fantasy play, and about the fate of those who are more interested in dressing down rather than dressing up. The relation between the home corner and the stage on which the drag queen dances are discussed, as is the possible relation between the fantastical worlds of magic horses and drag queens versus the everyday. In the closing session, more questions were raised than answered, as is perhaps fitting for an event such as this, but we were nevertheless left with a clear image of the powerful connections between the exigencies of the global/political stage and the intimate space of fantasy play.

Conversation with Judith Butler I

Compiled by BRONWYN DAVIES

This part of the symposium began with a question to Butler about address—what it meant for us each to address the other in the space in which we had agreed to converse about the intersections in our work. The question was asked by Bronwyn Davies in her position as convener of the symposium.

Bronwyn Davies: As you pointed out in *Precarious Life*, "there is a certain violence in being addressed, given a name, subject to a set of impositions, compelled to an exacting alterity." We have you here, captive, in this moment, for these two days, greeting you *as Judith Butler*—each with our own idea of what that might mean—and we ask you to make not only an account of yourself but of how the words you have spoken and written have addressed us, captured us, made a different kind of thought possible. It is a moment that could be painful on both sides, an unwilling capture by an exacting alterity. Yet we have all agreed to be here, more with love in mind, perhaps, than capture. More with a mind to expanding thought and moving across old borders. Can you tell us how it is to be you sitting there, face to face with us, at the beginning of these two days?

Judith Butler: There are going to be questions of translation that emerge for us. I'm, of course, informed by philosophy; I

1

was drawn to philosophy as a very young person, and it's what actually helped me live, even breathe. I realize that for some, the philosophical medium is considered disembodied, abstract or difficult or not immediately available; they have other languages or other expressive media with which they work. So my immediate concern is how I both honor my own language—my own way of working—and, at the same time, find out what the sites of intersection might be with each of you. I'm in favor of philosophical work being appropriated outside the walls of philosophy; I also think philosophy is enriched by its engagement with social critique. So my first question is about what kinds of translations can and must be made for this exchange to work.

The next question took up the interaction between Bronwyn Davies as a reader of Butler's texts and the strongly interactive position that she has been developing in books such as *Precarious Life*, in which she works on what she calls "the struggle at the heart of ethics."

Bronwyn Davies: In *Precarious Life* you invite me unequivocally into the text. I am your anonymous other and you depend on me. You tell me you cannot will me away[1]. You are perhaps afraid of me. In acknowledging your vulnerability you become human[2]. In not taking your life, or the viability of your life, I grant it to you. And you, in not taking my life from me, grant me mine. It is this acknowledged possibility of our danger to each other, our vulnerability to each other, that "establishes," you say, the "struggle at the heart of ethics." The ethical position you trace out in that book is also rooted in an acknowledgment of the mutual need for recognition, an acknowledgment that also dislocates us from our existing positions. "If the humanities has a future," you write, "it is no doubt to return us to the human where we do not expect to find it, in its frailty and at the limits of its capacity to make sense." This is necessary for the project of reinvigorating critique, for understanding the "difficulties and demands of cultural translation and dissent" and creating a "sense of the public in which oppositional voices are not feared, degraded or dismissed, but valued for the instigation to a sensate democracy they occasionally perform" [2004b, 151]. I wonder if you could talk to us about the performance of that sensate democracy?

Judith Butler: When we think about democracy, about democratic theory, for the most part we accept that one precondition of a democracy is participation. Democracy must be participatory, and, at a very basic level, entails a capacity to know the world, to judge the world, to deliberate upon it, and to make decisions that are based upon an apprehension of the world. I want to suggest that there are a number of structures—the media, in all its senses, that are working on our capacities for apprehension: restricting them, enabling them, organizing them in various ways. That's inevitable. There's no nonstructured apprehension. But given that we accept this, the question is, How we do we come to apprehend the larger social and political world? It seems to me that we have to be able to *see* images and *hear* voices, even to smell and to touch a world that we are asked to fathom. And it seems to me that all the senses are at work in such moments.

One of the problems with living in a first world country—if it suffices to call the U.S. a country, given its own disregard for national boundaries—living in the empire, is precisely the way in which the outsourcing of violence and the representation of violence can actually produce a very restricted sense of what the war in Iraq is, and what the contours of our political world are. The state enforced restrictions on the media, as well as those restrictions that the media willingly takes on, work to restrict a capacity to see, to hear, to know, at a very basic level. This is not only an effect of deliberate or overt censorship, but it makes our judgments, our capacity to deliberate extremely limited and extremely parochial. And I would say this is true also of Australia as I understand the government's attempts to control information here as well.

What I experienced immediately after 9/11 in the U.S., for instance, was the sense that certain questions could not be raised in the public sphere. I remember having a meeting in New York in October of that year with some friends. We were at a table trying to talk about how 9/11 was being taken up, about the media and censorship and what's happening in the new nationalism, and we realized that our words were regarded in a scandalized way by others in the same room. We felt ourselves to be compelled to conduct the conversation underneath the table in muted tones. At that moment, I asked myself, Where am I living? It wasn't as if the police were going to come to get us but, rather,

the people at the next table were going to start an alter-
cation. A certain restriction took hold on what could be
heard, spoken, uttered; and in public discourse more generally, you have to be careful about what kinds of positions
you espoused, and there was an active question, and surely
remains one, whether a critique of U.S. retaliatory measures
and further military aggressions could be dissociated from
the actions of Al Qaeda. Accordingly, it was not just what
could be said that was restricted, but an entire sense of the
public and shared world, an extraordinary restriction of spatial relations, of a sensate world, of the domain that could be
apprehended, noticed, remarked upon, and subject to critical commentary. That kind of knowing and critical deliberation on how the world has been formed, and how the world
might yet be formed, is one of the very basic prerequisites for
a democratic politics. We have to be able to apprehend the
world as it is currently being structured, and we have to consider how best to evaluate those structures and their effects.
And even though we may always be to some extent unknowing about the various social structures and conventions that
form our positions of knowing, we have to know at least that
such structures are not systemically and tactically occluded
from view by state controls.

Another meaning of *sensate democracy*, I would add, is
a capacity for grief. On the one hand, we had many, many
monuments for many of the people who died in the World
Trade Center on 9/11. The public obituaries told us their
names, their hobbies, their dogs, where they lived, their aspirations, and whom they left behind. In this sense they were
humanized or, perhaps, rendered superhuman if not carica-
turish through the narrative and visual frames of the public
obituary. Of course, those deaths were terrible and worthy
of public note and public grief. That those people died was
radically objectionable, and there is no question about it.

But it must be possible to object unequivocally to the
destruction of those lives at the same time that one conducts
a critique of the form that this public grieving assumes.
There was an amplification of grief around those lives, lives
that could be made to emblematize national ideals and values, and so fortify nationalism itself, and there was a radical
muting, even an absolute unspeakability of grief for many
other lives: illegal workers in the building at the time, foreign

nationals, gay and lesbian peoples. And then there are, and remain, all the other lives, especially in Afghanistan at that time, that were killed, that were destroyed, for which there were no pictures or names, for which it was obligatory to supply no narrative or visual frame.

So the *frames* that I am referring to count as some of the structures that decide our capacity to apprehend the political and social world affectively and determine whether or not we live in a sensate democracy.

Moreover, I would suggest that in the U.S., since 9/11 though surely before, we suffer a strange melancholy: we know that there have been losses, but we cannot name or know them. And this not naming and not knowing are essential to our national self-definition. At the same time that the deaths that the U.S. has caused have remained unnamable—non-narratable, outside all visual frames—we name and narrate and see U.S. deaths in a hyperbolic way. This selective amplification of the U.S. victim as grievable not only kept a massive public grieving alive but nourished an unbridled nationalism with that amplified grief and its corollary, revenge. If we ask how grief is being regulated in the service of nationalism and violence, we see that certain nationalist frames that produce and disavow the grievable life are very much at work.

To return, then, to your question about sensate democracy, I would suggest that certain primary affects were regulated—amplified or muted—and certain sensations were either sensationalized or deadened to the point of unspeakability. As a result, our idea of the world—that is, the idea of what can be narrated or shown or framed as the world—is a way of regulating affect and has a direct bearing on what we take the world to be, and the kinds of political judgments we can make about it. This kind of restriction and amplification of what counts as political reality is prior to any judgment we might make about that reality: it constitutes the basis on which we come to know, and ultimately the basis on which we form opinions and deliberate on our views. In this way, it is a restriction that establishes a certain conception of the public sphere and that delimits in advance the kinds of political views we might be able to articulate and espouse. We have to understand this restriction of what is knowable as the public sphere as crucial for thinking about the demarcation of the sphere of politics—and, hence, the circumscription, even the skewing, of democracy.

The many threads of conversation that emerged during the two days of the symposium looped back over each other in ensuing conversations. Fiona Jenkins, for example, later questioned Butler, asking her to take further what she had said here about grieving.

Fiona Jenkins: I wanted to just take up some of the things you were saying about grief, post-9/11. There was a sense in which you could be heard saying there shouldn't be too much or too little grief, that you are arguing for a kind of moderate grief. Now I take it that this isn't what you want to say—I take it you want to say something about the stark asymmetry of grievable and ungrievable lives—but the question that raises for me is how we use this to judge the two undesirable alternatives of the sensationalisation of sensation versus the deadening of sensation. I guess there's three things I want to say there. First, what is democratic about that judgment— going back to your idea of the sensate democracy? Second, how would it be related to the idea of error in accounting for oneself if one failed to engage in some way that asymmetry of grievability and the asymmetry of attribution of violence? And third, how do you engage the dilemma of singularity versus substitutability within that, for a sense of personal grief is perhaps bound in some ways to be excessive, to be immoderate, to fail to make that kind of balancing gesture which would incline us toward a sense of substitutable lives?

Judith Butler: Some of these questions I don't have answers to, but they're very good questions. To begin, I don't mean to suggest that one could determine what constitutes too much or too little grief, though I can see where you might derive such a conclusion on the basis of what I have suggested. Rather, what interests me is how grief is regulated in order to keep certain notions of the national polity intact. You know, that's true in Plato's *Republic* as well. There are a couple of great moments where Plato talks about why the poets have to be banished. He says that the poets are just glutinous in relation to grief, that unrestrained grief will produce disorder in the soul, and that what happens at the level of the individual soul directly affects the harmony and order of the polis itself. You cannot have an ordered polity on the basis of unrestrained grief. This leads him not only to banish the poets, but to commend restrained grief as a precondition of a workable polity.

In my work on [Sophocles'] *Antigone*, what interested me was the way in which Antigone's grieving for her brother was publicly proscribed. In that case, Creon literally forbids public grieving for the brother, Polyneices, who was considered an enemy of the state. But perhaps we can think about such prohibitions as operating in a more diffuse way, without being explicitly articulated, and without the idea of the king or sovereign subject who dictates such a prohibition. For instance, I think politically this is a salient point and also resonates for me with what has happened in the continuing AIDS crisis. Certain lives initially were not grievable publicly, and then there was a mobilization to make such lives grievable, and this altered the public sphere, at least within certain nation-states. But even that political intervention to demand the grievability of those lives remained uncritical about the global dimensions of the epidemic. And it may be that the domestic success of naming and framing those lives who were lost within the U.S. came at the cost of not acknowledging what's happening in Africa, where those tremendous losses remain for the most part unmarked and ungrieved. Did the gay movement in the U.S. develop a set of icons or conventions for the victim of AIDS that did not work to include those who are outside the implicit national framing at work in those conventions? Instead, the deaths in Africa are still regarded within the mainstream media as a nameless mass of people who are dying but about whom we know nothing and for whom we have limited, if any, responsibility. So, I remain interested in how politically grief becomes exploited or foreclosed depending on what notion of nationalism or national profile of the polity is at stake. Can we think public grieving and transnationality together? What would it look like?

Regarding grief, I don't have an idea of what measured and appropriate grief would be. In fact, I don't think grief works like that. Grief is not a quantity of affect, but a process that undergoes shifts in unexpected ways. Public grieving tends toward iconicity, and that has to be contested in order to allow grief to follow its course. So I'm much more concerned with prohibitions on grief, on the one hand, and the relationship between grief and outrage on the other, which is something I write about briefly in *The Psychic Life of Power*. When I refer to a sensate apprehension of the world, I'm not referring to a judgment about the world. Such an apprehension is not itself a judgment, though it is surely the precondition of judgment, including political judgment; such an apprehension is a necessary, though insufficient, condition for political judgment.

In order to make political judgments, we need to be able to make reference to a world, and this means that we are subject to a certain media understanding of the world, by which I mean a way that the world is given over to the senses. So I don't want to say that a sensate apprehension is the same as those kinds of judgments that are crucial to democratic institutions, but that media presentations form the necessary background and horizon for what is generally understood as the free flow of information without which democratic life cannot exist. The problem runs deeper than any notion of *information* can convey, however. We have to consider carefully what is meant by *information*. Information is not just getting facts about what's happening in Iraq—though it surely includes that. Information presupposes the ability to apprehend what is being presented, and if that ability to apprehend is systematically destroyed or limited or skewed, then our capacity to receive information is accordingly undermined. There are conditions of mediated world-making under which information about AIDS in Africa becomes difficult, if not impossible, to know. The way AIDS in Africa falls off the map in the U.S. is just astonishing; we nevertheless make all kinds of political judgments about the world without knowing what the world is, on the basis of an idea of the world based upon the nearly total foreclosure on an entire continent's massive suffering.

In response to your second question about error in the account that I give of myself, I would say that error is inevitable. I'm not interested in a true account of myself; I think there has to be error, and that in showing you my errors, I give something of myself that is rather different than *an account*. I try to approach the question of what it is to give an account of oneself not by way of a notion of a true and false account, but through the notion of an opacity without which no subject can emerge. There will always be mistakes I make, failings I make, precisely because I cannot take into account all the conditions that make my life possible. My unknowingness about these conditions is part of what constitutes me as a human subject. I'm not a translucent subject with respect to the conditions of my own emergence, and if I were, I would not be recognizable as human.

Third, what happens in public grieving is very interesting on the question of singularity and substitutability. After 9/11, the *New York Times* tried to run a story on every single person who had died, although some people, of course, could not be found or named, could not be located in terms of communities or even identities. But the ones who were found—or selected—each got a picture and a paragraph in what seemed to be a public moment for apprehending the loss of this singular life. In fact, the obituary form turned out to be a repeatable genre, and so the singular lives turned out to be quite substitutable; you could find certain phrases and narrative trajectories repeated again and again. And this suited the nationalist goal of the obituary, since a common national identity was literally wrought from the genre that sought to singularize each life.

But there is another way to approach public grieving. One could ask [Adriana] Cavarero's question of each photograph: Who are you? When the *New York Times* is done, can we still ask who this person might have been? In a way, that is the question that emerges from those *précis*. We got the happy family, the dog in the suburb of New Jersey, then later, we got stories on the web, like, *One day she opened his drawer and found the letters to his lover and she realized that for all those years ...* or, *The phone bill came that she'd never looked at and it turns out he was gambling.* But that's not part of the life that's being acknowledged, that's not what a grievable life looks like in the *New York Times* at this moment of building nationhood. It is a life stripped of errancy, whose only failing is imposed from the outside.

Perhaps we think a life must become singular in order to be grieved; I think that would probably be Cavarero's position, and I think there is something to that. However, there's also something to mass grieving, to grieving people one never knew and could never have known. There has to be a way of doing this without summarily positing all those lives as manifestations of a single national ideal or character. There's a very interesting book by Edith Wyschogrod on mass death, a consideration that makes use of [G. W. F.] Hegel and [Martin] Heidegger, in which she talks about the problem of grieving innumerable others. And I think there is a kind of grief that pertains to the innumerable others that's not about making them radically singular but neither is it about a full-scale substitutability, either. I don't yet know how to think about that; that part of your question stops me and I'm aware that that's work I've yet to do. The problem seems terribly important.

Butler's apparent determination to take thought where others may be afraid to take it opens thought up, not just to the asking of those questions deemed to be unaskable and unspeakable by government or by one's fellow citizens, who may be caught up in heightened patriotism that precludes the asking of some difficult questions. It takes her, and takes us as her readers, to questions that the desire for acceptable, recognizable, linear, noncontradictory thought might have made unaskable. Butler's writing takes us repeatedly to the heart of contradictions, and she works there to break it open, to see what becomes thinkable if one dwells in that conceptual space. For example:

> As a form of power, subjection is paradoxical. To be dominated by a power external to oneself is a familiar and agonizing form that power takes. To find, however, that what "one" is, one's very formation as a subject, is in some sense dependent upon that very power is quite another. (1997a, 1–2)
>
> That my agency is riven with paradox does not mean it is impossible. It means only that paradox is the condition of its possibility. (2004c, 3)
>
> I find that my very formation implicates the other in me, that my own foreignness to myself is, paradoxically, the source of my ethical connection with others. (2004b, 46)

In order to ask her about this practice in her thinking and writing, Davies began with the story of a dream she had had when trying to frame the question she wanted to ask about the way Butler works in the face of contradiction.

Bronwyn Davies: The dancing particles of my body open up a space to let the speeding car drive through. The tires screech toward the sickening thud of impact. My skittering heart lurches me into wakefulness and I lie there, the weight of my body under the feather warm doona, apprehending the light that flows through the dancing particles. This drum, my heart, contemplates this dangerous gap. The itching skin on the surface of my body is being obsessively and pleasurably scratched by my strong fingers. I am all surfaces; I am the muscle beneath the surface; I am the hand scratching the skin, bringing it to the surface of consciousness. I drift back to sleep, and my bladder insistently holds my brain in sporadic wakefulness. This graphic space of the solid vulnerability and the multiple mobile invulnerability—or is it the other way round?—is the unspeakable paradoxical space that Butler's writing enables me to enter. In the space of madness, of a bad dream, of being a woman, I stagger up out of bed to find pen and paper. Can't let the image slip away into the dark night's dreaming. So what was the question?

Your writing enters, again and again, the impossible space of contradiction, that space we have learned too well to shy away from. Can you talk about the pleasure you take—and perhaps also the pain—in entering the space of contradiction, opening up for inspection what is more usually closed down?

Judith Butler: Let me ask you about something in your dream, if that's okay. Tell me how you move from the dream to the paradox, because, for you, it's in the paradoxical experience of the body as both vulnerable and mobile.

Bronwyn Davies: The fact that I experienced my body as something that a car could move through and also something that was deeply vulnerable to the car hitting me and killing me, so it's this sense that I'm absolutely mobile and not solid and I'm absolutely solid and human and subject to death. I'd been looking around for an image that enabled me to express to myself what paradox is, what the impossibility is of the kind of spaces that your writing takes me into.

Judith Butler: Let me say two things about this. I fear that I don't have an answer to whether there's pleasure or pain in marking a paradox as such. I have a willingness to give up a romantic idea of the body as a source of emancipation, but at the same time I do not want to succumb to a kind of determinism or fatalism that would make the body into a pure effect of a prior power. Perhaps I am trying to rid myself of the romantic idea that there might be emancipatory potential to the body as a matter of course, without falling into a fatalism that would make of social forces a kind of car crash and determinism, where I'm just the plaything of whatever inscription is in operation. So there's perhaps a postromantic agency that I'm always struggling to achieve, which maybe has a realism and a hopefulness and an irony to it. Writing allows me the capacity to hold contradictions together, and make them mobile, rather than be felled by them.

Now, your example is an interesting one to me, because, of course, there are two bodies at issue—the figure of one's body in a dream and then the waking to the body in the bed, and there is an extraordinary kind of discontinuity between the two: that was my body in the dream, that was not my body in the dream, this is my body on the bed, but what body was that in the dream? Of course, many common-sensical people will tell you to understand the body in the bed as the real one, and suggest that the body in the dream is merely psychic or phantasmatic. But do we know how a body becomes real?

When [Sigmund] Freud talks about the *bodily ego* he refers to the bounded sense of our bodies as established and elaborated through a projection of a surface. It seems to me he's suggesting that there's always a psychic dimension to our understanding of our *proper* morphology, that we couldn't even have our discrete and bounded sense of self without a psychic elaboration of this kind. This would suggest, then, that there is a linking of the body in the dream to the body in the bed. To what extent does the dream body underwrite the body that we wake to? The fact that you choose to write the dream already transfigures it, since in writing you effect a further agency, and so work against the passive situation of the body in the dream. Moreover, the writing seeks to alter the psychic reality of the dream. It's in the manner of, I'm going to make meaning out of this dream rather than live with its residue to no avail. But I think it's very complicated, because though one could say that the body is merely passive in the dream, the body is being elaborated phantasmatically in the dream, too. So the dream has its own agency, one that should be thought of in terms of an orchestration, which is also strange, and so the dream is a kind of activity or doing that may well appear as the impasse of agency itself. So I would be interested in thinking of agency, passivity, reality, and phantasm in the transition between dreaming and waking, and whether those are as distinct as they might seem in that transition or whether they actually are mutually implicated in some other way.

Bronwyn Davies: I saw the dream as doing the work of enabling me to ask the question about how it is that you engage with contradiction.

Judith Butler: Well, that's great.

Bronwyn Davies: So the body and its muscles and its skin were what I used to organize my material body to put the words on the page that made the link between the dream and the question I was struggling to ask.

Judith Butler: Yes, I just hope that I'm not the crash! [*Laughter.*]

Butler's joke about the car crash and the laughter that followed signaled, perhaps, one of those areas of tension between social science and philosophy, where the interests of one may be incompatible with the interests of the other. Davies's desire that Butler give a reflexive account of herself engaged in the work of philosophy demanded a reflexivity that may be at odds with the work she's actually doing. She later commented that the kind of reflexivity demanded by the question that I asked about how she felt when working with contradictions may actually prevent her from getting on with the particular innovation that she is engaged in.

Judith Butler: I actually have mixed feelings about the notion of reflexivity. Because, on the one hand, we take it as a good that we account for our practices, situate ourselves in them, and have a heightened self-consciousness about what we do so that we're able to explain it to others. But on the other hand, it seems that reflexivity always runs the risk of [disciplinary] recodification, and that if I had to explain what I'm doing I would probably cease to do it. My doing it actually demands a certain kind of forgetfulness about the reflexive dimension in order to allow it to move forward. And I just worry about how heightened self-consciousness not only yields to recodification but can actually stymie a certain kind of innovation.

For most of the scholars engaged in this conversation, this was the first time they had encountered "Judith Butler" face-to-face. Davies's next question expressed her puzzlement at the way Butler's writing had been accused of somehow omitting "the body." She asked Butler if she could speak of how she read that accusation of the absent body.

Bronwyn Davies: Until now, most of us have related to you through the words you have written. In the past I exercised my power to bring your words to life on the page—through my body, through the cells of the body and their memories of being.

I am puzzled at the inability of other readers to find your body/any body in your texts. They ask, Where is the body in the writing?

[Roland] Barthes [1989] suggests that we take as our primary research focus the text that is written rather than the (real) person who writes it. In privileging the texts of our writing, Barthes enjoins us to give birth to ourselves in our writing—that is, to know ourselves as coincidental with our writing. I find myself finding you in the texts you write. Since I do not imagine a disembodied you, I find you as embodied. What is it, do you know, inside or outside the text that these readers, who say they cannot find the body, are looking for?

In her reply, Butler pointed out that looking for the body in the text is based on some wrong assumptions about the possibility of a stable object to be found, and it also comes from a particular approach to feminism that she finds oppressive.

Judith Butler: I have a couple of quick answers to that. The first is that even if someone were to say that they find my body in my text, they'd just be terribly wrong and I would be slightly offended by the claim. The idea that I should somehow make my body manifest in my text is also offensive to me. And I think that it's something that is asked of women. It may well involve a presumption about feminine speech, a highly normative one, that women should speak a certain way and write a certain way, but also make their bodies available to others as a defining gesture of femininity. That the body should be available regardless of whatever she happens to be doing or saying worries me, for both feminist and philosophical reasons.

To the extent that I accept that writing and speaking involves the body, involves sitting or standing, involves breathing, involves hands, then yes, the body is always there in a matter of fact way. There are always opaque ways in which bodies make themselves known in language, but I don't think there's any easy hermeneutic through which that decipherment can take place. I actually think we need to respect that about each other, that that opacity is there as something to be honored, rather than something to be forcibly exposed. So I would hope that I—or *my body*—could not be found. I would hope that there is some question that would remain an open and permanent question about where or who this *I* is. I would not be able to answer that question nor would I feel compelled to answer it.

I think there is, in addition, a problem with thinking about women philosophers as if philosophy is by definition abstracted and disembodied. I don't think that's necessarily true. Philosophical reflection can be a precondition or instrument of desire and embodiment for many, but it depends on what does it for you. I find it terribly presumptuous to imagine that abstraction somehow equals disembodiment. I'm also worried that there are strong, specific social norms of what embodiment is, and how it is gendered. What would it mean to hold each other to such norms or measures? Such a procedure strikes me as very unreflective about the state of the norms that govern recognizable embodiment, and the norms that demand an exposure of embodiment in order to legitimate a knowledge inquiry. I suppose as well that some people understand that there is a *real person* who is somehow lurking behind the written words on the page and the text of the author. Even if there is such a real person—a notion that disturbs me—I'm not sure why the reality of a person is equated with a body, where the body is somehow separable from psyche, from expression, from forms of presentation and cultural and social norms. If we were to talk about the real person, I think we'd have to talk about the whole array of sleeping, dreaming, waking, eating, writing, fucking, running, swimming, sitting on the bus, sitting in the doctor's office, being stung by a bee, writing a text, computing a math problem, listening to music, everything. How would we construe such moments of a life in order to discern some *reality*? Anyway, I'm not sure you could say that any of these moments is more real than any other, or that some of them are embodied and others are abstract. How would we decide which moments are *real* and which constitute some kind of cover or displacement? Who would decide, and according to what measure? Frightening questions, no?

When and if the body makes itself known, it makes itself known through expressive media. Can we say that song or touch or the things that we think of as immediately bodily are without their syntax, their logic, their structure and also their sociality and historicity? What would it mean to dissociate the body from the larger structures of signification in the world? That a math problem comes from a body, as it were, is an infinitely interesting problem, and we cannot understand it without recasting the body as an expressive medium along the lines that [Maurice] Merleau-Ponty has proposed.

Further, we are governed—though not determined—in normative ways, and the body is given and received on the basis of certain kinds of norms. This is as true in a medical setting as it is in love-making. If I say to someone, I love you, or, I want you, the language of desire, which we think of as so proximate, as expressing a body that is singularly mine, is a language that simultaneously foils me, dispossesses me, since I am entering into a language heavily trafficked and used, and I am hardly singular when I wield the utterance. Denise Riley's work formulates this, of course, beautifully and trenchantly. I am dispossessed at that moment in which I seek to express my innermost self. So though I realize that some people might want to know how I am expressed in my language or what self is expressed there, I am myself, as it were, much more interested in the question of how the language I use dispossesses me in the direction of the other or in the direction of the sociality that is not of my own making. This latter question introduces a very different framework, a very different hope, and a very different aspiration than the former one. I don't think it's more or less embodied than some other mode.

Perhaps we could account historically for something like an *embodiment effect* that follows from certain kinds of writing practices, and which leads audiences to conclude that they are somehow in the presence of a body in the text. I wonder to what extent certain modernist or surrealist fiction produced this effect, and whether the valorisation of what

Freud calls *primary process* within feminist writing, especially in some French feminist writing, produced this effect as well, one that worked in concert with a certain norm of feminine desire. It's unclear to me that any reader is actually closer to the body of the author by virtue of that kind of writing, though many become convinced that they are. We would have to inquire into the conditions of that kind of persuasion, and it would be interesting to account for through historical inquiries into reception theory.

Of course, the conceit that is produced as a result of that kind of effect is that one can actually qualify as an appropriate feminine subject or as a recognizable icon of embodiment if and only if you learn to write in such a way that produces that effect. Is this any less coercive as a formula than what one learns in introductory logic about proper sentential propositions? You know, I remember my first job was teaching what was called *French feminism*—there actually is no such monolith—by which was meant a certain kind of *écriture feminine*, and there were all these fabulous orgasms described on the page that lasted for centuries and covered several continents at a time and I just thought, My god, what an overwrought, oppressive notion of sexuality this is. Let me just return to my local pleasures and familiar neuroses! I mean, for some it was just incredibly liberating and for others it was surely, This is as far from my experiences as any other. [*Laughter.*] You know, we're all supposed to live up to this? Anyway, that's my answer.

Bronwyn Davies: I love that answer and I'm sorry I had to offend you to get there. [*Laughter.*]

Judith Butler: I'm not offended.

NOTES

1. "One insight that injury affords is that there are others out there on whom my life depends, people I do not know and may never know. This fundamental dependency on anonymous others is not a condition that I can will away. No security measure will foreclose this dependency; no violent act of sovereignty will rid the world of this fact" (Butler 2004b, xii).

2. "'Violence, mourning and politics' … pursues the problem of a primary vulnerability to others, one that one cannot will away without ceasing to be human … impressionability and violability are ineradicable dimensions of human dependency and sociality" (Butler 2004b, xiv).

CHAPTER 1

"An Account of Oneself"

JUDITH BUTLER

University of California–Berkeley

In a less well-known set of lectures on morality, Theodor Adorno offers the modest claim that there can be no morality without an "I," a first-person perspective through which one poses the question, "What ought I to do?" or, indeed, "what have I done?". He writes, for instance, that "it will be obvious to you that all ideas of morality or ethical behavior must relate to an 'I' that acts" (Adorno 1997, 28). And yet, it is equally clear to him that there is no "I" who can fully stand apart from the social conditions of his or her emergence, no "I" that is not implicated in a set of conditioning moral norms that, as norms, have a social character that exceeds a purely individual meaning.

The question of morality presupposes that I stand before a set of norms and decide among them, but Adorno cautions us against taking this scene as a description of ontology. The situation is misleading, since the "I" does not stand apart from the prevailing matrix of ethical norms and conflicting moral frameworks. In an important sense, this matrix is also the condition for the emergence of the "I", even as the

19

"I" is not causally induced by those norms, even though we cannot conclude that the "I" is simply the effect or the instrument of some prior ethos or some field of conflicting or discontinuous norms. When the "I" seeks to give an account of itself, it can try to start with its own singular past and origins, but it will find that this self, both as a narrating vehicle and as a subject to be narrated, is already implicated in a social temporality that exceeds its own capacities for narration; indeed, when the "I" seeks to give an account of itself, an account that must include the conditions of its own emergence, it must, as a matter of necessity, I want to suggest, become a social theorist.

The reason is that the "I" has no story of its own that is not at once the story of how the "I" is conditioned and produced within a matrix of conventions and norms governing the formation of the subject. And though many contemporary critics worry that this means there is no concept of the subject that can serve as the ground for moral agency and moral accountability, this conclusion, in my view, does not follow. The "I" is always to some extent dispossessed by the social conditions of its emergence. This dispossession does not mean that we have lost the subjective ground for ethics. On the contrary, this dispossession may well be the condition for moral inquiry, the condition under which morality itself emerges. If the "I" is not at one with the moral norms it negotiates, this means only that the subject must deliberate upon these norms, and that part of deliberation will entail a critical understanding of their social genesis and meaning. In this sense, ethical deliberation is bound up with the operation of critique. And critique finds that it cannot go forward without a consideration of how the deliberating subject comes into being and how a deliberating subject might actually live or appropriate a set of norms. Not only does ethics find itself embroiled in the task of social theory, but social theory, if it is to yield nonviolent results, must find a living place for this "I."

There are a variety of ways to account for the emergence of the "I" from the matrix of social institutions, ways of contextualizing morality in its social conditions. Friedrich Wilhelm Nietzsche underscored the violence of "bad conscience," which brings the "I" into being as a consequence of potentially annihilating cruelty. The "I" turns against itself, unleashing its morally condemning aggression against itself, and reflexivity is inaugurated as a result. This is, at least, the Nietzschean view of bad conscience. I would suggest that Adorno (1997) alludes to such a negative view of bad conscience when he maintains that an ethics that cannot be appropriated in "a living way" by individuals under socially existing conditions "is the bad conscience of conscience" (Nietzsche 1969, 15).

We have to ask here, however, whether the "I" who must appropriate moral norms in a living way is not itself conditioned by norms—norms that establish the viability of the subject. It is one thing to say that a subject must be able to appropriate norms, but it is another to say that there must be norms that prepare a place within the ontological field for a subject. In the first instance, norms are there, at an exterior distance, and the task is to find a way of appropriating them, taking them on, establishing a living relation to them. The epistemological frame is presupposed in this encounter, one in which a subject encounters moral norms and must find his way with them. But did Adorno consider that norms also decide in advance who will and will not become a subject? Did he consider the operation of norms in the very constitution of the subject, in the stylization of its ontology, and in the establishing of a legitimate site within the realm of social ontology?

It would seem that before we can ask about what a subject is to do, we have to understand how morality more generally functions as a forcible framework within which the subject is formed. For a subject produced by morality must nevertheless find her way with morality, and there is no willing away this paradoxical condition for moral deliberation and for the task of giving an account of oneself. Even if morality supplies a set of norms by which a subject is produced in her intelligibility, it also remains a set of norms and rules that a subject must negotiate in a living and reflective way.

In *On the Genealogy of Morals* (1969), Nietzsche offers a controversial account of how we become reflective at all about our actions and how we become positioned to give an account of what we have done. He remarks that we become conscious of ourselves only after certain injuries have been inflicted. Someone suffers as a consequence, and the suffering person—or, rather, someone acting as his advocate in a system of justice—seeks to find the cause of that suffering and asks us whether we might not be that cause. It is precisely in the interests of dealing a just punishment to the one responsible for an injurious action that the question is posed and that the subject in question comes to question himself. "Punishment," Nietzsche tells us, is "the making of a memory" (1969, 80). The question posits the self as a causative force, and it also models a specific mode of responsibility. In asking whether we caused such suffering, we are being asked by an established authority not only to establish a causal link between our own actions and the suffering that follows but also to take responsibility for these actions and their effects. It is in this context that we find ourselves in the position of having to give an account of ourselves.

We start to give an account only because we are interpellated as beings who are accountable to a system of justice and punishment. This system is not there from the start, but becomes instituted over time and at a great cost to the human instincts. Nietzsche writes that, under these conditions, people "felt unable to cope with the simplest undertakings; in this new world they no longer possessed their former guides, their regulating, unconscious, and infallible drives: they were reduced to thinking, inferring, reckoning, coordinating cause and effect, these unfortunate creatures; they were reduced to their 'consciousness,' their weakest and most fallible organ!" (1969, 84).

So I start to give an account, if Nietzsche is right, because someone has asked me to, and that someone has power delegated from an established system of justice. I have been addressed, even perhaps had an act attributed to me, and a certain threat of punishment backs up this interrogation. And so, in fearful response, I offer myself as an "I" and try to reconstruct my deeds, showing that the deed attributed to me was or was not, in fact, among them. I am either owning up to myself as the cause of such an action, qualifying my causative contribution, or defending myself against the attribution, perhaps locating the cause elsewhere. These are the parameters within which my account of myself takes place. For Nietzsche, accountability only follows upon an accusation or, minimally, an allegation, one made by someone in a position to deal a punishment if causality can be established. And we become reflective, accordingly, through fear and terror. Indeed, we become moral as a consequence of fear and terror.

Yet, let us consider that being addressed by another carries other valences besides fear. There may well be a desire to know and understand that is not fueled by the desire to punish, and a desire to explain and narrate that is not prompted by a terror of punishment. Nietzsche did well to understand that I only begin my story of myself in the face of a "you" who asks me to give an account. Only in the face of such a query or attribution from an "other"—"Was it you?"—do any of us start to narrate ourselves, or find that, for urgent reasons, we must become self-narrating beings. Of course, it is always possible to remain silent in the face of such a question, where the silence articulates a resistance to the question: "You have no right to ask such a question," or, "I will not dignify this allegation with a response," or, "Even if it was me, this is not for you to know." Silence on these occasions either calls into question the legitimacy of the authority invoked by the question and the questioner or attempts to circumscribe a domain of autonomy that cannot or should not be intruded upon by the questioner. The refusal to narrate remains a relation to narrative and to the scene of address. As a narrative withheld, it either refuses the relation that the inquirer presupposes or changes that relation so that the one queried refuses the one who queries.

Telling a story about oneself is not the same as giving an account of oneself. And yet, we can see in the example above that the kind of narrative required of an account we give of ourselves is one that accepts the presumption that the self has a causal relation to the suffering of others (and eventually, through bad conscience, to oneself as well). Not all narrative takes this form, clearly, but the narrative that responds to allegation must, from the outset, accept the possibility that the self has causal agency, even if, in a given instance, the self may not have been the cause of the suffering in question.

Giving an account thus takes a narrative form, depending not only on the ability to relay a set of sequential events with plausible transitions but also drawing upon narrative voice and authority, and it is directed toward an audience with the aim of persuasion. The narrative must then establish that the self either was or was not the cause of that suffering, and so supply a persuasive medium through which to understand the causal agency of the self. The narrative does not emerge after the fact of causal agency, but constitutes the prerequisite condition for any account of moral agency we might give. In this sense, narrative capacity constitutes a precondition for giving an account of oneself and assuming responsibility for one's actions through that means. Of course, one might simply nod or make use of another expressive gesture to acknowledge that one is indeed the one who authored the deed in question. The nod functions as an expressive precondition of acknowledgment. A similar kind of expressive power is at work when one remains silent in the face of the query, "Do you have anything to say for yourself?" In both examples, though, the gesture of acknowledgment makes sense only in relation to an implied story line: "Yes, I was the one who occupied the position of the causal agent in the sequence of the events to which you refer."

Nietzsche's view does not fully take into account the scene of address through which responsibility is queried and then either accepted or denied. He assumes that the query is made from within a legal framework in which punishment is threatened as an equivalent injury for the injury committed in the first place. But not all forms of address originate from this system and for this reason. The system of punishment he describes is based on revenge, even when it is valorized as "justice." It does not recognize that life entails a certain amount of suffering and injury that cannot be fully accounted for through recourse to the subject as a causal agent. Indeed, for Nietzsche, aggression itself is coextensive with life, and if we sought to outlaw aggression, we would effectively be trying to outlaw life itself. He writes that "life operates essentially, that is in its basic functions, through injury, assault, exploitation, destruction and cannot be thought of at all without this character." "Legal conditions," he adds, "constitute a partial restriction on the will of life," a will that is defined by struggle. The legal effort to obliterate struggle would be, in his words, "an attempt to assassinate the future of man ..." (1969, 76).

At stake for Nietzsche is not simply the prevalence of a morality and legal order he opposes, but a coerced crafting of the "human" in opposition to life itself. His view of life, however, assumes that aggression is more primary than generosity and that concerns for justice emerge from a revenge ethic. The self as "cause" of an injurious action is always retroactively attributed—the doer is only belatedly attached to the deed. In fact, the doer only becomes the causal agent of the deed through a retrospective attribution that seeks to comply with a moral ontology stipulated by a legal system that establishes accountability and punishable offenses through locating a relevant self as a causal source of suffering. For Nietzsche, suffering exceeds any effect caused by one self or another, and though there are clearly instances when one vents aggression externally against another, causing injury or destruction, there is something "justifiable" about this suffering to the extent that it is part of life, and constitutes part of the "seduction" and "vitality" of life itself. There are many reasons to quarrel with this account, and I will make some of my own differences clear as I proceed.

What seems important to point out first, though, is that Nietzsche restricts his understanding of accountability to this juridically mediated and belated attribution, not understanding, it seems, the other interlocutory conditions in which one is asked to give an account of oneself. He focuses instead on an original aggression that is part of every human and, indeed, coextensive with life itself. Its prosecution under a system of punishment would, in his view, eradicate this truth about life itself. The institution of law compels an originally aggressive human to turn that aggression inward, to craft an inner world composed of a guilty conscience and to vent that aggression against oneself in the name of morality; he notes that "in this psychical cruelty there resides a madness of the will which is absolutely unexampled; the will of man to find himself guilty and reprehensible to a degree that can never be atoned for" (1969, 93). This aggression that Nietzsche regards as native to every human animal and to life itself is turned against the will and then assumes a second life, imploding inward to construct a conscience that yields reflexivity on the model of self-beratement.

That reflexivity is the precipitate of the subject, understood as a reflexive being, one who can and does take him or herself as an object of reflection.

However, Nietzsche does not consider other linguistic dimensions of this situation. If I am held accountable through a framework of morality, that framework is first addressed to me—first starts to act upon me—through the address and query of another. Indeed, I come to know that framework through no other way. If I give an account of myself in response to such a query, I am implicated in a relation to the other before whom and to whom I speak. Thus, I come into being as a reflexive subject in the context of establishing a narrative account of myself when I am spoken to by someone and prompted to address myself to the one who addresses me.

In *The Psychic Life of Power* (Butler 1997a), I moved perhaps too quickly to accept this punitive scene of inauguration for the subject. According to that view, the institution of punishment ties me to my deed, and when I am punished for having done this or that deed, I emerge as a subject of conscience and, hence, a subject who reflects upon herself in some way. This view of subject formation depends upon an account of a subject who internalizes the law or, minimally, the causal tethering of the subject to the deed for which the institution of punishment seeks compensation.

One might expect that this Nietzschean account of punishment became crucial to Michel Foucault's account of disciplinary power in the prison. It surely was, but Foucault differs explicitly from Nietzsche by refusing to generalize that scene of punishment to account for how a reflexive subject comes about; the turning against oneself that typifies the emergence of Nietzschean bad conscience does not account for the emergence of reflexivity in Foucault. In *The Use of Pleasure*, the second volume of *The History of Sexuality*, Foucault turns to an examination of the conditions under which a self might take itself to be an object for reflection and cultivation, concentrating on premodern formations of the subject. Whereas ethics seemed derivable from a terrorizing scene of punishment for Nietzsche, Foucault moves with the final reflections of Nietzsche's *Genealogy* to focus on the peculiar creativity that morality engages, and how it is, in particular, that bad conscience becomes the means for the manufacturing of values. For Nietzsche, morality emerges as the terrorized response to punishment. But this terror turns out to be strangely fecund; morality and its precepts (soul, conscience, bad conscience, consciousness, self-reflection, and instrumental reasoning) are all soaked in cruelty and aggression turned back upon itself. The elaboration of a morality—a set of rules and equivalences—is the sublimated (and inverted) effect of this primary aggression turned against oneself, the idealized consequence of a turn against one's own destructiveness and, for Nietzsche, one's own life impulses.

Indeed, whereas Nietzsche considers the force of punishment as instrumental to the internalization of rage and the consequent production of bad conscience (and other moral precepts), Foucault turns increasingly to codes of morality, understood as codes of conduct—and not primarily to codes of punishment—to consider how subjects are constituted in relation to such codes that do not always rely on the violence of prohibition and its internalizing effects. Nietzsche's masterful account in *On the Genealogy of Morals* shows us how, for instance, rage and spontaneous will are internalized to produce the sphere of the "soul" as well as a sphere of morality. This process of internalization is to be understood as an inversion, a turning of primarily aggressive impulse back on itself, the signature action of bad conscience. For Foucault, reflexivity is elaborated in the taking up of a relation to moral codes, but it does not rely on an account of internalization or of psychic life more generally, and certainly not in a reduction of morality to bad conscience.

When one reads Nietzsche's critique of morality, one might derive a fully cynical view of morality and conclude that human conduct that seeks to follow norms of prescriptive value is motivated less by any desire to do good than by a terrorized fear of punishment and its injurious effects. What seems important here, however, is to see how strongly Foucault wants to move away from this particular model and conclusion when, in the early 1980s, he decided to move away from Nietzsche's position to rethink the sphere of ethics. His interest shifted to a consideration of how certain historically established prescriptive codes compelled a certain kind of subject formation. Whereas in his earlier work he treated the subject as an "effect" of discourse, in his later writings he nuances and refines his position so: The subject forms itself in relation to a set of codes, prescriptions, or norms, and does so in ways that not only (1) reveal self-constitution as a kind of poiesis, but (2) establish self-making as part of the broader operation of critique. As I've argued elsewhere, ethical self-making in Foucault is not a radical creation of the self ex nihilo, but a "delimit[ing] of that part of the self that will form the object of his moral practice" (1985, 28). This work on the self, this very act of delimiting, takes place within the context of a set of norms that precede and exceed the subject, and these are invested with power and recalcitrance, setting the limits to what will be considered an intelligible formation of the subject within a given historical scheme of things. There is no making of oneself (*poiesis*) outside of a mode of subjectivation (*assujettissement*) and, hence, no self-making outside of the norms that orchestrate the possible forms that a subject may take. The practice of critique will thus expose the limits of the historical scheme of things, the epistemological and ontological horizon within which subjects come to be at all. To make oneself, then, in such a way that one exposes those limits is precisely to engage an aesthetics of the self that maintains a critical relation to existing norms. In the 1978 lecture "What is Critique?" Foucault writes, "'Critique would insure the desubjugation of the subject in the course of what we could call, in a word, the politics of truth.'"[1] (1991c, 194)

In the introduction to *The Use of Pleasure*, Foucault makes clear that moral conduct is not merely a question of conforming to the prescriptions entailed by a given code, nor is it the internalization of a primary prohibition or interdiction. He writes that

> for an action to be "moral," it must not be reducible to an act or a series of acts conforming to a rule, a law, or a value. Of course all moral action involves a relationship with the reality in which it is carried out, and a relationship with the self. The latter is not merely "self-awareness" but self-formation as an "ethical subject," a process in which the individual delimits that part of himself that will form the object of his moral practice, defines his position relative to the precept he will follow, and decides on a certain mode of being that will serve as his moral goal. And this requires him to act upon himself, to monitor, test, improve, and transform himself. There is no specific moral action that does not refer to a unified moral conduct; no moral conduct that does not call for the forming of oneself as an ethical subject; and no forming of the ethical subject without "modes of subjectivation" and an "ascetics" or "practices of the self" that support them. Moral action is indissociable from these forms of self-activity.... (1985, 28)

Nietzsche laments that the internalization of morality takes place through debilitation of the will, even as he understands that this internalization constituted "the womb of all ideal and imaginative phenomena" (1969, 87) that would include, presumably, his own philosophical writing, including this very account. For Foucault, morality is also inventive, requires inventiveness, and even, as we shall consider later, comes at a certain price. However, the "I" engendered by morality is not conceived as a self-berating psychic agency. From the outset it is a challenge, if not an open question, of what relation the self will take to itself, how it will craft itself in response to an injunction, how it will form itself, and what labor it will perform upon itself. The injunction compels the act of self-making or self-crafting, which means that the injunction does not act unilaterally or deterministically upon the subject; it sets the stage for the subject's self-crafting, one that takes place always in relation to an imposed set of norms. The norm does not produce the subject as its necessary effect, and neither is the subject fully free to disregard the norm that inaugurates its reflexivity; one struggles invariably with the conditions of one's own life that one could not have chosen. If there is an operation of agency or, indeed, freedom in this struggle, it is one that takes place in the context of an enabling and limiting field of constraint. This ethical agency is neither fully determined nor radically free, but is one whose struggle or primary dilemma is to be produced by a world even as one must produce oneself in some way. This struggle with the unchosen conditions of one's life, a struggle—an agency—is also made possible, paradoxically, by the persistence of this primary condition of unfreedom.

Whereas many critics have claimed that the view of the subject proffered by Foucault—and other poststructuralists—undermines the capacity to conduct ethical deliberations, and to ground human agency, Foucault turns both to agency and to deliberation in new ways in his so-called ethical writings, and offers a reformulation of both that deserves a serious consideration. In a more fully developed reflection on these writings, I conduct a closer analysis of his attempt to provide an account of himself, but here I would like to turn to the more general question: Does the postulation of a subject who is not self-grounding, that is, whose conditions of emergence can never fully be accounted for, undermine the possibility of responsibility and, in particular, of giving an account of oneself?

Is it really true that if we are, as it were, divided, ungrounded, or incoherent from the start, it will be impossible to ground a notion of personal or social responsibility on the basis of such a view? I would like to rebut this view in what follows and show how a theory of subject formation that acknowledges the limits of self-knowledge can serve a conception of ethics and, indeed, of responsibility. If the subject is opaque to itself, not fully translucent and knowable to itself, it is not therefore licensed to do what it wants or to ignore its obligations to others. The contrary is surely true. The opacity of the subject may be a consequence of the subject conceived as a relational being, one whose early and primary relations are not always available to conscious knowledge. Moments of unknowingness about oneself tend to emerge in the context of relations to others, suggesting that these relations call upon primary forms of relationality that are not always available to explicit and reflective thematization. If we are formed in the context of relations that become partially irrecoverable to us, then it would seem that opacity is built into our formation and follows from our status as beings who are formed in relations of dependency.

This postulation of a primary opacity to the self that follows from formative relations has a specific implication for an ethical bearing toward the "other." Indeed, if it is precisely by virtue of one's relations to others that one is opaque to oneself, and if those relations to others are the venue for one's ethical responsibility, then it may well follow that it is precisely by virtue of the subject's opacity to itself that it incurs and sustains some of its most important ethical bonds.

Although we are compelled to give an account of our various selves, it will turn out that the structural conditions of that account make a full giving impossible. The singular body to which a narrative refers cannot itself yield to a full narration, not only because it has a formative history that remains irrecoverable from the point of view of reflection but because primary relations are formative in ways that produce a necessary opacity in our understanding of ourselves. The account of oneself is always given to another, whether conjured or existing, and this other establishes the scene of address as a more primary ethical relation than the reflexive effort to give an account of oneself. I consider as well that the terms by which we give an account are social in character. Even the terms by which we make ourselves intelligible, to ourselves and others, are not of our making, thus establishing social norms as a domain of unfreedom and substitutability on the basis of which our "singular" stories are told.

With the help of Foucault's self-criticism, it may be possible to show that the question of ethics emerges precisely at the limits of our schemes of intelligibility—the site where we ask ourselves what it might mean to continue in a dialogue where no common ground can be assumed, where one is, as it were, at the limits of what one knows and still under the demand to offer and receive acknowledgment: someone else there to be addressed and whose address is there to be received.

For Foucault, the question of self-constitution, which emerges most centrally for him in the 1980s, is one in which a regime of truth offers the terms by which self-recognition is possible. These terms are outside the subject to some degree, but they are also presented as the available norms through which self-recognition takes place, so that what I can "be," quite literally, is constrained in advance by a regime of truth that decides in advance what will and will not be a recognizable form of being. The regime of truth decides in advance what form recognition can take, but it does not constrain this form fully. Indeed, *decide* is perhaps too strong a word, since the regime of truth offers a framework for the scene of recognition, delineating who will qualify as a subject of recognition and offering available norms for the act of recognition itself. But in Foucault's view, there is always a relation to this regime, a mode of self-crafting that takes place in the context of the norms at issue and, specifically, negotiates an answer to the question of who the "I" will be in relation to these norms. In this sense, we are not deterministically decided by norms, although they do provide the framework and the point of reference for any set of decisions we subsequently make. This does not mean that a given regime of truth sets the invariable framework for recognition; it means only that it is in relation to this framework that recognition takes place or the norms that govern recognition are challenged and transformed.

Foucault's point, however, is not only that there is always a relation to such norms, but that any relation to the regime of truth will at once be a relation to myself. An operation of critique cannot take place without this reflexive dimension. To call into question a regime of truth, where that regime governs subjectivation, is to call into question the truth of oneself and, indeed, to question one's ability to tell the truth about oneself, to give an account of oneself.

Thus, if I question the regime of truth, I question, too, the regime through which being, and my own ontological status, is allocated; critique is not merely of a given social practice, or a certain horizon of intelligibility within which practices and institutions appear, but critique also implies that I come into question for myself. Self-questioning becomes an ethical consequence of critique for Foucault, as he makes clear in "What is Critique?" But it also turns out that self-questioning of this sort involves putting oneself at risk and imperiling the very possibility of being recognized by others, since to question the norms of recognition that govern what I might be—to ask what they leave out, what they might be compelled to accommodate—is, in relation to the present regime, to risk unrecognizability as a subject or at least to become the occasion for posing the questions of who one is (or can be) and whether or not one is recognizable.

These questions imply at least two kinds of inquiry for an ethical philosophy. The first is, What are these norms to which my very being is given over, that have the power to install me or, indeed, to disinstall me as a recognizable subject? Second, Where and who is this "other," and can the notion of the other comprise the frame of reference and normative horizon that holds and confers my potential for becoming a recognizable subject? It seems right to fault Foucault for not making room explicitly for the other in his consideration of ethics. Perhaps this is because the dyadic scene of self and other cannot describe adequately the social workings of normativity that condition both subject production and intersubjective exchange. If we conclude that Foucault's failure to think the other is decisive, we have perhaps overlooked the fact that the very being of the self is dependent not just on the existence of the other, in its singularity (as Emmanuel Lévinas [1974] would have it), but also on the social dimension of normativity that governs the scene of recognition. This social dimension of normativity precedes and conditions any dyadic exchange, even though it seems that we gain contact to that sphere of normativity precisely in the context of such proximate exchanges.

The norms by which I recognize another or, indeed, myself, are not mine alone; they function to the extent that they are social, exceeding every dyadic exchange that they condition. Their sociality, however, can be understood neither as a structuralist totality nor as a transcendental or quasi-transcendental invariability. Although some would likely argue that norms must already be in place for recognition to become possible, and there is doubtless truth to such a claim, it is also true that new norms are brought into being when unanticipated forms of recognition take place.

It will not do to collapse the notion of the "other" into the sociality of norms and claim that the other is implicitly present in the norms by which recognition is conferred. It is sometimes by virtue of the unrecognizability of the other that the norms governing recognition come into crisis. If and when, in an effort to confer or to receive a recognition that fails repeatedly, I call into question the normative horizon within which recognition takes place, then this questioning is part of the desire for recognition, a desire that can find no satisfaction, and whose unsatisfiability establishes a critical point of departure for the interrogation of available norms.

In Foucault's view, this opening calls into question the limits of established regimes of truth, where a certain risking of the self becomes, as he claims, the sign of virtue (Foucault 1991c). What he does not say is that sometimes calling into question the regime of truth by which my own truth is established is motivated precisely by the desire to recognize another or be recognized by one. The impossibility of doing precisely that within the norms that are available to me compels me into a critical relation to those norms. For Foucault, the regime of truth comes into question because "I" cannot recognize myself, or will not recognize myself, within the terms that are made available to me. There is an effort to escape or overcome the terms by which subjectivation takes place, and my struggle with norms is my own. Foucault's question effectively remains, "Who can I be, given the regime of truth that determines ontology for me?" But he does not precisely ask the question, "Who are you?" nor does he trace the way in which a critical perspective on norms might be elaborated from either of those questions.

The first-person perspective assumed by the ethical question, as well as the direct address to a "you," are disoriented by virtue of this fundamental dependency of the ethical sphere on the social. Whether or not the other is singular, the other is recognized and confers recognition through a set of norms that govern recognizability. So whereas the other may be singular, if not radically personal, the norms are to some extent impersonal and indifferent, and they introduce a disorientation of perspective for the subject in the midst of recognition as an encounter. For if I understand myself to be conferring recognition on you, for instance, then I take seriously that the recognition comes from me. But in the moment that I realize that the terms by which I confer recognition are not mine alone, that I did not single-handedly devise or craft them, then I am, as it were, dispossessed by the language that I offer. In a sense, I submit to a norm of recognition when I offer recognition to you, which means that the "I" is not offering this recognition from its own private resources. Indeed, it seems that the "I" is subjected to that norm at the moment it makes such offering, so that the "I" becomes an instrument of that norm's agency, and the "I" seems invariably used by the norm to the degree that the "I" tries to use the norm. If I thought I was having a relation to "you," I find that I am caught up in a struggle with norms. But could it also be true that I would not be in this struggle with norms if it were not for a desire to offer recognition to you? How do we understand this desire?

If the social theory of recognition, however, insists upon the impersonal operation of the norm in constituting the intelligibility of the subject, it remains equally true that we come into contact with these norms mainly through proximate and living exchanges, through the modes by which we are addressed and asked to take up the question of who we are and what our relation to the other ought to be. If these norms act upon us in the context of being addressed, then it would seem that a return to the problem of singularity is required to understand the specific occasions of address that make these norms into issues for a living appropriation of morality. In a Levinasian vein—though perhaps more decidedly Arendtian—Adriana Cavarero argues that the question to ask is not "what" we are, as if the task were simply to fill in the content of our personhood (Caverero, 2000). The question is not primarily a reflexive one, one that we pose to ourselves, as it is for Foucault, when he asks, "What can I become?" For Cavarero, the very structure of address through which the question is posed gives us the clue to understanding the significance of the question itself. The question most central to recognition is a direct one, and it is addressed to the other: "Who are you?" This question assumes that there is an other before us, one whom we do not know, cannot fully apprehend, whose uniqueness and nonsubstitutability cannot be captured by the operation of any impersonal norm.

In *Relating Narratives,* Cavarero underscores the kind of action that this speech act performs. To this end, she quotes Hannah Arendt's *The Human Condition*: "'Action and speech are so closely related because the primordial and specifically human act must at the same time answer to the question asked to every newcomer: "who are you?"'" (Arendt, quoted in Cavarero 2000, 20) In stark contrast with the Nietzschean view that life is essentially bound up with destruction and suffering, Cavarero argues that we are beings who are, of necessity, exposed to one another in our vulnerability and singularity, and that our political situation consists in part in learning how best to handle—and to honor—this constant and necessary exposure. In her view, I am not, as it were, an interior subject, closed upon myself, solipsistic, posing questions of myself alone. I exist in an important sense for you, and by virtue of you. If I have lost the conditions of address, if I have no "you" to address, then I have lost "myself." In Cavarero's view, one can only tell an autobiography to an other, and one can only reference an "I" in relation to a "you": without the "you," my own story becomes impossible.

For Cavarero, this position implies a critique of conventional ways of understanding sociality, and in this sense she reverses the progression one can discern in G. W. F. Hegel's *The Phenomenology of Spirit*, in which the scenario of the dyad gives way to a social theory of recognition. For Cavarero it is necessary to ground the social in the dyadic encounter. She writes,

> The "you" comes before the we, before the plural you and before the they. Symptomatically, the "you" is a term that is not at home in modern and contemporary developments of ethics and politics. The "you" is ignored by individualistic doctrines, which are too preoccupied with praising the rights of the I, and the "you" is masked by a Kantian form of ethics

that is only capable of staging an I that addresses itself as a
familiar "you." Neither does the "you" find a home in the
schools of thought to which individualism is opposed—these
schools reveal themselves for the most part to be affected by a
moralistic vice, which, in order to avoid falling into the deca-
dence of the I, avoids the contiguity of the you, and privileges collective, plural pronouns. Indeed, many revolutionary
movements (which range from traditional communism to the
feminism of sisterhood) seem to share a curious linguistic code
based on the intrinsic morality of pronouns. The we is always
positive, the plural you is a possible ally, the they has the face
of an antagonist, the I is unseemly, and the you is, of course,
superfluous. (Cavarero 2000, 90–91)

For Cavarero, the "I" does not only encounter this or that attri-
bute of the other, but the fact of this other as fundamentally exposed,
visible, seen, existing in a bodily way and of necessity in a domain of
appearance. It is, as it were, this exposure that I am that constitutes
my singularity. I cannot will it away, for it is a feature of my very corporeality and, in this sense, of my life, and yet it is not that over which
I can have control.

Cavarero's argument not only undercuts the Nietzschean account
of aggression and punishment; it also offers direction for a different
theory of recognition that is in some ways distinctly non-Hegelian.
There are, at least, two points to be made here. The first has to do
with our fundamental dependency on the other, the fact that we cannot exist without addressing the other and without being addressed by
the other, and that there is no wishing away our fundamental sociality. (You can see that I resort here to the plural we, even as Cavarero
advises against it, precisely because I am not convinced that we must
abandon it.) The second, however, limits the first point. No matter
how much we each desire recognition and require it, we are not therefore the same as the other, and not everything counts as recognition
in the same way. Although I have argued that no one can recognize
another simply by virtue of special psychological or critical skills, and
that there are norms that condition the possibility of recognition, it
still matters that we feel more properly recognized by some people
than we do by others. And this difference cannot be explained solely
through recourse to the notion that there is a variable operation of the
norm at work in these instances. Cavarero argues for an irreducibility
to each of our beings that becomes clear in the distinct stories we
have to tell, so that any effort to fully identify with a collective "we"

will necessarily fail. As Cavarero puts it, "[W]hat we have called an altruistic ethics of relation does not support empathy, identification, or confusions. Rather this ethic desires a you that is truly an other, in her uniqueness and distinction. No matter how much you are similar and consonant, says this ethic, your story is never my story. No matter how much the larger traits of our life-stories are similar, I still do not recognize myself in you and, even less, in the collective we" (2000, 92). The uniqueness of the other is exposed to me, but my uniqueness is also exposed to her, and this does not mean we are the same, but only that we are bound to one another by what differentiates us—namely, our singularity.

And though Cavarero thinks we might give a narrative account of this singularity, I want to suggest something different. Indeed, we might try to give a narrative account of this singularity, but the norms of narration in making the singular self recognizable also make it, more or less, substitutable. If we want to know what is nonsubstitutable in the other, it seems that we must founder on the limits of narrative itself. Caverero insists on a proliferation of unique stories, but this is, in my mind, to separate the life story from the social norms that make it intelligible as a story of a life. Whereas I agree with her that exposure to the other is fundamental to an ethical relationality, I would insist that this exposure is not precisely narratable. I cannot give an account of it, even as it structures any account I might give. The norms by which I seek to make myself recognizable are not precisely mine. They are not born with me; the temporality of their emergence does not coincide with the temporality of my own life. So, in living my life as a recognizable being, I live a vector of temporalities, one of which has my death as its terminus, but another of which consists in the social and historical temporality of those norms by which my recognizability is established and maintained. These norms are, as it were, indifferent to me, to my life and my death. Because norms emerge, transform, and persist according to a temporality that is not the same as the temporality of my life, and because they also in some ways sustain my life in its intelligibility, the temporality of norms interrupts the time of my living. Paradoxically, it is this interruption, this disorientation of the perspective of my life, this instance of an indifference in sociality, that nevertheless sustains my living.

Foucault put this point dramatically in his essay, "Politics and the Study of Discourse," when he wrote, "I know as well as anyone how 'thankless' such research can be, how irritating it is to approach discourses not by way of the gentle, silent and intimate consciousness which expresses itself through them, but through an obscure set of anonymous rules" (1991a, 70–71). He continues, "Must I suppose that, in my discourse, it is not my own survival that is at stake? And that, by speaking, I do not exorcise my death, but establish it; or rather, that I suppress all interiority, and yield my utterance to an outside which is so indifferent to my life, so neutral, that it knows no difference between my life and my death?" (1991a, 71). These rhetorical questions mark a sense of inevitability in the face of the fact that one's own life cannot be redeemed or extended through discourse (even though it tacitly praises discourse as that which finally has a life that is more robust than our own). For those who believe that language houses an intimate subjectivity whose death is overcome there as well, Foucault writes, "they cannot bear—and one can understand them a little—to be told: discourse is not life; its time is not yours ..." (1991a, 71–72).

So this account of myself that I give in discourse never fully expresses or carries this living self. My words are taken away as I give them, interrupted by the time of a discourse that is not the same as the time of my life. This "interruption" contests the sense of the account being grounded in myself alone, since the indifferent structures that enable my living belong to a sociality that exceeds me.

I give an account to someone, and the addressee of the account, real or imaginary, thus interrupts the sense of this account of myself as my own. If it is an account of myself, and it is an accounting to someone, then I am compelled to give the account away, to send it off, to be dispossessed of it at the very moment that I establish it as my account. No account takes place without a structure of address, and in this sense no account belongs to the person who offers it. The address establishes the account as an account, and so the account is completed only on the occasion when it is effectively exported and expropriated from the domain of what is my own. It is only in dispossession of myself that I can and do give any account of myself.

Can I take account of this very exposure implied by address in the course of my narrative? This is an exposure that takes place in spoken language and, in a different way, through written address as well, but I am not sure I can give an account of this exposure.[2] Is it there, as it were, as a condition of my narration, one I cannot fully thematize within any narrative I might provide, one that does not fully yield to a sequential account? There is a bodily referent here, a condition of me that I can point to, but that I cannot narrate precisely, even though there are no doubt stories about where my body went and what it did and did not do. The stories do not capture the body to which they refer. Even the history of this body is not fully narratable. To be a body is, in some sense, to be deprived of having a full recollection of one's life. There is thus a history to my body of which I can have no recollection.

If there is, then, also a part of bodily experience—what is indexed by the word *exposure*—that cannot be narrated, but constitutes the bodily condition of one's narrative account of oneself, then exposure constitutes one among several vexations for the effort to give a narrative account of oneself. Exposure, like the operation of the norm, constitutes the conditions of my own emergence as a reflective being, one with memory, one who might be said to have a story to tell (these postulates from both Freud and Nietzsche can be accepted even if the formative role of punishment and morality in those accounts is disputed). Accordingly, I cannot be present to a temporality that precedes my own capacity for self-reflection, and whatever story about myself that I might give is one that has to take this constitutive incommensurability into consideration. It constitutes the way in which my story arrives belatedly, missing some of the constitutive beginnings and the preconditions of the life it seeks to narrate. And this means that my narrative begins *in medias res*, when many things have already taken place to make me and my story possible in language. I am always recuperating, reconstructing, and I am left to fictionalize and fabulate those origins I cannot know. In the making of the story, I create myself in new form, instituting a narrative "I" that is superadded to the "I" whose past life I seek to tell. The narrative "I" effectively adds to the story every time it tries to speak, since the "I" appears again as the narrative perspective, and this addition cannot be fully narrated at the moment in which it provides the perspectival anchor for the narration in question.

My account of myself is partial, haunted by that for which I can devise no definitive story. I cannot explain exactly why I have emerged in this way, and my efforts at narrative reconstruction are always undergoing revision. There is that in me and of me for which I can give no account. But does this mean that I am not, in the moral sense, accountable for who I am and for what I do? If I find that, despite my best efforts, a certain opacity persists and I cannot make myself fully accountable to you, is this ethical failure? Or is it a failure that gives rise to another ethical disposition in the place of a full and satisfying notion of narrative accountability? Is there in this affirmation of partial transparency a possibility for acknowledging a relationality that binds me more deeply to language and to the other than I previously knew? And is this relationality that conditions and blinds this "self" not, precisely, an indispensable resource for ethics, of being there, as it were, for the other?

NOTES

This essay is an adapted and shortened version of my chapter by the same title in *Giving an Account of Oneself* (Butler 2005).

1. Foucault's "What is Critique" was originally a lecture given at the French Society of Philosophy on 27 May 1978; it was subsequently published in the *Bulletin de la Société Française de Philosophie* 84, no.2 (1990): 35–63, and later translated into English and published in David Ingram, ed., *The Political* (see Foucault 1991c). See also my commentary on this essay (Butler 2002b).
2. See Felman 2002.

Forgiving, Given Over, Given Away: A Response to Judith Butler

FIONA JENKINS

Australian National University

GIVING ONESELF AWAY

What life of the gift or of the given is revealed in the reflection Judith Butler offers us here on "giving" an account of oneself? At least in one sense this is a tale of multiple dispossessions, though at the same time the reflection invites us to acknowledge that what we seem to have lost we never truly owned. Thus, if I give my story to another, it is a gift of narration that was never purely mine to give, and over which I cannot exercise full control, claim full knowledge, or promise as a purely representational truth; for rather than disposing willfully of the terms of language in which I would speak of who I am, I must "recuperate" or stage my relation to the modes of recognition that language affords me, receiving and transmitting what is at once given and compelled by a normative order. Nor can I appropriate a position of epistemic authority with respect to my story, for "my narrative begins in medias res" and I appear neither as origin nor as master of it. I am already made by that which will exceed the possibility of my taking it fully into account or becoming accountable for it; and yet the "I" itself is revealed and becomes possible in and through this impossibility. Thus it is that in every fictionalizing and fabulating attempt to cover over the lack of coherence and completion in my narrative, I give myself away in my paradoxical truth as incoherent and incomplete, as ruptured in my being and open. My gestures both betray me and confer a certain irreducible fidelity of relation between giver and given, testifying to the bind of exposure in which I am made and undone.

How, then, does this being dispossessed of what one never fully had speak of ethics and its particular responsibilities? On the account Butler gives us here, one gives an account because one must respond—"I only begin the story of myself in the face of a 'you' who asks me to give an account". The gift is not free but compelled by the other. But to what order of insistence does this "must" belong? One thrust of Butler's discussion of Friedrich Wilhelm Nietzsche's story about the formation of the accountable subject aims to contest the claim that what compels the offer of oneself as "I" is an interrogation delivered by authorities and backed up by a threat of punishment. She points out that the scene of address is broader and contains more possibilities than this. If I must respond then this is not necessarily, or foremost, because I am overtly terrorized into assuming the position of the "I"; nor because I internalize that threat in bad conscience. Rather, and this is where Butler suggests that Michel Foucault goes beyond Nietzsche, I must respond because there is no "I" without the active taking up of a relation to a moral code.

So if the subject is in excess of the forces acting to shape it, this is because to be a self involves taking up a relation to prescriptive codes, and in this sense being at once compelled and self-making. If I respond (rather than simply freewheel) I am in relation to something other that delimits and constrains the terms of the encounter; I respond "within the context of a set of norms that precede and exceed the subject". And yet I do respond, and am active and self-forming *in* and *as* response. The norm lives through its reiteration, in and through its being taken up, followed, and reenacted. It confers the place of a subject but also is animated by a practice, and from this it follows that the response I am compelled to make is also the place of potential critique—of an expected response refused, of an initiative that contests a regime of truth, of a response that may in turn compel response, altering the terms of future encounter.

The self Butler shows us, then, is in an important sense structured by the compulsion of response, and this situates the self both ethically and politically in terms that challenge every assumption of self-identity. Elaborating G. W. F. Hegel's *ek-static* notion of the self, Butler poses as fundamentally undecidable the question of *where* and *when* the self is—"It is the self over here who considers its reflection over there, but it is equally over there, reflected, and reflecting. Its ontology is precisely to be divided and spanned in irrecoverable ways.... To be a self is, on these terms, to be at a distance from who one is, not to enjoy the prerogative of self-identity". On this account, the self is the compulsion of response—"the self never returns to itself free of the Other, [so] that its 'relationality' becomes constitutive of who the self is" (Butler 2004c,148). Such a self cannot incorporate the other or reduce it to the same (for all that it might wish to be able to do so) for, as constituted in and through alterity, in and as the compulsion of response, its being is always inescapably dependent, "given over" to another in a fundamental vulnerability that is the condition and the risk of recognition. In Butler's view this is never a strictly dyadic scene but is preceded and conditioned by a normative field inscribing this uncertain time of encounter within a social temporality. Equally, however, sociality is enacted in this ruptured dyadic moment, between this self and this other, and implies the possibility of a response in which established norms might come into crisis or unanticipated forms of recognition take place The ethical relation founded on the compulsion of response thus occurs at an open-ended place of unknowingness; "the site where we ask ourselves what it might mean to continue in a dialogue where no common ground can be assumed, where one is, at it were, at the limits of what one knows and still under the demand to offer and receive acknowledgment: someone else there to be addressed and whose address is there to be received".

We might also say that the self constituted in the compulsion of response is captured by an open-ended desire—a desire for recognition that can find no satisfaction, for it lives in the to and fro, the in-between, the here-as-over-there of relational being. But what then will mark the difference between the "I" and the "you," if not the self-identity of each? Refusing a positive account of singular life as the subject of a unique narrative, Butler allows only that the self appear in its singularity at the limits of the narratable and as the failure of all accounting. I am compelled to respond, and in responding, to give myself away, exposed as the paradoxical place where self-identity founders on the conditions of its own making. The "I" as Butler renders it can become the *subject* of its own account only in and as a certain operation of idealization, only then out of a helpless yet often violent gesture to refuse as "not-me" the historicity, embodiment, and sociality of self.

To this thought correlates the complementary claim that the "I" (now no longer assumed to be the subject) is *revealed* (given away) only in dispossession, only in and as the failure of idealization and the impossibility of any account being fully owned. This scene has the potential to humble or to humiliate depending on the manner in which I attempt or am brought to come to terms with the "being me" that is ever vulnerable to becoming suddenly, unaccountably "undone," flushed with shame, fallen in love, helpless with laughter. But this scene is not only the revelation of my singularity on terms of ultimate abandonment. For if the "I" is the moment of failure in every effort to account for oneself, the ethical question becomes not simply how to act but how to act *this scene*—that is, how to mobilize an understanding of the rhetoricity of self-accounting, the moment of address in which the difference of "I" and "you" is marked and engaged, in which the claim and desire that lies between us becomes open to the work and transformation of language or gesture.

A gift, then—perhaps the gift of my account—may be given or received in many ways; all that is certain is that it is given away and thus its "life" exceeds anything I can hold to be fully mine or fully yours. It is the dispossessing scene not only of an exchange but of a sharing in which the "I" and "you" partake, only to be remade. And if, as Butler also insists, this dyadic scene is itself interrupted by a wider life of normative claims, what is shared is not only a social and political struggle that concerns the given terms of recognition but also a sociality that irreducibly constrains even as it sustains our being and over which none of us is ever fully in control. As social critics, our ethics give way onto an interrogative politics. The self that is the subject of a claim and demand to account for itself may—indeed must—also ask, "Who are you?" "Who speaks to me?" "To whom do I speak when I speak to you?" (Butler 2005, 134). This gesture may be rendered in several ways, bearing among other valences a sharply critical force; but in its ethical sense and in the mode of generosity, the question gives back the opening residing in the incompletion of address. The nonviolent ethical response returns to the other an acknowledgment and promise of a world shared—that is, a world divided and between us. In this space of freedom, the best gifts—unknowing and exposed—will make of ethics something surprising and unanticipatable, an action that is passion and undergoing and as such goes beyond, even as it begins in, what may be demanded or compelled.

FORGIVING FAILURE

This brings us, however, to the question Butler repeatedly confronts throughout her discussion. Can failure—the failure of the gift to be a pure gift, the failure of the given to fully retain its meaning and integrity, the failure of the "I" to control and dispose of the narrative that is most properly its own—be thought as the site of an ethical disposition, as a relation to language and the other in which the bind of ethical existence (its sustaining and compelling power) lies? Butler's claim that it might be so seen is framed in dispute with the view that a reduction in moral responsibility and accountability occurs in and through the thesis that the "I" is conditioned and produced by normative life, such that the subject is never a pure origin of action, never at the origin of its own story. This thesis, which recurs throughout Butler's oeuvre, has brought familiar charges of moral and political nihilism to her door, as claims that the normatively constituted self lacks agency and accountability. She has addressed the former point by elaborating how the constitutive failure of norms to reproduce themselves "ideally" itself allows for agency, this being conceived as a resignifying practice that is a perpetual potential of the embodied life norms both regulate and are animated by. In this present work, a failure or impossibility is again thematized as the site of possibility, such that we are at once enabled and bound by that which, according to the claim made upon us by a dominant scheme of thought, we disavowed and sought to transcend. Butler's thought on ethics is thus situated in a deconstructive relationship to a normatively "naturalized" model of moral agency and responsibility, one that presumes as ideal the transparency of the self to itself and the ability to assume responsibility for what one is, even if it is acknowledged (as it surely most often is) that such conditions are rarely if ever fully met. From the conventional view, the failure that afflicts our ability to give an account of ourselves—in all the ways that Butler details—limits and disables a responsibility assumed to belong paradigmatically to the subject of a freedom connoting self-origination, mastery, and causal power, and threatened by deterministic or external forces as well as by its own internal weakness. Butler's rearticulation of the meaning of failure turns first around the insight that such a subject is not only fictional, but compelled to disavow its *constitutive* dependency upon and relationality with others; and second, around undoing what underpins this disavowal—a metaphysics that posits freedom precisely as transcendence, and binds disavowal of relation with the individualization of the subject before the law in the figure of autonomy.

It is therefore important to avert an interpretation that might readily be made of Butler's thought on ethics whereby her point about the irreducible dependency of the subject upon a matrix of norms and conventions, or her thought about the constitutive relation to others in which the self is formed, would be taken as indicating that our freedom is always limited or contaminated by elements we should learn to affirm. For her point, I take it, is not that the ways in which we fail to ground ourselves as self-originating subjects of judgment demands a generosity or forgiveness with respect to inevitable failure in a sense that would still remain sustaining of the ideal by which failure is judged; but rather, that the ideal itself must *give way* to modes of thinking and being that it has actively sought to disqualify.

There are remarks in *Giving an Account of Oneself* that might indeed seem to lend themselves to the former interpretation, as when Butler writes that the necessarily partial and failed account of myself that constitutes my final "irresponsibility" is "one for which I may be forgiven only because I could not do otherwise" (Butler 2005, 78–79). Yet forgiveness itself occupies an interesting position in Butler's ethical thought, appearing not simply as that response that might follow on a certain admission of failure but as that which precedes and conditions the terms on which the admission offers itself. Forgiveness seeks not to "allow" for failure but to prevent the very instatement of a self-punitive consciousness premised on a "grandiose notion of the transparent 'I'" (Butler 2005, 80). Forgiveness occurs as a yielding to the other (Butler 2005, 125), as the pledge of ethical life to which I take Butler to allude when she writes, in the closing line of her book, that when we seek to speak from the place in which we are "undone" by the other, vacating our position in the imaginary space of an ideal self-sufficiency, "we will not be irresponsible, or, if we are, we will surely be forgiven" (Butler 2005, 136). The claim here is surely not that to be "undone" by the other—perhaps in the sense of feeling our affective bond to them as determinative for us—somehow guarantees a good faith in our action for which, should what we do prove to have been inadvertently irresponsible, we would deserve forgiveness. Rather, forgiveness anticipates a moment of irresponsibility inseparable from responsibility, in the sense that it anticipates and welcomes the unknowingness that conditions ethical relation as the chance of an opening, of averting the closure of judgmental violence, and thus a chance of "becoming human" (Butler 2005, 136). Similarly, the failure to account for oneself marks the site of an "I" who might forgivingly welcome the alterity interrupting all self-narration, not simply because this cannot be avoided, but as offering the opportunity to reflectively begin again.

It is perhaps worth considering what model is implied here of the kinds of encounter in which the ethical relation to others might not only be undergone but come into question. If Emmanuel Levinas seems to emphasize only the first element of this in his insistence upon one's "persecution" by the other, thereby articulating a fundamental passivity that Butler takes most seriously, Butler also sees and welcomes a validation of critique and exploration as constitutive elements of ethical life, occurring in Foucault's late work on the care of the self. In the essay given here, Butler points to a limitation in Foucault's thought insofar as his account is focused upon the problem, "Who can I be, given the regime of truth that determines ontology for me?"—thus failing to do justice to the way in which a regime of truth can come into question through another, as the desire to recognize or be recognized by someone I encounter. Elsewhere, however, she insists upon the importance of aspects of Foucault's thought that resonate closely with her own insofar as he not only acknowledges a passional life of the self as "recalcitrant to self-reflection and self-making" but elaborates how self-examination takes place "in the form of address to another, after having been addressed (pedagogically) by another" (Butler 2005, 128).

Such self-examination is distinguished from later practices of confession in that it presents a care for oneself—that is, the work of freedom undertaken by one deliberating on matters of comportment in relation to the various possibilities of taking up a socially available set of norms. This contrasts with the internalized and moralized relation to the self as the subject of conscience, who would offer to a confessor secret faults or shameful desires in the hope that the articulation of these "truths" might allow them to be forgiven. Telling the truth about oneself in a sense that assumes the expressive character of this act, its ability to identify what one is, necessarily fails to interrogate the regime of truth in which such an act takes place, thus overlooking the forming of the self even in the act of self-relating that the demand for truth compels. Further, the desire for forgiveness, so construed, situates the other to whom the account is delivered in a position that is first that of judgment, not only demanding but confirming the givens of the self's true nature. Forgiveness in the confessional scene follows on the failure that attends the desiring creature man is, and does so in the mode of judgment and attestation of identity. According to a Foucauldian account of the scene of ethical life, however, the rhetoricity of this situation and the performative constitution of selfhood that it implies comes to the fore. Forgiveness in this other scene anticipates the pain of struggle with the dispossession that "I" am, yet offers its gift only on terms that throw into question the relevance of established terms of judgment and, indeed, works to disable the judgmental relation.

The reflective scene of ethical life is described when Butler writes of how a certain "failure" of full identification with moral norms becomes a condition of possibility for their critical engagement:

> If the "I" is not at one with the moral norms it negotiates, this means only that the subject must deliberate upon these norms, and that part of deliberation will entail a critical understanding of their social genesis and meaning. In this sense, ethical deliberation is bound up with the operation of critique. And critique finds that it cannot go forward without a consideration of how the deliberating subject comes into being and how a deliberating subject might actually live or appropriate a set of norms. Not only does ethics find itself embroiled in the task of social theory, but social theory, if it is to yield nonviolent results, must find a living place for this "I."

Elsewhere—in an essay on Foucault's "What is Critique?"—Butler interprets Foucault as answering that critique is always particular and cannot be generalized: it is always a "critique of some instituted practice, discourse, episteme, institution" and cannot be abstracted from this operation as a generalizable practice. Moreover, the specificity of this response is not captured by the notion of judgment but only by what is itself also a specific practice. In offering a critique, then, we do not stand outside a practice as its external judge; rather, we offer a responding practice. That we respond, indeed, precludes in effect the very possibility of judging; thus, for Foucault, critique is "precisely a practice that not only suspends judgment ... but offers a new practice of values based on that suspension" (Butler 2002b, 212). In discerning the dependency of any practice upon certain constitutive limits, critique frames judgment as a problem; yet the sense of those limits as also constituting an opening is instated in Foucault's appreciation of an ethical practice of response, with the doubled valence of self-making and unmaking. Both these gestures occur in the movement outside an established regime of truth; and both are engaged when the task is not to judge what is good or bad but to bring into relief the very framework of evaluation according to which such judgments might be passed, to discover this practice of values in its specificity, and, in that space of suspension to counterpractice (respond with) a "virtue" inseparable from critique itself.

The "I" of ethics, for reasons that correspond to the reflections above, is the "I" of response before judgment, yet an "I" whose living place is maintained through an operation of critique. The greatest specificity of critique will thus concern the self and its own grounds of intelligibility—"critique is not merely of a given social practice, or a certain horizon of intelligibility within which practices and institutions appear, but critique also implies that I come into question for myself". I risk unrecognizability as I begin to interrogate the holding conditions of my being, asking, "Who are you, demanding of me that I account for myself?" and "What constrains the very possibility of my appearance as a subject—as one who must render an intelligible account?" To pose such questions is to open to critique two scenes, respectively that of address and that of judgment. Butler's faulting of Foucault might now perhaps be more precisely phrased, as turning on his failure to invoke the generous moment of the question "Who are you?"—the moment when, instead of concerning oneself only with the problem of one's own being ("Who can I be?") the opening of address is given back to the other. One might call this the *moment of forgiveness* that would perhaps delineate a specifically ethical gesture within a socially and politically resonant questioning. The failure of self-narration—upon which the bind of ethical existence depends—is here inflected not only by the impossibility of its own integrity, but also by lying irrecoverably between us. Here, neither party can be the judge or the forgiver of the other; rather, a forgiving (or "fore-giving", the space created by the gift preceeding and exceeding exchange) is inscribed in the encounter we share.

This scene of ethical encounter can be understood as nonviolent: first, in the sense that it breaks with the judgmentalism of the morality of conscience, and second—and more precisely—in the sense that in the moment of uptake of the demand for an account the generosity of incompletion is returned. Only in this way can the relation of address be maintained in excess of the moment of judgment. The problem of how a "living relation to norms" is possible, as a chance marked first in the failure of self-accounting, is marked again in the question of how "we let the Other live, since life might be understood as precisely that which exceeds any account we may try to give of it" (Butler 2001, 27). In this scene of desire (a desire, recall, that is constitutive of the self as relational) to want the other to respond to the question "Who are you?" is to want to set in play a question that must remain open, already forgiven only in and as an apprehension of the limits of knowledge: "[S]o if there is, in the question, a desire for recognition, this will be a desire that is under an obligation to keep itself alive as desire, and not to resolve itself through satisfaction" (Butler 2001, 27). Such is the nonviolence of a desire that maintains the space of our difference without resorting to the unforgiving claim to identity—"Oh, now I know who you are"; for with the latter gesture the relation of address gives way to the closure of judgment.

It is perhaps worth remarking, however, that this need not be an unduly cautious encounter, as though to acknowledge the vulnerability of the other were to avoid at all costs imposing anything of oneself upon them. There is a risk in speaking of the limits of knowledge that we start to think of the other's "unknowability" as itself substantial, a space of privacy and self-enclosure with vulnerable boundaries that ethics enjoins us not to violate. To respect the other in this sense might well be conceived as a matter of recognizing the other's "right" to full control over the terms of self-narration. But this would seem to entirely miss the point of Butler's decentering of identity and of the questions she raises about the communicational forms that seek to confirm or certify who we are. A better model, perhaps, is offered by the rare and astonishing conversation, which—unfolding in unpredictable ways, breaching psychophysical integrity, neither aiming at a good nor confirming our identity—leaves us both transformed through the manner in which we have found ourselves exposed.[1]

This is not a comfortable space, though at times, and at best, it may be an exhilarating one. Perhaps it is also the fundamental character of the scene of love—marked not by perspicacity but blindness, not by self-control but enthrallment to the other, not by self-preservation but vulnerability to devastation (Butler 2005, 102). It is not that we have no rights to preserve ourselves against such vulnerability, but only that what moves us to affirm the right already testifies to such being given over to the other as to nullify the full security the right would claim. Here the ethical bind appears as double, as one's right to preserve oneself, which fails and founders on the desire and need of its own undoing—"One seeks to preserve oneself against the injuriousness of the other, but if one were successful at walling oneself off from injury, one would become inhuman" (Butler 2005, 103).

This version of the bind constitutes our ethical predicament, as "impingement is inevitable: there is no 'right' we might assert against this fundamental condition. At the same time, surely we can, and must devise norms to adjudicate between its inevitable and insuperable dimension, on the one hand and its socially contingent and reversible conditions, on the other" (Butler 2005, 107). Thus, we are returned by our ethical bind to a need for judgment. Judgment, however, is framed and ruptured by the scene of address, by the unavoidable insistence that sometimes we must not and sometimes we cannot seek to preserve ourselves—for, as Butler reads Theodor Adorno, and expanding the terms on which she understands *critique*, "our responsibility is not just for the purity of our souls but for the shape of the collectively inhabited world" (Butler 2005, 110).

Likewise, our forgiving failure does not secure the purity of an abstract and idealized subject but appears as an endless questioning and equally endless renewal of the desire that at once sustains us and exposes us to injury.

Unreasonable Interruptions

It is important, then, to see that Butler's ethical thought not only situates a set of preconditions for morality in the relationality and normative dependency of the self but offers a specific critique of the "morality system" that overlays and exploits such conditions in turning both the vulnerability and compulsion at the heart of ethics into a system of violence. Rejecting in Nietzsche's powerful elaboration of the violence of the morality system his tendency to celebrate the aggressive forms of life such morality would claim to restrict, Butler here attempts instead to elaborate a structure of resistance premised on what is revealed in the disavowed testimony of aggression. Her critique of violence is worked around what violence "gives away" of itself, the trace of perpetual vulnerability it reveals. This allows her, contra Nietzsche, to elaborate a more nuanced account of that life that morality "deadens," to imagine how nonviolence might articulate one possibility of response, and to elaborate an image of the self as self-making and exposed to the other, in a sense that renews the promise of its ethical being precisely by refusing the deadlock of its prior ontological inscription as free or determined, master or slave, originary or dependent.

Yet the analysis Nietzsche gives of the force—or rather, genealogically, of the multiple, overlaying, and competing forces—of morality takes Butler a long way before she turns to specify the limit of his critique as unduly restricting the scene of address to "a legal framework in which punishment is threatened as an equivalent injury"—that is, to a constitution of the subject through an address construed only in the mode of judgment, rendering the self morally responsible and legally culpable for a suffering of which it is alleged to be the cause.

In many respects the Nietzschean account of morality frames the nexus of problems Butler addresses here. The subject of responsibility as an isolatable causal agent—one figure of freedom of which he is highly critical—is also, Nietzsche argues, the subject inscribed in a world rendered intelligible to instrumental reason alone, as remarked in the "reduction" of man to "thinking, inferring, reckoning, coordinating cause and effect" (Nietzsche 1969, 84). The instrumentality of such consciousness will thereafter dog the attempt to give an account of the relation to others that does not make them means to egoistic ends or, more subtly, into that which unavoidably threatens the ability to preserve oneself, thus constructing the other as a hostile threat. The demand that we manifest and maintain self-identity (an impossible demand for a temporal being, as Butler remarks) is one that Nietzsche insightfully thematizes as a key requirement of a morality system that thinks of responsibility as requiring the governance of action by an imaginary, atemporal point of stability, the "doer" behind the deed. This is a subject whose existence in time and multiple lineage must necessarily be disavowed; a subject whose ideal of being must be located outside life itself, and thus whose "fallen" and imperfect status inscribes it as ontologically guilty within an economy of infinite retribution. It is in critique of such an account of responsibility that it becomes important to undo this nexus of claims around self-identity and the fundamentally hostile posture such a self is forced to adopt toward the world, a task Butler develops by linking the inherent resistance to self-identity in the subject of any account (its non-narratability), to a relationality that, coming prior to and rupturing all intentionality, might begin in the enthrallment of love not in threat and fear.

So the post-Nietzschean stakes of the problem of accounting for the very possibility of ethical life, on terms other than those offered by the morality system of self-righteous violence, punitive judgment, and bad conscience, might be said to be (1) how to give an account of the relation to the other that is not inherently hostile; (2) how to locate responsibility in its temporal and material inscription and thus beyond the figure of ideal self-identity and stability; and (3) how to think ethics beyond a guilt that "deadens" life. Butler's response to these issues is worked in part around their reframing along lines that pose the subject as a problem for ethics rather than as its ground (Butler 2005, 110). Thus, ethics does not begin in the problem of moving from an egotistic "I" to the world of others; rather, attachment to and immersion in the world of others is primary, and the problem of ethical life will be how to remain true to this, how to negotiate and honor it, how not to perform the violence against oneself and others of disavowing it. Responsibility, likewise, will not require the conceit of a mastering subject, fully transparent to itself; rather, to the extent that I know myself I do so through a practice of critique that fully implicates me in my relations to others and as a being constituted through norms of recognizability. Moreover, the limit of my self-knowing alludes to the preontological space in which the self is formed in radical passivity, attached, claimed, impinged upon, demanded of, elicited, as a responsibility that is unknowing and unfree. Such a conception of responsibility directly resists the effort to think ethics on the basis of a subject who is the cause of injury and must assume the burden of payment for it; for this conception of one who owns her actions is itself formed in resistance to the irreducible vulnerability of a constitutive relationality; on the basis of the idealization it offers, one seeks (and fails) to foreclose the rupture and open-endedness of the self. Butler suggests that if one seeks only to secure one's rights against the other, one finds that, even in the best case—that of their reciprocal granting and respect—something importantly "gratuitous" has been missed: the "given" conditions under which we assume responsibility, our being given over to others whom we did not choose. These conditions are honored best in the nonviolent response of forgiveness, in returning to the other an acknowledgment and promise of a world shared. Thus, to think ethics beyond the frame of a guilt that "deadens" life is precisely to acknowledge an insistent resistance to the primacy of self-preservation in moral life—an ethical resistance to that which would justify me in killing the one through whom my life is threatened; a resistance coming through an interminable vulnerability to which the act of violence itself testifies and which constitutes its ever-present point of failure (Butler 2005, 100).

It is not the case, I think, that Butler aims to resolve this tension fully on the side of a willingness to "undergo violation" as though this could be a prescription or imperative. Her point, rather, is to articulate the space of a dilemma in which we return to the problem of judgment and the question of how to act informed by a deliberation on the space of possibility opened by resisting the compulsion to simply repeat a defensive gesture. If our vulnerability clearly provides apt occasion for making self-preservation the highest goal, it appears also as the sign of a "difficult, intractable, even sometimes unbearable relationality" (Butler 2005, 100); and this, the mark of our inherent sociality, cannot be foresworn but only (and necessarily repeatedly) refused.

Yet, is this the only way in which we might formulate the terms of a nonhostile relation to the other? Immanuel Kant might seem to pose an alternative through his simple prescription that we relate to others as ends in themselves, never as means to our own ends. This formula explicitly refuses instrumentality in the relation to the other and does so through a mode of recognition that posits the equality of autonomous freedom, whether in my own person or in that of another. Yet this account only resolves the problem of the hostile relations of egoistic subjects by figuring the law of impersonal reason as both judge and police of desire. With Kant, a key question for morality becomes the freedom of the subject from that heteronomy of influence that would corrupt a respect for the impartial law of autonomy. Kant's ethics is thus paradigmatic of a thought worked around the ideally self-founding subject of freedom, whose inevitable failure to manifest a perfectly "good will" is anticipated, but figured as the challenge the moral subject must constantly strive to overcome. It is telling here that moral law in Kant's sense produces fear and respect but is wary of love except in the abstract sense of a "love of humanity." Love of the other has no moral value in itself; only love checked by law—only "reasonable" love—can be admitted into morality. Thus, in Kant's ethics, fear and distrust of the particular other to whom we may be bound in ways we cannot ever fully fathom or analyze persists; respect for the other as end, not means, is coupled to a repudiation of all the terms of relation that precede judgment and requires a willing subordination to an infinitely demanding law. It is clear that if, with Kant, we resort to locating each subject of desire before the law we do not undo but only limit in effect—and this, at best—the fundamental presupposition of hostility between individual egos; and this, as Walter Benjamin points out in his "Critique of Violence," will always allow that the relation to the other as end not means can be trumped by the justifiability of violence in the name of self-preservation.

According to Butler's account, such justification might indeed be given but will fail at the point at which it betrays its formalism, its willingness in the name of an unquestioned right of self-preservation to write a blank check for violence; this is the character of a right of self-defense "that, precisely because it achieves a permanent moral justification for retaliation, knows no end and can have no end" (Butler 2005, 101). Butler's point, I take it, is not to rule out a priori the very possibility of justifying self-defense but, to insist that the burden of justification must be assumed in all its weight, as a justification addressed to the particular other that not only anticipates and heeds the other's unanticipatable response but does not know in advance where its conclusion must lie. The question of how to respond to the other's violence remains an open question, one to which we must find rather than presume an answer, thus suspending the compulsion of violence as an act that dictates its own repetition. This suspension of violence testifies to an unreasonable and ambivalent order of love at the scene of self-constitution; on the one side, that "being given over" to the other that precedes the very possibility of judgment; on the other side, that forgiveness that interrupts and refuses every judgment that seeks to strip away the structure and the question of address.

Butler leaves us, then, with no calculus, no obvious means of answering in practice the ethical problems posed by our irredeemable vulnerability; rather, she allows this mode of being its voice of unreasonable interruption. How can the primary vulnerability of our constitution in relations that always precede and exceed ourselves come to be seen not as the constant stumbling block of morality but as the binding place of ethical life? How, in the exposure to violence that we risk here, might we avert immediate recourse to that further and inflationary violence of subjecting all our relations to the force of law? How might reaction pause and take on the burden of opening the space of forgiving? Butler's point, in a sense, is simply that we find ourselves already and inescapably in the bind that requires us to bear the practical responsibility of accepting these as our questions. Nothing is resolved, and so we are compelled to respond, to give account of ourselves to the others we address, at once in our resolve and again in our interminable irresolution.

NOTES

The author wishes to gratefully acknowledge financial support from the Equity and Diversity Unit of Australian National University, which facilitated attending the University of Western Sydney symposium with Judith Butler.

1. Here I draw on Alphonso Lingis's description of conversation (2000, 85–101), discussed further in Jenkins (2002).

CHAPTER 2

Passionately Attached: Academic Subjects of Desire

EVA BENDIX PETERSEN

Monash University

What breach of order is it possible to commit in solitude?

—**Gustave de Beaumont and Alexis de Tocqueville,**
*On the Penitentiary System in the United States
and Its Application in France*

How do discursive constructions take hold—take hold of the body, take hold of desire? And how are certain discursive constructions appropriated while others are discarded, relegated as irrelevant or even as life-threatening? And how is it that these embodied appropriations come to work, and sometimes work quite "affectively"; making us make faces, tap our feet, bob our feet irritably, make us blush, make our hearts beat faster? How do we become passionately attached to particular ideas about who we are; about right and wrong; about good and bad; competent and incompetent? Or, how do these desires come to make *us*? And how is it that some of these passionate attachments become *stubborn* attachments, persistent, enduring, rigidly colonizing the flesh, while others can be more easily exceeded or turned down? How is the desiring subject produced, and how is *desire* done?

In my study on the discursive constitution of "academicity" among Danish and Australian researchers within the social sciences and humanities (Petersen, 2004), I became curious about this—for lack of a more (in)appropriate word—*level* of subjectification. The notion of *academicity* as I have conceptualized and developed it draws directly on Judith Butler's (1990a) concept of performativity, where being/doing the culturally intelligible academic is understood as a citational and reiterative discursive practice within multiple and contradictory power-knowledge relations. I became quite obsessed with Beaumont and Tocqueville's question about the breaches of orders that academics may commit all by themselves; I became interested in these curious cultural beings as subjects of desire and of *certain* desires, and in their both stubborn and flimsy passionate attachments.

In this essay I will ponder Beaumont and Tocqueville's question and explore some ways that Butler helps me consider it in relation to academic subjects of desire. The question is interesting, I think, to link with the concept of *subjectification*. It addresses the tacit performativity of power—indeed, the psychic life of power (Butler, 1997b); it asks questions about the possibility of transgression, and about different forms of transgression; about the operation of the hailing law; about the possibility of desubjectification; and it compels us, or at least researchers like me, to think about particular historical actualizations of desire: how desire emerges and operates, and how it works in the processes of maintaining, policing, or challenging operative constructions of legitimate academicity.

I would like to begin with an event. As Michel Foucault wrote about "eventalization" as a procedure of analysis,

> What do I mean by this term? First of all, a breach of self-evidence. It means making visible a singularity at places where there is a temptation to invoke a historical constant, an immediate anthropological trait, or an obviousness which imposes itself uniformly on all. To show that things "weren't as necessary as all that"; it wasn't as a matter of course that mad people came to be regarded as mentally ill; it wasn't self-evident that

the only thing to be done with a criminal was to lock him up; it wasn't self-evident that the causes of illness were to be sought through the individual examination of bodies; and so on. A breach of self-evidence, of those self-evidences on which our knowledges, acquiescences and practices rest: this is the first theoretico-political function of "eventalization," (Foucault 1991, 76)

Imagine sitting alone in your office at work tapping away on your keyboard (there is, after all, nothing like a bit of phenomenology or, indeed, metaphysics of subject and presence, to get things started). The door is closed or slightly ajar; this is a time and space for writing. You are writing along when suddenly you come to a halt: "Nah, that's too ..." with a frown, perhaps, or a slight tension of the neck muscles. Without finishing the thought, your mind is already working on finding an alternative, something that would not be "too...." Something that would be "more ...," something "not so...." You catch your finger pressing down on the backspace key, deleting, mending the transgression, making space for the more appropriate enactment. How could we think about this activity, this incident, this historical event?

One could see it as an everyday uneventful event for the researching academic—nothing much, nothing big, nothing like the big-picture course review meeting taking place tomorrow where it is to be decided (not in those terms, of course) which of the disciplinary paradigms within the department is to control the teaching of X course for the next couple of years. Or it hardly compares with the meeting you had with the department head yesterday in which he "advised" you, in his words, to "ease your ideological crusade." Nor is it on a par with yet another of the government's stupefying anti-intellectual ventures into performance-based funding. It's hardly a political activity, that slight, trivial movement of the finger.

However, we could also conceptualize the event as nothing short of an awesome historical accomplishment. We might think of it as an operation of those infinitesimal mechanisms of power that Foucault (1980) urges us to look at, where the subject—you, me—enact, serve as vehicles of historically contingent, complex, and microphysical power-knowledge relations. And we could let ourselves be stunned by its breathtaking (political) implications. As Foucault writes, "I don't believe that this question of 'who exercises power?' can be resolved unless that other question 'how does it happen?' is resolved at the same time ... for we know perfectly well that even if we reach the point of designating exactly ... those 'decision-makers,' we will still not really know why and how the decision was made, how it came to be accepted by everybody, and how it is that it hurts a particular category of person, etc." (Foucault 1988, 103–4).

Whatever might have been "too …" about that which prompted reflex edification it constituted something that the subject somehow has come to recognize as, know as, feel as placed *outside* the boundary separating legitimate from illegitimate academic performativity. In that light, the finger on the backspace key could signify that the subject has somehow caught herself in a zone of uninhabitability. She finds herself not getting it right, or not getting it quite right, enacting relative "abjectivity." The abject, as Butler writes, "forms the constitutive outside of the domain of the subject" (1993a, 3); it constitutes the defining limit of the subject's domain ("I would rather die than be that!").

How did it come to this? How did the subject come to know what to let remain in sentences and paragraphs and, indeed, in *academic* sentences and paragraphs, arguments and papers, and what to delete, erase, expunge? How did she come to know/feel that that word, or that phrase/reference/notion/argument, does not belong on this kind of page—or, at least, not on the kind of page that "I," in this context, have come to want to be the author of? "I" have come to desire other words and phrases, and I have come to desire them in a way that makes those Other words look and feel like monsters, monstrosities, or embarrassments—or sins that I can commit all by myself.

Before proceeding with this line of thought it might be worth calling attention to the fact that this essay in a certain sense, and especially given its debt to Foucault, has a fundamental problem; or rather, it enacts an investigation that potentially grounds further some assumptions that need radical historicization. By attempting an analysis of a concrete body of desire, the metaphysics of the subject that Foucault so vehemently attempted to trouble may be reinstalled, further romanticized, reassumed. One would hope, however, that the focus on an *enactment* of desire displaces those problematic assumptions while at the same time insisting on investigating current conditions of subjective being/performativity. As Butler writes, "The temporal paradox of the subject is such that, of necessity, we must lose the perspective of a subject already formed in order to account for our own becoming. That 'becoming' is no simple or continuous affair, but an uneasy practice of repetition and its risks, compelled yet incomplete, wavering on the horizon of social being" (1997b, 30).

Returning to the question of how our subject came to push the backspace key. In *The Subject and Power* (1982), Foucault writes that he has been interested in studying the modes by which human beings, in our culture, are made subjects. He presents the notion of the subject as a subject of power: "There are two meanings of the word subject: subject to someone else by control and dependence, and tied to his own identity by a conscience of self-knowledge. Both meanings suggest a form of power which subjugates and makes subject to" (Foucault 1982, 212).

In *The Psychic Life of Power* Butler (1997b) elaborates on this double movement of power and the paradox of subjectification, where that little *of*, as in "of power," becomes pivotal. She writes,

> Power acts on the subject in at least two ways: first, as what makes the subject possible, the condition of its possibility and its formative occasion, and second, as what is taken up and reiterated in the subject's "own" acting. As a subject *of* power (where "of" connotes both "belonging to" and "wielding"), the subject eclipses the conditions of its own emergence; it eclipses power with power. The conditions not only make possible the subject but enter into the subject's formation. They are made present in the acts of that formation and in the acts of the subject that follow. (14)

Much has happened *prior* to the event in which our subject reaches for the backspace key (with *much* being the most ludicrous understatement ever). Throughout her process of becoming an academic subject—and recognizable to the extent that she is granted a university office designated for academic staff and a computer, and (a ridiculously small amount of) time to "do her research"—she has been subject to, and vehicle for, a myriad of discourses and subject positions (Davies and Harré, 2000). These discourses and positions have been made available to her and she must have appropriated and performed actualizations that were recognized not only as viable but as acceptable enough to deem her relevant enough to endow her with all sorts of symbolic and material arrangements and privileges—such as a strip of aluminium for the office door with her title and name on it—that work to uphold this relevance. Her particular actualizations as a relevant academic subject also consist of simultaneously mastering discourses of culturally intelligible femininity, ethnicity, class belonging, and sexuality—did I forget any of those social categories that we have come to agree *matter*?—including (or not) those particular challenges that the *combination*, or lived intersection, of various social categories may bring about for subjects in an academic context (Petersen 1999; Søndergaard 2005a, 2005b).

The stories that follow are conglomerates of stories that are meant to illustrate some of the dynamics depicted.[1]

Story 1

She kept struggling to get her head around this new perspective. She kept stuffing up in her writing. Her supervisor kept telling her that she was almost there but not quite. Red scribbles all over her text as if it was about to bleed to death. He told her that she kept using words that made him doubt whether she'd really comprehended the theory. Slipping, sliding, slipping, sliding. Her supervisor suggested that she made a list of words *not* to use in her writing and pin it up on the board next to her computer. "Influence" was on the top of the list ("constitute," the desirable substitute, was written in parenthesis after it). "Influence" was wrong, belonged to other people, not us, not me. She wanted to get it right—not to please him, no, but to get it right full stop.

Through initial submission, our backspace-key-pushing subject has become a subject of knowledge, desire, and agency. She has come to know certain things to be "true," she has come to know certain things to be true about herself ("I am this, *this* sort of academic person, not *that* sort"), she has come to desire to do, to master, to know and will certain things—for instance, "the truth"; she has become *passionately attached* to certain ideas about what constitutes "good scholarship," what constitutes a "rigorous academic argument" or a "speculative opinion piece." She has become passionately attached to notions of "competent" or "incompetent" writing, of "precise" or "imprecise" concepts; of "methodological consistency" or "inconsistency." As Butler writes, "In each case, power that first appears as external, pressed upon the subject, pressing the subject into subordination, assumes a psychic form that constitutes the subject's self-identity" (1997b, 2). Our subject can recognize, for example, "patriarchal," "condescending," or "imperialist" academic subject positions, and she can desire not to be recognized as enacting *those* in her writing, as being *that*, monitoring her words and sentences carefully: "Could that construe me as *that*, am I being adequately *not that* here?" She has come to be able to master complex webs of knowledge relations among paradigms, metaphors, books, people, institutions, and titles—all placed in relative hierarchical position to each other—and these knowledges and their complementary discursive rationalities are actively at work in the sentences and paragraphs that she writes and that write her. They are alive in the moments of hesitation—"Is this word me?"—in the fuzzy split second before deleting or writing on, constituting and constituted. In her office, all by herself, she is working and policing the boundaries of the categories *academic* and *myself as this particular kind of academic in this particular context*, and the policing, we could say, the self-regulatory work "precisely because it is a bodily act, is not always 'knowing' about what it says" (Butler 1997a, 141).

So, through years of coming to mastery and agency through submission to discourses she never initially chose but now *can* choose, discard, make objects for reflection, resist or attempt to alter, she has become passionately attached to an intricate and fluid complex of power-knowledge relations with her body (what we have come to know as nervous system, muscles, sweat glands, pulse, etc.) (re)acting as a barometer of transgression, indicating that something is not quite right. Along the way our subject and her body might even have become quite stubbornly attached to the idea that the kind of position she inhabits, the kind of academicity she enacts and shares with others, is a completely legitimate and relevant one. And was someone to maintain that her academic practices and desires were illegitimate, indeed unacademic, she would most likely have come to know *not* to express it in those ways, yet she may feel like spitting at the person in question, or crying, or engaging in other such activities. Her body performing and bearing witness to the passions and desires she has come to consider her own.

Story 2

Her pulse stepped up a pace when she saw the email from the editor. Finally! And yep, there was an attachment there. She read the e-mail ... her mouth dried up. *Ask you to resubmit ... reviewer asks for major revisions....* What, only one reviewer? *Please let us know when to expect ... yours sincerely ...* She opened the attachment. What? A sick feeling in her stomach. What the ... how, how could they say that? Her eyes sped over the lines, ablur in tears, hurt; rage; muscles tightening around her lungs, difficult to breathe.

Taking seriously the passionate attachments involved in subjectification enables an understanding of how exclusion, denigration, and indeed "hate speech"—and academia has its own more or less sophisticated forms of that (Petersen, in press)—can be understood not merely in terms of abstract deprivations of cultural articulation or credibility or as some sort of abstract delegitimization of our subject position and of the position we share with others, but, as Butler suggests (1997a), sometimes quite literally, as blows to the body: painful, paralyzing, debilitating blows; bending the spine, making us lose our footing and our ability to speak. Similarly, more inclusionary positionings may affect the body by affording sensations of solace, jubilance, and pleasure; even—in Barthes's (1975) terms—bliss.

Being a subject *of* power, a subject whose agency depends upon discourses she never chose, how can we make sense of the need, the desire, to amend the violation that the finger on the backspace key could be construed to profess?

The notion of performativity entails that culturally acceptable academicity is not something once achieved and then safely established but, rather, something that requires continual intelligible repetition. While the internationally known, widely published and cited sixty-year-old white male Oxford educated Harvard professor may need to engage in less explicit acts of reassurance than other academics, he is still subject to the conditions of maintaining cultural intelligibility. (Behaving "oddly" over a period of time might not immediately subject him to forces of exclusion, as there are readily available discursive links to be made between the categories *professor* and *odd*, yet were he to engage, and get caught, in multiple cases of severe "academic misconduct"—acts finding their way to that classification and not merely to "odd"—such forces of exclusion and delegitimization could gain force.[2]) Thus, although our backspace-key-pushing subject has been endowed with an office, a title, and a strip of aluminium for the door, she needs to continue to reachieve the recognition as a legitimate and relevant subject in the academic context. As Butler writes, "The subject is compelled to repeat the norms by which it is produced, but that repetition establishes a domain of risk, for if one fails to reinstate the norm 'in the right way,' one becomes subject to further sanction, one feels the prevailing conditions of existence threatened" (1997b, 28). In this light the finger on the backspace key might be read precisely as an act to mend the act of failing to reinstate a certain kind of norm. But where is this "norm" located?

Certainly we could say that the breach of order that our academic caught herself enacting could be felt *in relation to* the possibility of somebody—perhaps significant and institutionally powerful somebodies—catching her not getting it right. Given that she needs to reachieve recognition as culturally intelligible and competent, she does become vulnerable to others, both in an abstract and a corporeal sense (see also

Davies et al. 2001). Every article, every phrase, every lecture, every walk down the hallway, every collegial conversation is a repetition that involves an aspect of risk of social exclusion. In a dramatic sense the "too ..." poses a threat to the continuation of her social existence, her continued viability as an academic subject. Not that one act of transgression, violation or failure would kill her off straight away, but it would most likely be read as a glitch that needs some sort of explanatory or restorative work (she was probably tired; she's not normally one to ...), and if the ogres happen to outshine the non-ogres in her writing, and in her academic performativity more generally—that is, if the associative link between her and the category "competent and relevant" can not be successfully sustained over time—her continued existence in this institutional context will be threatened.

Story 3

She was up for promotion and she had been told that it was almost just a question of paperwork. She had to apply for the associate professorship, though, so that the faculty could officially say that it had been subject to open competition. She was invited to have an interview. At the interview, in front of the dean and everybody, the head of her department said that he was a bit worried about the direction her recent research had taken. It almost sounded like a threat, and they all looked at her, waiting for her to explain, to account for herself. The department head continued, noting that the panel had discussed whether or not her research really fell within the discipline anymore. She panicked—was she in trouble, was she about to lose her job? The department head suggested that in future she got more in line with the core areas and methods of the discipline and make sure not to get lost. They all laughed when he said that, although it wasn't funny. She'd laughed too.

So while there certainly is a vulnerability to the judging other— who can judge and prompt rectification without being physically present—the norm that the "too ... ," if not amended, risks to fail to reinstate has also come to reside *with* our subject herself. As noted, she has become passionately attached to particular forms of practices and values, or they have become attached to her; she has developed a *taste* for some things and a distaste for others, and she has come to know certain things and actions to be in relative alignment with her own desires—thus they more easily get a hook in; she can unproblematically take them up and make them part of her repertoire—and other performances as in relative opposition to, irreconcilable with, her own appropriations, with what and who she "is" and desires to be. Foucault writes, "This form of power applies itself to immediate everyday life which categorizes the individual, marks him by his own individuality, attaches him to his own identity, imposes a law of truth on him which he must recognize and which others have to recognize in him. It is a form of power which makes individuals subjects (1982, 212).

Through her subjectification as an academic subject she has become attached to her own identity; a law of truth has been imposed on her so that she cannot persist as "herself" if she does not amend the transgression of her "own" embodied norm. As Butler states, "To desire the conditions of one's own subordination is thus required to persist as oneself" (1997b, 9). Our subject would not "be her," or be "true to herself," to what she has become; she would not recognize herself as herself if she did not actively regulate her actions (and her actions regulate "her"—and the nonhuman actors such as the backspace key make this particular form of regulation possible as well) to become what she has come to desire to be: all by herself she can risk "herself." The law that she can fail to reinstate is embodied; she continuously interpellates herself—"Hey you there, you are not getting it right, *that* way does not belong to what you do and are." Notably, however, as Butler points out (2001), *accounting* for one's desires—for example, explaining *why* you choose to erase this and keep that in your writing—will not give access to these desires in any prediscursive form or shape. More important, the very discourses, story lines, or metaphors taken up in this process of accounting or explaining or analyzing "oneself" constitute a further formation of that which is said to originate it. Accounting for oneself will always be a further formation of that self, if not an inauguration of that self—and, of course, a further continuation of historically viable/unviable possibilities of and rules for accounting for oneself. In a discussion of memory/Eurydice/knowing oneself, Butler (2004c) complicates both the self-turn and the (historical practice of the) "need" for this self-turn. She writes, "We turned around, needing to know, but it was this need to know, to know with certainty, that undid us, for we could not capture [Eurydice] that way. And when we sought to have her through knowing her, we lost her, since she cannot be had that way" (2004c, 96).

On her journey of subjectification, our subject has also come to understand that one can be more or less "true to one self" (Foucault, 1982), that one can *lie* to oneself, and that it is, above all, desirable to stay true to oneself.[3] As it is continuously repeated, a "worthy" subject is a subject who fares with "integrity," who is rational and noncontra-dictory, and so on and so forth *ad infinitum*, and these constructions are not only prevalent, they are formative, constative. Our subject is desiring and enacting (within) a web of discursive continuities, and one of these discursive continuities—generated, sophisticated, and carried by psychodynamic/folk-psychological thinking and practice—is that the subject must perform herself in ways that others and herself can recognize in terms of some sameness and continuity in the enactment of desire; that is, she is to perform an "identity." It is part of the his-torical requirement of staying culturally and subjectively intelligible. "Such attributions or interpellations, notes Butler, "contribute to that field of discourse and power that orchestrates, delimits, and sustains that which qualifies as 'the human'" (1993a, 8). Those who do not appear to be doing what is recognized as an appropriate form of self-coherence are pathologized if not ostracized, reeling on the boundary between the human and the monstrous. The breach of order com-mitted in solitude can in that way be understood as a transgression of, or a violation of, embodied desires to persist as worthy, relevant and competent—and in alignment with oneself. The death potentially courted dangerously (Butler, 1997b, 28) in the act of transgression is thus both, and simultaneously, a social and an individual death.

Story 4

She went to a meeting about faculty early-career researcher grants. There were five other so-called early-career researchers there. The professor calling the meeting told them that the seed grant was meant to install in them a "generic awareness of grant writing." He was very keen for them to apply, sooner rather than later; it was a way of ensuring continuing funding, he said. He went through the guidelines: Remember to write in font size 10 when it says so, because the committee will always be looking for things to reject you on. Find the hooks; make a compelling case; use that rhetoric. Take a sexy stance; sell it; make them an offer they can't refuse. There was laughter ("we are playing"). There were some questions: a $2000 grant and no, it can't be used for buying out teaching; it's for equip-ment, travel, transcription, that sort of thing. She thought about the amount of time it would take her to put together a (sellable and "sexy") application, and the amount of time it would take her to find an appropriate research assistant, and the amount of time it would take her to get that person into her head space—or even just find that person a desk. There was too much work to be done using time she already had much too little of. An "investment" with no actual "outcomes" for her in terms of the quality of her work, she thought. She raised this concern to the professor: "Tell me why I should spend my time doing this, spend this time that I could use writing a good article." She could hear one of her colleagues sigh deeply, irritated, saying between her teeth but audibly enough, "Oh for God's sake, you're not the only one; you know, we're *all* busy, let's just get on with it." The professor looked at her with some surprise—was it annoyance, or interest? "Well," he said, "It's developmental, it's a requirement, it's part of your job, it's a way to get you on board, to begin a track record, making you more competitive for other grants, increasing productivity—for promotion, ultimately. It's the name of the game." There was no mention of doing good work. As the meeting went along it became clearer and clearer to her: to survive working in present day universities you have to enjoy playing this so-called game—if you enjoy playing and winning it—seeing that "Yes, I can successfully 'jump through the hoops,'" another image tossed around, and, "Yes, I can get on board (and that is just *super*)." You'll survive this, she thought, maybe even enjoy it. If you desire the promotion, and desire getting a track record, desire winning the game (whether grant game or publishing game, really) you'll be right. She felt it—*that* was the person she needed to become. There was no doubt in her mind that she could play that game quite successfully if she wanted to: hook up with some quantoids, mobilize some serious risk discourses, construct gaps and flaws, seduce, seduce, seduce. If she could only want to win, if she could only desire to be promoted, she could be the person they wanted her to be, that she's supposed to be. There was no excitement though, just numbness.

The slight movement of the finger could in that way be said to be an enactment of astounding complexity, a massive whirlpool of historical and subjective possibilities and impossibilities. Much has happened prior to the event and climaxes in that event—*in every event*. However, the pressure of the finger on that button on the keyboard, as subjectification and category boundary work, has a future dimension to it as well. The act, as a single note in an amazing cacophony, enables and constrains future actions and enactments of desire. It participates in the continuation of some discourses, in the possibility of some utterances and subjectivities and, potentially, in the discontinuation of others. The politics involved here are immense.

In this essay I have attempted to illustrate a possible way of running with Foucault and Butler's thoughts on subjects and power; on the psychic, passionate, corporeal, and material life of power. In this attempt I have taken *Homo academicus* (Bourdieu, 1988), this creature who in puzzling and vexing ways at times insists that s/he inhabits a culture of no culture (Traweek, 1988), and caught her in the act of opaque and sweaty desire (beyond the capital-maximizing kind). It is a take-up that insists on the always political and ethical of the nitty-gritty and of historical enactments of passionate attachments.

Notes

I would like to thank Professor Dorte Marie Søndergaard and Dr. Gabrielle O'Flynn for their productive feedback in the preparation of this essay. Also, a warm thank you is due to the reviewers.

1. The stories I have included here have been created from material generated through fieldwork and interviews with Danish and Australian academics in the social sciences and humanities (for elaboration on specific creata-generating endeavors see Petersen 2004). The stories are mostly conglomerates of several stories: fictionalized facts, factionalized fictions. They are meant to vivify some of the dynamics I am attempting to depict. The hope is that an accentuation of their construed nature displaces the troublesome notions of authenticity and pure presence, which seem to continue to be a remarkably persistent methodological desire in the social sciences (see Lather 2000).

2. This notion of the movement of relative inclusionary and exclusionary forces is inspired by Søndergaard (1994).

3. The interesting thing—and where it gets particularly complicated—is that this self one must be true to shifts, can be talked about in different ways, and is subject to contradictory governmental rationalities. In other words, we have come to know that the subject can choose to stay true to the self who wants to keep a job (persist as an eating and rent-paying self), rather than the self who says, "I cannot persist with professional and personal integrity here!"—and such "choices" can be rendered legitimate through mobilizing a number of discursive rationalities.

Found/Wanting and Becoming/Undone: A Response to Eva Bendix Petersen

SHERIDAN LINNELL

University of Western Sydney

So Eva, here you have us, or me at least. My stomach is a little tight as I'm taken, by association with the stories in your essay, into anticipation of a meeting where I will attempt to work out—with my workload supervisor, who is, after all, sympathetic, but who is also caught in a network (a *whirlpool*, did you say?) of contradictory and competing claims—how I might claim the "right" to spend a little of my time on research. I'll attempt to work this out without it impacting on my teaching load or that of my colleagues; without incurring the need to "buy in" teaching because then it has "budget implications"; without—and here's the crunch—destabilizing the delicate balance by which the course in which I teach (a course that trains artists to be psychotherapists, of all things![1]) continues to survive within an environment of increasing pressure to move toward hard science and even harder cash.

And then, too, I wonder what I am doing here at all. How did I come to be one of the ones interpellated by the intricate webs of discourses and practices invoked in your essay? For that matter am I—and

69

if so, *how* am I—called upon by your essay itself? On what ground do I stand, here, given not just the radical groundlessness of being, but far more immediate and pragmatic issues of entitlement, and from where can I respond? Why would I, a clinician, a therapist, and teacher of therapists, a sometimes and would-be poet but surely not an academic, be slinking along these increasingly narrow paths overarched with a tangle of neoliberal jargon and requirements, one path called *candidature*, and another that once was called a *tenured academic position* but is now ominously signposted *ongoing employment*?

Should I reach for the backspace key right now—not just to elide that last metaphor (not a *path*, surely—how hackneyed, what an unreconstructed humanist trope), but to remove myself from a potentially scandalous moment when all my pretensions fall away and I stand here (or maybe sit—that feels a bit better) exposed to you all?

Yet at the moment of writing this I do not stand before you. I am sitting at my computer early one Sunday morning, as Petersen might put it, "all by myself." (The grammatical construction of that phrase rather beautifully suggests a spacialization of *self* and an embodiment of reflexivity, even while the limits of reflexivity are in question here.) I have been trying to work my way toward this precious space and time for writing—not in an office as such, but in a corner of my studio. I am sitting at a long paint-stained bench, with books and two filing cabinets (a locked one for client notes and an unlocked one for teaching and research materials) at one end, paints and brushes and fine art papers at the other, and, in the middle of these, a place for writing. There's a bit of metaphysics of the subject and presence for you, or at least an opportune map of my positionings in between practices of reading, writing, teaching, therapy, and the visual arts.

To what extent do I sit here "all by myself"? Can there be solitude without solicitude (see Atwood and Beaulieu 1998)? And would such a solitude be an unbearable loneliness? In what place am I, who forgets her body sitting before the computer screen and projects an imagined self into an unseen room with high ceilings and long reflecting windows admitting light—a Hegelian room? (Butler 2001)—in the ghostly company of others at once like and unlike myself? In what time am I, who imagines the future scene of disgrace, or who hopes to make some small but meaningful and dignified, even dignifying, contribution to the dialogue that is yet to come? Who is it who works hard to see this opportunity as a conversation perhaps different from—but surely no more significant than—those conversations in her therapy room, but who nevertheless invests the imagined scene with power to do her violence or grant her sanction? And if she, the imagined one, could look back at me sitting here, what might she see? Would her look be deadly? (Butler 2004b). What might she say? Would she ask, "Who are you?" (Butler 2001). And who would be there, who would there be, to reply?

In one sense I am sitting here with Eva Bendix Petersen, or with how I imagine her, because through the structure of the symposium, the request of the convenor, and the urgency and significance of Petersen's essay, I am both formally and ethically obliged to respond to her address. As to what constitutes (because it certainly more than "influences") an appropriate response in this context, the guidelines are clear: I am to "interrogate what is being presented in the essay, with the aim of elucidating, clarifying and extending the ideas presented there." (We in academia have ways of making you talk!) Furthermore, I can "bring in some of my own work and thinking in constructing the reply, but holding in mind the overall task of elaborating what Judith Butler's contribution to thought has been" (Davies 2005b).

That's right, Judith Butler is going to be there. Somehow I've managed to push that into the background. Sorry, Eva, the "I and thou" relation that had somehow survived poststructural critique to this point has just been eclipsed by a greater concern. Is this even imaginable, that "Judith Butler" is not just a series of books and journal articles read and reread in reading groups, lounge chairs, and bed late at night? This is not going to be like reading Michel Foucault, when my first Ph.D. advisor said to me, "You need to put your postmodern methodology out of mind while you look at the object of research— even though I know you don't believe in an object of research, and if Foucault were here in this room he would agree with me," and I quipped, "Well, we can scarcely dig him up to ask him what he'd say, can we?"[2] No. Judith Butler, while she most emphatically deserves recognition—even though she suggests that an act of recognition may not be fully possible (Butler 2001)—does not warrant excavation. She is a real, live person (whatever that means), with a body, a wardrobe, and a life, or maybe several lives. What will she be like? What will she think of all these willy-nilly appropriations and possible distortions of her ideas? Can I tell from her books and essays?

I go back to the first thing of Butler's that I ever read, that most of us ever read—to those opening words about her childhood (I am a therapist, after all): "To make trouble was, within the reigning discourse of my childhood, something one should never do precisely because that would get you in trouble. The rebellion and its reprimand seemed caught up in the same terms, a phenomenon that gave rise to my first critical insight into the subtle ruse of power: the prevailing

law threatened one with trouble, even put one in trouble, all to keep
one out of trouble. Hence I concluded that trouble is inevitable and
the task how best to make it, what best way to be in it" (Butler 1999a,
xxvii).

Great; she's a troublemaker. And reading on, I am reminded that
the kind of trouble she makes or gets herself into is my kind of trouble:
feminine trouble, troubling the feminine, engendering desire, undoing gender, contesting boundaries, that sort of thing.[3] Of course, even
back then she was quick to point out that this childhood story is an
allegorical construction of sorts, although based in memory. And so
are the stories in Petersen's essay and in this response. But as Foucault (2001) might have it, just because everything we write is a fiction
doesn't mean it isn't the truth.

As I browse through her later writings, I notice that Butler is not
especially prone to indulge in personal disclosure, although when she
does it is both salient and memorable,[4] and moreover there is a "presence" of sorts, a "voice" of personal and ethical concern, in her texts.
What will she think, then, of these Antipodean and Scandinavian
habits of storytelling as data (Davies et. al. 1997; Davies, Flemmen,
Gannon, Laws, and Watson 2002; Petersen 2004)? Is it comparable
with the worst excesses of autoethnography (Gannon 2006), or does it
serve a more discursively acceptable purpose?

I come to "giving an account of myself" (Butler 2001). Mmmm;
sounds like Butler has more than a theoretical knowledge of the transference. I wonder if she's done therapy; hasn't everyone in the States?
Here's the bit I've been looking for, about accountability; she writes,
"I would have to say that I can tell the story of my origin and even tell
it again and again, but the story of my origin I tell is not one for which
I am accountable, and it cannot establish my accountability. At least,
let's hope not, since, over wine usually, I tell it in various ways, and the
accounts are not always consistent with each other" (Butler 2001, 26).

Good; let's get through the day as quickly as possible and retreat
from the reflective light of my imagined symposium room into the
plush of a dimly lit bar, where we can drink a bighearted Western Red,
forget about the embarrassments of the day, and tell stories for which,
strictly speaking, none of us can be held accountable.

How can I understand the anxiety that so far has driven the performance (and perhaps in some sense the performativity) of this response?
I could understand it, following Petersen's eloquent and provocative
taking up of Foucault and Butler, as an embodied and citational articulation of passionate attachments: of being passionately attached to an
academicity that in my case has not yet accomplished even the myth

of its achievement, and which moreover will never be fully achieved but must be constantly reiterated, within increasingly unfavorable historical conditions of possibility. I could understand it, following the Foucauldian tendencies of narrative therapy, as an individualized emotional response to modernist prescriptions for failure (White 2002), in which there are a myriad ways to fail at the project of fulfilling one's potential, achieving one's identity, becoming one's authentic self, and so forth, "academicity" being just one of them. I could also understand my anxiety, following varying emphases within psychoanalysis, as a response to the threat of my psychically unacceptable aggressions and longings (Freud 1926), or as a fear of the reiteration of an original separation, violence, or loss (Freud 1995)—hence a precursor to melancholy and, perhaps, to a (more social and mature) state of mourning (Bowlby 1960; Freud 1917). Or I could claim, following Butler, that this last reading does not invalidate the former two, but haunts them from the horizons, gesturing toward an originary vulnerability to the "other," a vulnerability that makes me always and inevitably a subject of both power and desire (see, e.g., Butler 1997c, 2004b).

How does Petersen's subject become "our" subject? How is the quickening pulse, the beating heart, the tapping foot intertwined with our bodies? How does what she, the imaginary subject, feels course through our blood, raise our temperatures, wrench our hearts, lift our spirits? Is this only because we, too, are subjects of academicity? How are we, who are constituted and reconstituted as autonomous, doomed to fail so miserably at this independence? Is it perhaps, as Butler might suggest, because we are always already linked to others through gratitude, through debt, through an embodied connectedness that predates and survives the myriad modern forms of constituting self and knowledge as singular and impregnable? Is our vulnerability a consequence of how we are formed in discourse, how we are obliged to repeatedly perform, each time risking that to which we have become passionately attached? Or are we vulnerable to our formation in discourse because life is precarious, even before our precarious subjectivity is precariously formed and performed? And if these positions are not mutually exclusive, and these questions not fully answerable, what are the ethics associated with such insights? (Butler 1997b, 1997c, 2001, 2004b).

I think of Petersen's essay as vigorously Foucauldian in its insistence on "the always political and ethical of the nitty-gritty and of the historical enactments of passionate attachments." Foucault emphasized that the positivity of contemporary criticism must entail "an historical investigation into the events that have led us to constitute ourselves and recognize ourselves as subjects of what we are doing, thinking and saying." As archaeology, this criticism will "treat the instances of discourse that articulate what we think, say and do as so many historical events." As genealogy, this criticism will "separate out, from the contingency that has made us what we are, the possibility of no longer being, doing, or thinking what we are, do, or think" (Foucault 1997, 315). Petersen takes up those aspects of Butler's work that elaborate and critically engage with Foucault's archaeological and genealogical investigations, aspects that further the possibilities of giving a poststructural account of the fraught processes of the becoming of a subject. Petersen is perhaps less concerned, in this particular investigation, with Butler's critical engagement with the limits of accountability itself. In extending my response into a consideration of the latter, I am cautious of the dangers of falling into yet another metaphysics of the subject or myth of origins. From my practice as a narrative and art therapist, interested in how therapy is itself implicated in the production of abnormal and pathological subjects, I am constantly reminded of just how much that appears either self-evident or mysterious about the processes of subjectification can be painstakingly historicized, narrativized, and thereby made available for question. Nevertheless, I am also interested in how the ethics of accountability and the genre of narrative may themselves shape subjectification, and from what borderlands they may be questioned.

Narrative therapy and psychoanalysis[5]—the main or at least the overt psychological discourses in the different areas in which I work as a therapist and educator—can themselves seem almost mutually exclusive, although there have been some reconciliatory moves (see, e.g., McFayden 1997, White 2004).[6] I find this polarization interesting given that both narrative therapy and psychoanalysis attempt to theorize a decentred subject and to understand the possibilities for subjective and social transformation inherent in this subject's instability. In both narrative and psychoanalytic therapies, *language, relationship,* and *embodiment* are key terms in the constitution and destabilization of the autonomous, self-identical individual.

Something like a Butlerian insight that the reiteration of the subject and of language is both citational and productive of difference (Butler 1997b) informs both narrative and psychoanalytic therapies, but it informs them very differently. Narrative work eschews a consideration of psychodynamics and transference, focusing instead on deconstructions and retellings of and audiences for people's stories in relation to other socially and culturally constructed and embodied/embedded narratives as a site for subjective and social transformation. Psychoanalysis, on the other hand, is concerned with the scene of therapy itself and with the therapeutic relation as a repetition and reparation of that which cannot be directly thought or remembered, cannot directly enter a time-based narrative.

In narrative therapies, the therapist as coauthor engages in a collaborative deconstruction and production of multiple narratives (White 1992; White and Epston 1990). She asks questions that help tease out, from the discursive complexities of the subject's formation in power, distinctions between that subject's constitution through dominant discourses and discursive practices and the subject's taking up of positions and narratives in ways that challenge or exceed dominant prescriptions. In psychoanalytic therapies, the therapist as ally and other makes herself available for projections and allows herself to become implicated, but not absorbed, in a different form of reiteration, whereby a ghostly realm of early connection and loss appears in the present narrative as a transference.

From the perspective of psychoanalysis, I would become obliged to question the kinds of reiterations produced within narrative therapy: to ask if the more active and questioning style of the narrative therapist could be defensive and likely to further the client's defences, if the collaborative position of the narrative therapist promotes an exclusively positive transference and maintains an illusion, and if the generation of a "preferred story" risks a "flight to health" at the expense of self-knowledge. And as a narrative therapist, I become obliged to question the sorts of reiterations produced within psychoanalytic therapies: seeing transference as an effect of a set of technologies of power (White 2000a) that produce the subject of therapy as regressed and resistant and privilege the therapist's knowledge of the shape, if not the content, of what the "patient" cannot, by definition, know. These examples not only highlight the incommensurability of different therapeutic ideas and practices; they also draw attention to the work that subjects do in policing the boundaries of their own and others' subject positions and subjectivities (Davies 2000).

Psychoanalysis, of course, is not somehow magically outside the discursive and narrative construction of knowledge and reality, simply because it posits a formative prehistory to the subject's formation in language. Psychoanalysis cannot be other than yet another story, one with powerful and suspect claims to universality. As Søndergaard (2002) has pointed out, perhaps it is precisely the theoretical and discursive dominance of psychoanalysis that makes its truths seem so self-evident. Moreover, psychoanalysis has the devastating trick of labeling as denial or repression any attempt to critique its truth status. Psychoanalysis is implicated in creating the normal through a production and abjection of the abnormal, and in problematizing instinct and desire, thereby giving rise to an expansion and consolidation of technologies of regulation, normalization, and self-government (Foucault 2003). In my areas of work I have had very good reason, faced with the normative and pathologizing practices of much analytically oriented therapy, to take up—in relation to psychotherapy, psychoanalysis, and my own profession of art psychotherapy—a Foucauldian critique of the repressive hypothesis and of juridicodiscursive power (Foucault 1978).

Similarly, narrative therapy is not, by virtue of taking up the narrative metaphor in its poststructural dimensions of multiplicity and indeterminacy, exempt from a poststructural critique of subjectification. Attempting to bring poststructural research methodology together with narrative therapy has led my colleague Carolyn Williams and myself to raise some questions about just who is the subject of narrative therapy. We suggest that "from a poststructural viewpoint, the privileging of a 'preferred story,' albeit from multiple narrative possibilities, is problematic" and ask if "the self as narrative coherence is the aim of such therapy" (Williams and Linnell 2007, 47). Even though we can see how this critique is anticipated and forestalled by many of the strategies of deconstruction and retelling within narrative therapy, as well as by how narrative therapy is theorized, we feel there remains an important and problematic sense in which narrative practice reconstitutes a predominantly volitional and agential subject, and hence a humanist one. Thinking this further through Butler's intervention, I begin to wonder whether this problem might flow from any therapeutic taking up of narrativity. Clearly *narrative* is not the sole province of narrative therapy: it was after all Anna O, a patient of Joseph Breuer, who first named "the talking cure" (Breuer and Freud 1895). In all therapies we have ways of making you talk, and to talk in ways we are trained to hear. When narrative therapy makes space for the wordless and metaphorical dimensions of the therapeutic encounter (White 1995, 1997, 2000b), it turns toward the liminal and the poetic, and this turn may mark a limit of narrative itself.

My acts, my speech, and my thoughts and feelings as a therapist are, in Butler's terms, citational, and even my sense of myself as an agential subject is itself a citation of predominantly humanist and modernist notions of agency. This suggests a limit not only to my reflexivity as a therapist, but to this response I am currently making—perhaps even a limit to all calls and all responses. I am of course not without the possibility—even the inevitability—of performing that which can be called agency, but is it the agency I think I have, and is it even the agency I unthinkingly assume? When I propose or assume that I can "exercise" even a poststructural version of agency, as perhaps I must propose in order to do my work, am I not already undone?

My effectiveness as subject of whatever order is always somewhat mysterious to me, displaced from intention, played out in layers of histories, memories, relations, and bodies. Having attempted to dethrone the self-identified agency of a phenomenological subject, I cannot rely on the intervention of a critical theory to pull the wool from my eyes. Sovereign theory is as problematic as any other sovereignty. The effect of this realization, as Butler points out, need not be nihilism, paralysis, unbounded relativism, amorality, or despair. Humility, connectedness, and open-endedness might rather be the implications of such radical uncertainty (Butler 2001). And perhaps I cannot even afford to be certain of uncertainty, or grounded in an assuredness of ungroundedness. At the limits of reflexivity I do not so much turn as become the turn itself, that which is always forming through turning toward the other, losing myself at the moment of self-consciousness, finding myself only in that which I must strive to, but cannot, know (Butler 1997c).

Butler's writing not only gives an intellectual account of, but enacts, discursive agency together with an ethics of vulnerability, accountability, and gratitude to the other. Butler's engagement with a Western philosophical tradition, according to her own theories, can be seen as inevitable and citational. Her painstaking reiterations and questionings of philosophical and psychoanalytic narratives produce possibilities of transforming knowledges and the subjectivities they shape. In this regard, following Butler, I think it becomes more difficult to simply take a position of refusing the foundational assumptions of, for example, certain psychoanalytic, Marxist, or humanist writings while appropriating particular concepts from those knowledges into a postmodern lexicon. It becomes also a matter of how, in turning seriously toward such knowledges, our misrecognitions, reiterations, and interpellations, as well as our interrogations, may transform the very terms within which "we" are continually producing and being produced.

There has not been time here to enumerate the numerous ethical practices by which one constitutes oneself as a particular kind of therapist within the broader context of the psy disciplines (Rose, 1998) or to attempt to understand how, like Petersen's subject of academicity, one comes to embody these ethics, let alone to consider the implications of such ethics for those who seek therapy and whom therapy calls into being as its clients. Rather, what might be interesting to consider is the persistence, even in this response, of a desire to be able to give a consistent account of myself.

At times this can even take the form of wanting to bring together divergent theories and practices once and for all into the instrumentality of an approach of which I am the self-identified practitioner. Yet, without arguing for a sloppy eclecticism, I simultaneously know this to be impossible, and to be deeply undesirable, since to form such an approach, worst still a model, would be deadly. Implicit in models of therapy are therapeutic norms that materialize individual pathologies as their "constitutive outside" (see Butler 1993a).

I am, it would seem, strongly inscribed within a narrative approach to therapy, and have taken myself up more passionately within this approach than any other. Yet I could not write the following stories of therapy within narrative therapy's conventions of coauthorship.[7] In this sense the writing of such stories, confabulated from some of my experiences and imaginings as both client and practitioner, may mark a limit in the ethical self-constitution of myself as a narrative therapist:

> She is sitting again in the consulting room at the back of the narrow inner city terrace, recalling the previous session. The white walls of the therapy room had become the hospital bed where her mother, an unmarried mother in the 1950s, had been in labor. She had felt the hush, the shame, the prohibition under which she herself had entered this world. She knows she couldn't possibly have remembered this; it was a physiological and developmental impossibility. And yet she remembers herself remembering, composing herself at that imaginary point of origin, pulling the bits and pieces together into a tentative, stammering confession.

> She is beginning to find words to tell the other how, following their last meeting, an exquisite and tortuous sadness had seeped into the texture of her week, when out of the blue her therapist says, "This is difficult, but I have to stop seeing you. This will be our last session. I'm sorry, but this is not something I could have anticipated." She is shocked of course, stunned into an initial and very awkward silence, but, somewhere almost inaccessible, she is not really surprised. It is a confirmation of something deeply held, though always held at a distance. She becomes solicitous, asks if the therapist is all right—she has noticed the other looking a little pale of late—knowing though that she will get no answer. She asks if this sudden ending applies to everyone the therapist sees or only to her, guessing that it must apply to everyone, and

yet feeling as if it applies only to her. The therapist suggests that she see someone else and tries to give her a list of names. She won't take them, thinking—and recoiling simultaneously from the ugliness of the thought—*Fuck you, don't expect me to say yes just so that you can feel better.* She is feeling huge and distorted, a woman with grossly ballooning arms and legs, a huge distorted belly and head, features stretched into monstrous unrecognizability. She floats toward the ceiling, looking down on the tiny therapist doll, who is mouthing something. She forces herself to hear it: *I wonder if you feel you have been too much for me.* She's back in her chair with a thud, deflated to a dense fiery coil. *Patronizing bitch.* She'd been wondering anyway whether to continue. Where had it got her. She hands over the ninety dollars, thinking how next week she'll be able to buy that new book on Gilles Deleuze that she hadn't been able to afford. As she walks out she's suddenly very sorry; has she been rude, has she made it harder? She wonders fleetingly if the therapist is sick and going to die; touches even more fleetingly on something comforting in that possibility. At the door, she leans toward the therapist and hugs her. Immediately she feels embarrassed, knowing she has breached some code even at the moment when such rules surely should have ceased to concern her. She feels how the other receives her embrace with equanimity, just as one who had practiced forbearance might receive a blow.

She must have this particular color: the red that comes in the tiny metal tube has the viscosity and hue of fresh blood. She spills it onto the white paper, into a white porcelain basin, onto white tiles, a white cotton sheet. There is a clawing inside, the incessant chatter of voices, a rope coiled in her stomach and pulling tight around her throat. She watches one hand take the blade and pull it across the other wrist. At first the line is bloodless like the scar it will leave behind. Then blood wells and spreads, becomes an outpouring. The little metal tube shines like a knife in her hand. At first she bleeds incontinently onto the page, week after week, the flow not so much lessening as finding the contours of a life, her life, running into crevices and gullies and pooling in the bottom of craters. She begins to spread it with the large brush, dragging the red across planes of luminous blues, blending to a purple starved of the oxygen of immediacy but pleasing in its sovereign dignity. Or she pushes it into a wet glistening yellow so that a promise of something begins to rise orange at the far edge of the page. Just behind her there is someone of whom she is barely aware, who slides fresh sheets of paper before her, who keeps the little tube knives full and flowing with lifeblood. And slowly, over months, as the blood is staunched on the page, the words begin to flow out of her and toward this other, in trickles and splashes and outpourings. Sometimes the other seems far from her, inaccessible, and she must try to soothe her hurt through a liberal application of paint. At other times she shrinks in fear or shame from an intrusive presence, retreating into the space of the paper, cupping her hand around the work so the other cannot see. Sometimes they feel so close it is almost unbearable. Their words and their silence flow into an intangible space stretched out between them, a valley, a fold of skin, warm, diffuse, there/here. *No wonder*, she says almost to herself, *no wonder, no wonder.* She whispers this refrain only to herself and wonders how the other can hear it. *No wonder I have felt, no wonder I have done, no wonder I could not....* Her tears drop clear onto a page thick enough to hold them. It's different from the chemical shock when she dabs her fingers in the red paint and takes them carelessly to her mouth, breaching the fiction. Her tears taste like her own blood, her own body, salty but without the red. Excrescence of her own impossible being—on her tongue.

Butler has claimed that her texts are addressed to those of us who are "beside ourselves" with rage, grief, passion, and so on (Butler 2004c). Another trajectory for this response might have been to explicitly take up, alongside or in excess of the notion of being "all by myself," the metaphor of being "beside myself" in order to suggest the displacing/transformative possibilities of affect. And, indeed, I did write these stories of therapy, much as I might paint, draw, or write poetry, in a condition of being "beside myself." Such stories can only be produced, I think, at some kind of juncture of poststructuralism, poetics/aesthetics and a non-normative (or perhaps a differently normative) psychoanalysis (see Butler 2000, 2004a; Ettinger 2004). If my current practice as a narrative therapist meets its limits in accordance with what Butler figures as the limits of narrative itself, perhaps a turn—or in my case, return—to the (im)possibility of psychoanalysis becomes a necessary fiction. In such a (re)turn, I know of course that it, that I, cannot be the same as I was; but then perhaps I have only lost what I never had (Butler 2001, 2004a).

At the limits of narrative coherence, one can perhaps "enact" or "write" (but scarcely "write about") openness to the other. It is this radical vulnerability that institutes/constitutes the psychic and the social as mutually imbricated and also confounds attempts at disembodied, conclusive, or "once and for all" knowledge. While sometimes the exigencies of therapeutic practice (as of any practice) demand that one "take a position," at least within certain contexts at certain times, therapy, like writing, is at best experimentation and performance, earnestly and playfully pursuing the fiction of truth while tolerating and even embracing indeterminacy and uncertainty. And writing, like therapy, is incomplete, faulty, fragile, dangerous, longing to love and to be loved, given over to the other, forever opening on "an other" possibility.

While this response has wandered from its starting point in Petersen's essay, I am still, at least in part, that subject she invites me to consider, sitting at my computer. I am tapping the keys, although there is no one key to be found, and pressing the backspace key, although what I try to elide may return anyway to haunt my attempts at "making sense." This is a subjectivity at once solitary and social. I am producing a text to which I am inevitably attached, and which I am also tempted to disavow. This text bears relation to and produces, but also exceeds and is discontinuous with, a biographical "self" to which I am also attached, also inclined to disavow. I address a "you" to whom I am somehow indebted, accountable, and vulnerable, but whom I cannot fully know. Perhaps Butler's work, in its insistent risking of itself through turning toward the other, its persistent dissolving of the binary of the psychic and the social, might provide me with a way of eating my words and having them too.

POSTSCRIPT

I hope that an ongoing engagement with Butler's thought will continue to inspire questions about how such binaries are created/reproduced, how regimes of power are thereby produced and maintained, and how I and others might think/feel/act/write beyond these.[8] In practice, this could mean embracing and researching the contradictions that continually emerge from multiple positionings: in the academy, the community sector, the arts, and independent practice; as a writer, student, researcher, supervisor, and educator; and as a practitioner within two apparently conflicting approaches to therapy. It could mean continuing to participate in, draw sustenance from, and contribute to communities of "like-minded" people while refusing to let collective preferences set into unquestioned norms. It could mean acknowledging and finding a sustainable relationship to discomforts and anxieties about acceptance and "belonging" that arise when practicing "immanent critique" (Butler 1999c, vii) within communities of shared concern (see Madigan and Epston 1995). It could mean finding ways to express thought in the process of its becoming, without resting in certainty. It could mean finding ways to act, individually and collectively, not in spite of, but with a sense of the necessary partiality/limits of knowledge and the vulnerability/opacity of subjectivities.

In these tentative ways, and in other ways I have yet to even imagine, I would hope to pursue a question that arose in conversation with other symposium participants at the margins of the formal event. We found ourselves asking, "Are the ethics expressed in *Precarious Life* (Butler 2004b), and elsewhere in Butler's writings, liveable?"[9] In one sense this is a nonquestion, since these ethics live, and are lived out, in the Butlerian text, and in infinite readings thereof. Yet the question also bears the urgency of our intentions, desires, and strivings for a more just and inclusive world at a moment of great injustices and exclusions. We can hope that our various contributions to this symposium and to the book arising from it, and the specific ways we take the knowledges so produced into ourselves, our communities, and all the different dimensions of our lives, may constitute a provisional response to this question.

In my specific areas of art therapy and narrative therapy, Butler's work assists me toward rigorously attentive readings of the theoretical antecedents, histories and current praxes of these therapies, so that critique arises out of close intellectual and ethical engagement. Her work makes it possible for me to regard my experience of a partial "standoff" between these different traditions and practices of therapy as testimony to deeply held convictions on both "sides," and as a specific instance of the effects and ongoing production of a binary of the psychic and the social. In its appreciation of the significance and limits of narrativity, Butler's work creates further ground for both the theory and practice of narrative therapy while offering a poststructural critique of its limits. To me, this kind of critique is crucial in sustaining narrative therapeutic practice as a form of enquiry rather than allowing it to solidify into received knowledge. Meanwhile, Butler's close questioning and "re-visioning" of the founding myths of psychoanalysis assist me to reconsider my ambivalent relationship to this tradition. It becomes possible to maintain a Foucauldian critique of how psychoanalytic discourse and practice enables normalizing power while simultaneously drawing upon the critical potential of psychoanalysis in order to trouble the figure of a self-identical, self-reflexive, and autonomous subject.

The discursive subject of narrative therapy appears far less at odds with the psychoanalytic subject from a perspective that analyzes the intricate mutual constitution of social and psychic realms and acknowledges intrapsychic suffering as an effect of power (Butler, 1997c). The deconstructive questioning associated with narrative therapy can make this mutual constitution and these effects of power available to the therapeutic conversation, at the same time that psychoanalytic and art psychotherapeutic practices provide space for the eruption, intensification, and containment of emotions and memories that appear "out of time." Although different therapeutic practices invite different narratives of self, and what is available to be "storied" changes across time and context, there is arguably always an excess to that which can be storied. Failure to recognize this implicates therapy in the reconstitution of the autonomous subject of rationality.

Although I do not have an answer to the specific question of how Butler's work might inform a dissolution of the apparent opposition of narrative therapies and art psychotherapy, the question invites me into some useful thought, not only in relation to the specific discourses and practices of therapy, but as to whether or not an ontology of the subject, albeit fictional, is necessary to a poststructural project of subjective and social transformation. Rather than attempting to reconcile art psychotherapy and narrative practice, I believe it is more a matter of allowing the tensions between these approaches (and the philosophies and histories that [in]form them) to play themselves out through specific instances of my work, through my writing, my art making, my therapeutic practice, my relationships with others, even in my embodied and psychic sense of who, and for whom, I might be. I would suggest the task is not to choose between or force a resolution of contradictions, but to experiment with what might arise from a refusal to foreclose on the radical and transformative possibilities of either/both.

I have belatedly noticed an irony in having originally ended this response with a conclusion, albeit a tentative and cryptic one. Such a rhetorical strategy might close down the ethical resources that inhere in unknowability,[10] thereby reconstituting the very binary I wish to challenge. The point at which the binary of the psychic and the social might dissolve and a "re-visioned" humanity become fully imaginable and possible is inevitably deferred, located in uncertain futures, and troubled by future uncertainties. And while it may be more useful to engage with the ethics of uncertainty as ongoing orientation and practice rather than as progress toward an end, any account of such an ethics is always, in its own terms, bound to be flawed and partial.

To "eat my words" is to taste the visceral pleasures of writing and speaking: to experiment, to blurt out an address to the other, to get it "wrong" and to take it back; to find sustenance in humility; to be—paradoxically—intellectually and ethically "nourished" by the inevitability of producing a partial and flawed account; to "have my words." But are my words ever my words? Do I have them, or do they have me? Nevertheless, to continue to respond, to speak, to write toward an ethics (of therapy, of writing itself) based in unknowingness, indebtedness, and vulnerability to the other—an ethics particularly inspired by Butler's intellectual work. And yet, who is "Judith Butler"? How can she "provide" me with anything? (She can incite me, excite me, perhaps—but *provide*?) As Butler herself has asked, "What am I calling on her to be? And how does she take up that call?" (2001, 33).

NOTES

I wish to thank Peter Bansel for reading, listening and "responding" to this response in draft, and to Bronwyn Davies for her feedback on the penultimate version.

1. For an influential introduction to art psychotherapy, see Case and Dalley (1992).
2. Of course, this is a relatively easy story to tell—even something of a "set piece." In fairness, given the trajectory of this essay, I should also tell how this same supervisor suggested that I would not be able to do without psychoanalysis!
3. In the 1999 edition of Butler's *Gender Trouble*, from which I have quoted here, the original 1990 preface containing these words was preceded by a new preface that reflected on the life of the earlier text and situated the book as a form of immanent critique that sought to promote more inclusive forms of feminist theory. This, then, is a particular type of "trouble" made in the service of expanding the possibilities of feminist theory, of social worlds, and, indeed, the categories of who and what can be regarded as "human."
4. For example, Butler partly locates her insistence on the "negative" and on survival as "simply what happens when a Jewish girl with a Holocaustal psychic legacy sits down to read philosophy at an early age, especially when she turns to philosophy from violent circumstances" (Butler 2004c: 195).
5. The narrative therapies referenced in this essay are those influenced predominantly by poststructuralism, textual theory, Batesonian family therapies and the interpretative, narrative, and performative turns in ethnography (see Williams and Linnell 2007), rather than by a theory of social construction. I have also chosen to write about art psychotherapy

rather than art therapy more broadly, although it has been persuasively argued that approaches to art therapy from humanistic, systemic, social constructionist, and behavioural frameworks also assume a notion of "the unconscious" (see Gilroy, 1997).

6. The apparent incommensurability of narrative therapy and psychoanalytic therapy has antecedents in the relationship of family therapy and psychoanalysis, and in associated disputes as to whether the individual or the family/social unit is the most effective and appropriate focus for therapy. McFayden (1997) suggests that the narrative turn in family therapy, toward a position of nondirectiveness and uncertainty and away from a focus on intervening in the family system, could herald a rapprochement with psychoanalysis. White (2004) draws on the alternative Jamesian tradition in psychoanalysis, and specifically the work of Russell Meares, in a discussion of narrative therapy in relation to the subjective effects of trauma, suggesting that there can be shared sentiments although divergent practices amongst practitioners from these different therapeutic traditions.

7. I did, however, write these stories in a manner that I hope is consistent with the ethical considerations usually followed in narrative therapeutic practice. I have drawn substantially on my memories of having been a patient in psychoanalytic therapy—a situation that I believe *produced* certain effects of transference—and also more generally upon my work with people who have experienced severe childhood trauma. The stories are fictionalized, but in the very few instances where it became apparent to me that I had drawn details directly from my work as a therapist, I either deleted that detail or negotiated closely with the relevant person as to whether and how I might include this material in the essay.

8. My mother once cautioned me not to explain my own jokes, but in this instance I am called upon to do so. This call comes from a reviewer to whom I am indebted for challenging me to elaborate upon the original concluding statement of my symposium essay. I would also like to acknowledge Bronwyn Davies's editorial suggestion that I respond to this request in relation to my contradictory positioning(s) between narrative therapy and art psychotherapy and with particular regard to how Butler's work might inform a dissolution of this apparent opposition.

9. This could be a "companion" problem to one raised throughout the symposium—that of "translatability" between disciplinary areas. I think such problems highlight a further and sometimes unhelpful binary: that of philosophical thought and its "application."

10. Butler expresses a concern with "the way in which narrative coherence may foreclose upon an ethical resource, namely, an acceptance of the limits of knowability in oneself and others" (2001, 34).

Conversation with Judith Butler II

Judith Butler: I'm struck, listening to both of you, about the possibilities that emerge from experimentation, and I'm also struck by the fact that Eva's work, this particular essay, is itself experimental. It doesn't push the backspace button; it does something else. It continues to write and continues to write about the possibility of pushing the backspace, and it may well be that the author pushed that backspace at some points, but we have no way of knowing. We don't know because what's erased is not explicitly set under erasure, but perhaps Eva writes through or against the backspace to talk about what it is to sit there, to handle that door, to take account of that life that has, at least in part, been made through a certain compliance with scholarly norms. Obviously we have noncompliance as well, because we have the paper, and that constitutes a completed act of some kind. We have in the paper an actual enactment of a compliance/noncompliance and then we are asked to consider whether it complies or does not comply with academic standards, and whether it would be publishable. Of course, it could get published (and doubtless will in the proceedings of this event), but does one get a so-called *point* according to the Australian research standards for this kind of published essay?

It seems to me that there's a fabulous contradiction at the heart of academic work—on the one hand, the best thing that could possibly be said about anybody's work is that it's innovative, that it sets a new standard, it's unprecedented, it's original and hasn't been done before. On the other hand,

I don't know about your points system is, but it seems to require that you write in ways that conform to already established norms and meet certain standards of peer review. So how is one supposed to get a point for being innovative, for revising or challenging those norms? [*Laughter.*] And hey, who is getting points for this conversation anyway?

Seriously, the problem, of course, is that the very same work that's lauded in some circles as innovative, unprecedented, and groundbreaking can be dismissed as impossible, unacceptable, inappropriate, excessive, and noncompliant in others, and sometimes within the same breath: *We would love to give you this job, we think the world of you, you impressed us with your originality, and we really couldn't bring ourselves to give you this job because what would we have said to the dean and how would that have looked to the committees that oversee the department? and thank you very much.* I was once denied a job on the most wonderful basis. They said, "We tried to consider you for this job but we could find no category under which to assess you." It was a great moment. "Thank you," I said, "thank you, this is a gift." There was no category into which I fit. That was a reason for not giving me a job, but, of course, it could have been a reason *for* giving me a job; it could have been a reason for lauding or not lauding—it could be both at once.

But it does strike me that this question of working with and against the policing function of academic norms— doubting oneself, tempting the limits, risking the limits—is posed in the context of experimentation. We might even see experimentation as a way of operating both with and against, through and beyond the norms. The *work* is in many ways a function of its reception. Depending on how it's worked, how it's delivered, for whom and in what context, it can turn out to be compliant or noncompliant, or both at once; it can change, it can maintain both of those valences, it can take on one valance over time and another in another time. So it seems to me that the academic training to which Eva refers doesn't just require a continual repetition, but also gives rise to a repetition that is a kind of experimentation, one that is knowing about the norms, even if not strictly obedient. After all, you don't suddenly abandon your training at the moment in which you question that training through experimental means; that training becomes a topic for you, a challenge, but it also becomes that through which you work. In other words, I'm not sure you could have produced this experimental piece without the training, without a firm grasp of the norms that you are trying to sidestep or question.

So I would caution against typologies here. Rather than distinguishing between work that is considered normative and other kinds of work that breaches the norm, it may help us to understand that the norm requires and produces the breach, that it actually *needs* the breach, since it could not renew its police function without the breach. It needs the undisciplined, unruly, noncompliant, the figure of the noncompliant, unruly piece of work in order to shore up and manage its own boundaries. This can be seen as well in the paradoxical logic by which it valorizes original work that breaks with existing norms at the same time that it degrades such work. It can't always give an account of why it valorizes one and degrades the other or why it valorizes the exact same thing that it also degrades. So perhaps I would stay away from typologies and think more about how the norm and its breach work together, and also how those who breach the norm require the norm as well in order to establish their radicalism. Where would you be without your *Homo academicus*? Would you be motivated to write your work? Your *Homo academicus* is a figure that goads you, excites you, motivates you, it …

Eva Bendix Petersen: It vexes me.

Judith Butler: It vexes you. You hate it, but at the same time you're passionately attached, and there is something in that that needs to be pondered. I very much like Sheridan's question, What am I doing here at all? I think that's a great question and we should all be asking it at this moment.

I also had the following idea—the way in which disgrace haunts these issues. Will I disgrace myself? *Have* I disgraced myself? An anticipation of a nonsurvivable social shame can haunt certain notions of academic performance; emerging through disgrace or emerging through the specter of disgrace is actually crucial in order to do critical work. One can't allow oneself to be bullied, policed by the conjectured or actual authority; and even though one is quite certain that one won't survive, one has to go through it and survive anyway. We might read this anticipation of shame in how the speculative and the conditional work in both Eva's writing and Sheridan's response. There's a lot of conjecture—what if it's this way? What if it's that way? We could ask here, How does conjecture actually provide a way to move to the side of the more dire situation in which one blindly cites authoritative practice, motivated by our fear of disgrace?

I'm interested as well in the question of narrative therapy that Sheridan proposes. I'm wondering why psychoanalysis almost always takes place in a bounded room with a closed door and how the spatiality of its scene, its conduct, produces a different kind of possibility for relationality than narrative does. Narrative is a temporal mode, and the office is also emphatically spatial. How does the bounded space work to produce a possibility for a certain kind of narrative even as the space itself is not primarily a narrative structure? It is the space for a certain speaking or a certain telling, and that speaking and telling may or may not be narrative in kind. If the space functions analytically along the lines of a Winicottian holding environment, then, the literal space of the room can function as a kind of psychic boundary, externally positioned and elaborated. The spatial holding, which would have to be elaborated in the transference and countertransference, would be the occasion for a certain psychic restructuring, and the analysand would, as it were, begin to carry the space internally at some point. That would be an example of how the psyche is formed through a spatially bounded relationality.

So I wondered about the way both of you grounded yourselves in talking about the space of writing, which is another kind of space, but still one that acknowledges something about the spatial conditions of a certain psychic transformation. I'm not sure what to make of that, but it seems important for considering what the conditions are for experimentation in writing. At the end of Sheridan's remarks, I was struck by the freedom she gives herself to move from one scene to the next: the whiteness of blood, the bleeding onto the page, the way in which bleeding and writing become really crucially intermixed there. There's no backspace key when we're talking about bleeding onto the page, although surely it's edited. It's not a purely immediate outwash but it somehow isn't thwarted by the backspace, if by that we mean the more paralyzing prohibitions of the academic norm. I presume that editing itself is not the problem, but rather the superegoic seizure of the editing function. My question, then, regards what kind of editing allows for the kind of writing that Sheridan gives us, given how it is beautifully crafted and hence edited, yet not superegoically expunged in a way that we might fear from the *Homo academicus* who appears in Eva's paper.

And just a final question of whether *Homo academicus* actually exists. I mean, you refer briefly to the sixty-year-old Harvard professor, Oxford trained—I don't know, does this person exist?

Eva Bendix Petersen: No.

Judith Butler: Okay, I just wanted to check. [*Laughter.*] Because if we accept that *Homo academicus* doesn't exist, that it's never fully or finally embodied, then there's a certain failure of embodiment across the board. I'm not sure anyone embodies the norm, or when they imagine they do, or are imagined to embody it, whether it can ever happen without a rather severe cost.

Eva Bendix Petersen: When we're in a situation where we call into question something, or when we're in a moment of transgression, what we are also doing is calling into question the degree of intelligibility, right? And so when we're verging on the social death, instead of only thinking about it as surviving social death in terms of compliance, we are also negotiating for, maybe, another grid of intelligibility and can push through to there, right? I'm thinking about *Gender Trouble*, you know, and I think of that as pushy, it's always pushy going the other way, and also in my own work when we talk about experimentation, the fact is that I actually do like the disgrace and committing the sin, also in public, in order to attempt to push the grid of intelligibility, right? So I actually caught myself a little bit by surprise having written a fairly conservative subject into existence and a compliant subject into existence.

Judith Butler: Well I think that's literally what happens in the paper because the paper enacts an experimentation that defies the thesis.

Eva Bendix Petersen: Yeah and I suppose that—but that was the idea, trying to get the paper to enact something.

David McInnes: I wondered whether Sheridan would respond to what Judith had to say about Winnicott, because I liked that a lot and you were nodding vigorously at that point.

Sheridan Linnell: The reason I was nodding vigorously at that point is that, in writing this response, which I'm very thankful to Eva for giving me the opportunity to do, I felt like I was writing my way back toward a more psychoanalytic position in relation to therapy. It crystallized something for me when Judith talked about Winnicott and the holding space of therapy. Narrative therapy contradicts just about everything that's taken for granted within traditional psychotherapy, including notions such as containment and holding, boundaries of time and place, and it vigorously attempts to decenter the position of the therapist. But in doing so, narrative therapy tends to relegate any kind of notion of an inner world, an intrapsychic space, to a very low level of consideration. Yet it seems to me that, as Judith seems to be saying, there's something non-narrativizable within the spatialization of self and other within a therapy room. In art psychotherapy you have the production of an artwork as a space for projection and you have that artwork being made in the space between two people; you have a regularity of time, you have regularity of place—or at least that is something you aspire to. It's as though you aspire to an embodiment of something symbolic, which then becomes symbolic again. And somehow having this metaphor of a holding space and a holding relationship is what, in a paradoxical way, enables people to move out from all kinds of tortures within themselves and to move toward another. So I'm coming more and more to appreciate and take up again some of those traditional positions within therapy.

Some of what I wrote about, that ended up in footnotes to my response, is the kind of policing that goes on within styles of therapy. A practice that is considered a preferred practice within one approach could actually have you disciplined within another. For instance, narrative therapists have developed certain practices of self-disclosure, as one way to displace the expert position of a therapist. If you do that within psychoanalysis, that's regarded as being extremely incontinent and inappropriate—as acting out rather than understanding the countertransference. Then in narrative therapy, if you use a word like *transference* or *countertransference*, people immediately exclude you from the notion of what it is to be a narrative therapist. And of course these ideas and practices become part of the ethical self constitution of therapists. There's something in this that relates to Eva's phrase "all by myself." I saw that phrase as capturing some kind of spatialization of self, too, a spatialization of self that makes possible an embodiment of *reflexivity*.

Very powerful regulatory divisions keep the social and the psychic separate within therapy practice. This is getting difficult for me because I work with both art therapists and narrative therapists, and I'm getting more and more interested in how I can break down some of the boundaries between narrative therapy and psychoanalysis. Some of my response was quite hard to write because there'd be moments when I was writing something that just wasn't identical with myself, or at least with myself as I am known within the narrative therapy community. I've been experimenting with bringing these things out in conversations with other therapists, and some people just look at me as though I've lost it, you know, I've gone somewhere different, I've gone over some edge.

CHAPTER 3

Sissy-Boy Melancholy and the Educational Possibilities of Incoherence

DAVID MCINNES

University of Western Sydney

This essay draws on Judith Butler's potent analysis of melancholy gender and refused identification (1997a, 132–66) in an examination of some Australian academic literature concerning masculinities. Substantial attention is given to the work of R. W. Connell because certain aspects of Connell's work have been used to shape a *pedagogical discourse of masculinities,* which is a *recontextualizing* discourse (after Bernstein 1996) generated by academic research about the experience of young men and boys in schools. This essay offers a critical conceptual analysis of aspects of this recontextualizing discourse. Further attention will be paid to the work of Wayne Martino, a major contributor to the discourse of masculinities. As a *pedagogical* discourse, the discourse of masculinities seeks to provide insights for educational intervention. Like Connell and others working from their positions as educational researchers, Martino's work has developed great authority and offers educational imperatives for school-based work (see Martino, Lingard, and Mills 2004 or Martino and Pallotta-Chiarolli 2001, 2003 for recent iterations of the discourse of masculinities and its educational imperatives).

Throughout this essay, I work within the terrain opened by Butler in *Gender Trouble* when she argues for the suspension of the "facticity" of the body (1990c, 129). I will accentuate the discursive production of the "natural" alignments between biological sex and gender. Enhancing and elaborating on the discursive production of gender in *The Psychic Life of Power*, Butler (1997c) contends that gender, as an "uncertain accomplishment" composed in part by a disavowed grief for same-sex desire, is constituted through melancholy. She proposes differences in the melancholic responses possible in excess of the most resolved kind demanded by heterosexuality. These less-than-successful forms of melancholic response permit different kinds of identity "resolutions." Further, differences in melancholic response open disruptive potentials because less resolved responses unsettle the fiction of normative gender, identity coherence and, therefore, can work to destabilize the underpinnings of such fictions. In what follows, melancholy, as metaphor and analytic/descriptive device, appears useful in arguing with the reality-sustaining effect of the discourse of masculinities. A critique of this discourse as a melancholic turning also offers insight toward ethical alternatives for both educational researchers and for educational intervention. Additionally useful and woven into this essay is Alexander Garcia Düttmann's (2000) analysis of the presumptive process of naming.

* * *

Marco stands 5 meters back from the top of the pitch. He hates this part. He has to run up and pitch the ball. Oh, well, here he goes....

It's over and it was a blur of nerves and uncontrolled movement. "Fucking sissy!" the batsman at his end of the pitch says. The teacher, acting as umpire, snickers, stops himself, and then declares, "No ball." Marco has to pitch again.[1]

Sissy boy is a nomination I use as an entry point into the analysis of gender and sexuality for young men and boys in school contexts

(McInnes 2002, McInnes and Couch 2004). I am not suggesting that *sissy boys*, or "boys who act like girls," constitutes a stable category; I am focusing on the iterative process of recognition/naming that constitutes gendered "others." Eric Rofes (1995, 79) provides a useful description of the sissy boy based on his own experience. The sissy boy is the boy at school who has a "gentle and sweet" voice, who "avoid[s] sports and all roughness" and who plays with girls. He cries a lot when he gets hurt, he can't throw a ball, and sometimes he likes to put on girls' clothing. This is a static description—it describes a type of boy based on attributes and behaviors. Rather than identifying the sissy boy as a type of boy, I ask the reader to join me in troubling the tension involved in the semiotic violence of recognizing the sissy. Troubling this moment of wounding involves paying attention to this semiotic violence and highlights the ethical potential within moments when a boy is declared "other" because he does not conform to gender norms.

How might a sissy boy become a sissy boy? It is not simply or easily about his quality of being girl-like. He becomes a sissy through processes of recognition and witness, processes that rely not only on social structures and discourses of gender but are (and *must be*, if they are to be effective) produced through complex social processes involving what boys do, what other people say about them and do in response to them, and how others bear witness to these sayings and doings. Marco is "othered" on the basis of perceived gender nonconformity. His performance of gender (how he acts, talks, walks, dresses, etc.) is problematic (because he has a "male" body, he should be boylike) and is used, as his fellow student does, as the basis of hate speech.

The moment recounted above is usefully considered a moment of recognition: Marco is recognized as "other" by the declaration *and* his status as "sissy," which is brought into being by the declaration from his fellow student. This is one axis of recognition that moves from what is understood to be the "authentic" form of the masculine to the "other"—the disordered, the problematic. The effect for the declarer is that, in declaring the other as disordered, incoherent, as not making the right kind of sense of a body/gender alignment, the declarer's position as masculine is reestablished, shored up as the coherent and ordered form of masculinity.

In addition to this authentic-to-other axis of recognition, there is also an axis of recognition that is produced by "witnesses"—that is, those who authenticate the "speakability" of the declaration by being witness to it. In this example, teachers and fellow students would be witness to the declaration. The declaration is made possible by citation; the declaration "fucking sissy" draws down and offers up into this moment the normative violence of gender, enacting assumptions about gender and body alignments. Declarers and witnesses comply with this iteration, leaving governing gender norms unquestioned and, therefore, apparently stable.[2]

What of Marco's recognition of himself? In the experience of being othered by a declaration such as this there is an experience of shame, of having one's interest in social connection and interaction thwarted because one doesn't fit the norm. This turns the declared back onto himself, and attenuates his interest. What Marco can do and/or wants to do in response to this may range across acceptance to hostility, to acting up or out, to quietly or more loudly producing over time a more "authentic" gender performance so as not to be shamed in this way. Marco may use another form of power, such as academic capacity or computer skill, to establish himself in a different but valuable way. There are, of course, many options besides these that could exploit the complex discursive territory of a sports field, classroom, or school. Elsewhere, I have outlined an account of the epistemophilic response to sissy boy hate speech and shame (McInnes and Couch 2004). Rather than considering what might be done to move from this process of shameful othering, we can consider what might be available for ethical response *at the moment of recognition*.

The matrix of declarations and witness explored here can be described as a *circuit of recognition*: declarer, declared, and witness are all involved in processes of self- and other recognition, enabled and constrained by the discursive possibilities offered by institutions and sociocultural context. At the moment of declaration and witness described there is, as always, a process of foreclosure that both threatens and makes possible the subject (Butler 1997b, 134–36): Marco is made recognizable by the declaration, but how he is recognized is foreclosed and foreclosing. If he goes on to experience further such declarations, he is likely to become the school "sissy." This provides Marco and others a way to know Marco, a category through which a restricted sense can be made of who or what Marco is.

Adding "girlness" (sissy) to "boyness" (boy) in the noun phrase *sissy boy*, and thereby attempting to link femininity with masculinity, underscores the "problem" or "disorder" being recognized and managed. There is a semiotic tension at work in all declarations.[3] Sustaining rather than foreclosing this tension offers the possibility of disruption. So, let's not assume that any 'boy' necessarily embodies or performs a kind of masculinity and, more dangerously, maybe we can suspend our belief in the category *boy*. What are we left with? Perhaps unknowingness, a moment when things don't cohere around bodies and make any "gender" sense. Perhaps we are left with noticing that in doing the semiotic violence of declaring Marco a "fucking sissy" his fellow student is attempting to name, shame, and tame Marco. He is naming and taming Marco's body—implying *it's a boy's body!*—and by naming and shaming Marco in relation to his performance of masculinity is also naming and taming the beastliness of gender, and doing so by making it mean certain things.

In thinking through the need for the conceptual intervention I offer here, it is useful to keep in mind the pedagogical impact of research and theorizing about boys and masculinities. More so than Connell, Martino has had an enormous impact on how educational processes might be rethought to deal with issues related to boys and masculinity. He explicitly offers educational imperatives (see, for example, Martino 2000). Following the work of Bronwyn Davies, in which she uses poststructuralist methods and insights toward the deconstruction of restrictions around gender and sexuality through "renaming," "repositioning," and "rewriting" (Davies 1989, 1993), Martino (2000) recommends pedagogy centered on self-problematizing strategies extant in the discourse of young men and boys aligned with more powerful forms of masculinity. His imperative, like Davies's (1993), is concerned with developing critical analytical skills and awareness of the production of norms in students (and in teachers; see Martino, Lingard, and Mills 2004).

Clearly there would be benefit in students developing such levels of awareness about how others are positioned or understood in school contexts, and working toward literacy practices that rewrite, rename, and reposition. This kind of strategy, of course, lends itself, as much poststructuralist discourse analysis does, to a critique centered on identifying what is good or bad about the way people are valued and developing discursive spaces/names/positions in which to locate difference. So, for example, Marco's schoolmate might be asked to see how he "hurts" or harms Marco through his hate speech. It would be assumed that his increased sensitivity to how Marco is positioned would allow the declaring student to be more sympathetic and therefore less hurtful to Marco in the future. Marco, as a 'kind' of boy, could then be seen as occupying a "different" position. This strategy, problematically, works from the perspective of the "authentic" and assumes that the direction of the recognition in this moment extends from the authentic to the other. It further assumes that the effect or impact of this recognition flows in this one direction.

I will return to this imperative and Martino's work later in the essay, following a consideration of Connell's work, which opens the conceptual space for the discourse of masculinities. For now I would like to suggest that rather than saying that processes of hurtful, violent, gender-based vilification are negative and that students need to be critically aware of the process of reproducing gender norms, we pause at the moment of recognition to consider what the intricacies in *circuits of recognition* might offer for a disruption of the very foundations of gender-based identification and the violence it produces. This, I will suggest, demands that we remain cognizant of, and ethically open to, the tensions woven into processes of recognition. It demands that we take a conceptual step back from, (1) the question of educational intervention and (2) the assumption of the existence of boys and/or types of boys. Further, it demands that we work against the "danger" within circuits of recognition whereby axes of recognition become solidified—that is, where a declarer (an *I*) like Marco's male classmate maintains and shores up their position by the declaration of "others" (*non-I*) and in which those witness to it affirm and support the declarations. This *pausing at the moment of recognition* might help avoid the foreclosures produced in all-too-rapid processes of recognition motivated by the educational and moral demand to accept or tolerate "others" or to provide them named, non-normative spaces or positions.

*   *   *

For Düttmann, "language is a constellation," an emergent, dynamic, and unstable array; it "is in no way the representation of a sublating [exact apprehending] movement which reaches a result." He contrasts the traveling and dispersed nature of the constellation with "language which denies the constellation and tries to name the name in an unthinkable immediacy" (2000, 1)—in other words, naming or *declaring* works to stabilize that which is dispersing. This would be the case if we assume that a "sissy" is a type of boy or a type of masculinity, among many other types of masculinity, and proceeded to deploy this label as researchers, teachers, or even self-problematizing students to account for young men who do not fit another of the categories of masculinity.

Düttmann (1997, 2000) also provides a contrast between recognition and "re-cognition," built on a morphological and semantic distinction available in German that is not available in English.[4] *Recognition* is a process whereby that which is without a name, emerging from the dispersed and dispersing constellation, demands recognition in the form of an acknowledgment that it without a pre-existing name. *Re-cognition*, in contrast, is the process whereby what emerges, demanding recognition, is *re-cognized* into and through a preexisting language. In the first, the process of acknowledgment is destabilized and oriented to developing an understanding of the emergent. "Why attach *sissy* to *boy?*" would be the question that emerges from this perspective. In the second form of recognition, the process of identification knows what it sees and has a name ready. This second process is one of sublation, of fixing, and it is a sublating move made possible by the declarer/declared axis of recognition—that is, the axis that proceeds from center to margin, re-cognizing *as* ...: "Oh, Marco's the school sissy." This second kind of recognition avoids the reflexive demand for recognition made by the unrecognizable, a demand that might be expressed as "What do I make of this, what does my naming of this mean for me?" "What are the ethical consequences of how I recognize?" These questions are intended to resist the push to recognition embedded into the English declarative mood. Pushing against the given axes of recognition naturalized into the declarative, these questions might affect a pause in the circuit of recognition, opening a space for an emergent sense of the self/narcissistic need also embedded into the grammatical (declarative) form. Of course, as Butler suggests, "the conventional and precritical needs of grammar trump the demands of critical reflection (2004b, 150); the questions do not ask for declarations of self or of other, and are not assumed to have fixed and stable answers. Instead, they seek to undo the declaring status of *the I/the self.*

Within the kind of questioning disposition to recognition (rather than re-cognition) there exists the possibility of a different kind of politics or ethics, one that Düttmann characterizes as an active politics of recognition. He writes, "A reactive politics of recognition seeks grounds which can be recognized as presuppositions and preconditions necessary for the formation of identity. *An active politics of recognition looks for the possibilities of a transforming praxis which turns all humans into beings without a presupposition*" (2000, 102; emphasis in the original).

The term *sissy boy* morphologically strains at the tensions in gender recognition. Frustrating and frustrated by the process of naming, it invites us to ask what is at stake, what is so vital in gender recognition that a noun phrase is produced and applied in order to re-cognize the constellation. Sublating moves are enacted through the use of terms like (*fucking*) *sissy* in response to and to make sense of disordered performances of gender.

* * *

Educational research, like any research, produces and distributes
knowledge through processes of recontextualization whereby knowledge produced in one field is translated and made meaningful in
another. In doing so, research processes of various kinds regulate the
production, transmission, and acquisition of knowledge (Bernstein
1996). The research of Connell and Martino contributes to the recontextualization of knowledge that produces the pedagogical discourse of
masculinities. Methodology, theory, data, analysis, and interpretation
and educational imperatives offered by these and other researchers are
all part of the complex process of recontextualization whereby what is
known, how it is known, by whom it is known, and—further—what
should be done in response to or with such knowledge is unevenly and
powerfully distributed.

In *The Men and the Boys* (2000) and in the introductory chapter
to a book titled *Male Trouble* (2003), Connell provides an account of
what constituted the masculinities framework.[5] There are two central
contributions that Connell has made to the study of masculinity: he
offers a deployment of the notion of hegemony to an understanding
of masculinity, and pluralizes the term. *Masculinities*, then, allows for
the description of multiple competing forms of masculinity that operate within hierarchies and at different times and in different contexts.
Connell explains that "it is clear from the new social research as a
whole that there is no one pattern of masculinity that is found every-
where. We need to speak of 'masculinities,' not 'masculinity,'" and
"masculinities do not sit side-by-side like dishes on a smorgasbord.
There are definite social relations between them. Especially, there are
relations of hierarchy, for some masculinities are dominant while others are subordinated or marginalized. In most of the situations that
have been closely studied, there is some hegemonic form of masculinity—the most honoured or desired" (2000, 10). Using the concept of
hegemony "deriving from Antonio Gramsci's analysis of class relations,
[which] refers to the cultural dynamic by which a group claims and
sustains a leading position in social life" (1995, 77), Connell suggests
that there is a more powerful or valued form of masculinity, the hegemonic, and cautions against global, unitary understandings of masculinity (1995, 76; 2003, 15).

The masculinities framework is built on a perspective of "gender relations": "'Masculinity,' to the extent the term can be briefly
defined at all, is simultaneously a place in gender relations, the practices through which men and women engage that place in gender,
and the effects of these practices in bodily experience, personality and

culture" (1995, 71). While using Gramsci, Connell omits any direct reference to Gramsci's discussion of the dynamic relation between the hegemonic and the counterhegemonic (Gramsci 1992; see also Laclau and Mouffe 1985), and in so doing opens the way for those that follow to transmute the dynamic relation into a binary of hegemonic/non-hegemonic, as we will see below.

Connell's initial set of findings were based on studies that "tried to identify groups of men for whom the construction or integration of masculinity was under pressure" (1995, 90). This idea of "groups" permeates Connell's work and, as a starting point, it figures the terrain it examines in a specific way. It makes young men and boys knowable as "types," rendering their genders and sexualities aspects of themselves that locate them within—and as like—others within groups. This must, necessarily, generate reduction and constraint about what can be seen and known about men and boys. This predisposition cannot pay attention to the iterative production of positions within the ongoing formation of orders of gender, the surveillance of performances and the tensions, anxieties and disruptions that might be enacted at moments of recognition.

* * *

Taking the metaphors offered by psychoanalysis, particularly Sigmund Freud's work on melancholy, Butler describes the organization of gender within heterosexuality as a *culture of melancholy*.[6] The prohibition that is exerted over the loving attachment to one's same-sex parent is so strong, Butler suggests (following Freud), that the love of this parent *must* be lost. However, this love is not only lost, but can never be acknowledged as existing. Instead, it must be doubly "lost": lost as a loving attachment, and then disavowed as ever having been a love because the strength of prohibition means that it should never have been a love. The experience of an unacknowledgeable loss of an unavowabale love is the source of melancholy because the loss of a love that cannot be declared can never be mourned. The effect of such a bind is a turn back to the self by the ego that generates rage and ambivalence directed toward the ego/self and to the once-loved object.

In Butler's account of the emergence of gender, "masculinity and femininity emerge as traces of an ungrieved and ungrievable love" and the maintenance of gender norms happens because "masculinity and femininity within the heterosexual matrix are strengthened through the repudiations they perform" (1997c, 140). The emergence and strengthening of masculinity and femininity through melancholy happens because "certain forms of disavowal and repudiation … organize the performance of gender" (145).

Gender is *melancholy gender* because it is a response to an unavowable loss—a loss that, because of social prohibition, cannot be mourned. It involves the incorporation of the lost object or ideal into the ego in order to preserve it: the boy takes the lost and unmournable father into his own ego; the girl takes the lost and unmournable mother into her ego. However, what the melancholic finds in the incorporation of what has been lost, and in his subduing of the desire for it, is that "the ego is a poor substitute for the lost object, and its failure to substitute in a way that satisfies (that is, to overcome its status *as* a substitution), leads to the ambivalence that distinguishes melancholia" (1997c, 169). This failure of substitution and the ambivalence it generates opens a critical space for disruption, because the failure of the incorporated to be satisfactory "exposes the faultlines in its [the ego's] own tenuous foundations" (169). In this way, Butler uses melancholy as "an account of how psychic and social domains are produced in relation to one another" and, "as such, melancholy offers potential insight into how the boundaries of the social are instituted and maintained" (167–68). Further, the ambivalence and rage that become aspects of melancholy afford a critical and disruptive disposition within what is meant to be a much more stable and resolved arrangement of identifications.

Gender melancholy is also, given the tense underscoring of same-sex desire it enacts, a way to account for "a foreclosure of possibility which *produces* a domain of homosexuality" (1997c, 135; emphasis added). The disavowal of homosexual attachment, through a process of foreclosure, *produces* the domain of homosexuality. This means that homosexuality can be "understood as unlived passion and ungrievable loss" (135). Further, "if we accept the notion that the prohibition on homosexuality operates throughout a largely heterosexual culture as one of its defining operations, then the loss of homosexual objects and aims, would appear to be foreclosed from the start" and it is foreclosed "from the start" because it "is a preemptive loss, a mourning for unlived possibilities" (139). Homosexual desire operates as a less-than-successful melancholy in that, through the dynamic that Butler charts, it can be understood as the speaking of that which should be repudiated and denied. It is, in effect, the presence of "the love that dare not speak its name." More so, it involves the grieving of a lost love that should never be mourned as it should never have been loved.

As I have proposed elsewhere, the "properly" masculine not only involves the repudiation of same sex desiring attachments, but it also requires the renunciation of a performative identity that might include aspects of what is understood to be "femininity" (McInnes 2004, 231). The repudiations that produce gender interweave desiring attachments and bodily performance and inscription. It is useful, I think, to consider how gender nonconformity might operate as part of these normalizing renunciations. Butler suggests that lesbians and gay men in the military disrupt the circuit of renunciation on which masculinity is built (1997c, 139). The declaration *sissy boy*, as a moment of linguistic and semiotic labor, also suggests that the gender-nonconforming boy disrupts the renunciations necessary to the production of gender norms. Like the military debate in the United States, where the labor of (dis)avowal involved in the complex "don't ask, don't tell" policies enacts the position of the homosexual other to the properly masculine in the very process of the violence it inflicts against those whose desire is non-normatively same-sex, so, too, does Marco's classmate's "fucking sissy" bring Marco's sissiness into being. Both, though, also inflict this violence in order to establish and make real the normative and more powerful performance of masculinity.[7]

I am working here with Butler's useful distinction of a more "complete" melancholia—that is, a more resolved and stable formation of ego that permits (apparently) less ambiguity/ambivalence (1997c, 146–47). By suggesting that there are more "successful" forms of melancholia, Butler implies that there are less successful forms of melancholia in which a less resolved, less stable ego would permit greater ambiguity and ambivalence. Hyperbolic identifications, those most resolutely identifiable (sublated) and shored up, depend on the most complete and successful repudiations of that which cannot be mourned because it cannot be lost, because it should not be desired or loved—these constitute the more successful melancholic "resolution" within ego formation. Exploring the less successfully melancholic and the relation between a necessary "other" (homosexuality, or the "sissy") in the formation of a self or central term (heterosexuality, or the "properly" masculine) and the associated necessity of the denial or repudiation of the possibility of this other is a dynamic that Butler usefully and provocatively applies across a range of contexts. She identifies the bringing into being of male homosexuality in the very act of its silencing (don't ask, don't tell) as a moment of simultaneous foreclosure and disruption precisely because it enunciates what is meant to be renunciated.

Further, the activities and interventions of Queer Nation, whereby gay men and other queers demand the space of mourning for those that they should never have loved, "call for being read as life affirming rejoinders to the dire psychic consequences of a grieving process culturally thwarted and proscribed" (Butler 1997c, 148).

The kind of acting out or acting up of those less resolutely identifiable (the less successfully melancholic) is precisely the kind of life-affirming and destabilizing rejoinder that I interpret the sissy boy as making possible in the order of the school. The sissy boy, as gender nonconformer, exists as a speaking of that which should be repudiated—the presence or performance of femininity on/by a male body. More that this, though, Butler's insights about gender melancholy provoke questions about the double movement underpinning such declarations as "fucking sissy": The declaration, as a moment within circuits of recognition, enacts a violence in order to make the normative appear real. The normative's realness is strengthened if the other's position is allowed to be both stabilized and sublated—that is, if it becomes a knowable, named, and fixed part of the constellation. This is precisely what would happen if *sissy* is accepted as an adjective/classifier to the noun *boy* and the phrase is entered into the taxonomy of "types" of masculinity. If this foreclosure is enacted, then we miss the opportunity to pay attention to the violence involved in naming/recognizing. This can be what happens if, in the terms of some educational imperatives, we identify others in order that we see difference in order that we tolerate those that are different. In enacting a foreclosure through naming kinds of boys, we also miss the opportunity for all terms/positions within the system to be a little or a lot undone by suspending such foreclosure through *queerer melancholic responses.*

*   *   *

Martino is a significant contributor to the work on masculinities and schooling in Australia (1997, 1999, 2000). His earlier work (which underpins his more recent work) developed from Connell's framework and was built on research conducted at a Catholic coeducational high school in Perth, Western Australia. For one particular piece of research, Martino interviewed boys from what he calls "distinctive peer group cultures." "Footballers" were the dominant group he interviewed, but he also interviewed two other boys, those he refers to as "non-hegemonic boys" (2000, 104). In this essay, his use of "peer group cultures" as a framing device lends his analysis (because it informs his data gathering) to the use of categories. His description of "footballers" and "other [nonhegemonic] boys" makes clear that the grouping and naming of "others" happens in terms used by the dominant kinds of boys, reenacting these sublations. The boys Martino describes as other or nonhegemonic are recognized by abusive practices. They act like girls or are feminized in their love of learning. The harassment they experience is about violently making intelligible—and simultaneously devaluing them as 'other'. The footballer group demonstrated an "imperative to act cool," and displayed a "regime of peer group self-monitoring practices." Martino suggests that "these boys are enmeshed in a regime of self-surveillance: Their masculinity is in opposition to the demeanour of a hard-working student," and "through a regime of abusive practices, a public hegemonic form of masculinity places certain boys on the outside as targets of harassment. The peer-group dynamic revolves around being able to get a laugh at the expense of boys designated as other because they fail to measure up to the norm of hegemonic masculinity" (2000, 105, 106). In deploying aspects of Connell's framework, predisposed as it is to the proliferation of types of boys/masculinities, Martino, here and in other essays (see, for example, Martino 1999), uses labels like *hegemonic masculinity, rebel masculinity, dominant boys, hegemonic boys, nonhegemonic boys, cool boys, party animals, squids,* and *poofters,* and as such fixes the constellation of dispersed gender performances through the giving of names, apprehending and making a particular sense of gender and its relation to bodies. These abusive practices Martino describes can also be interpreted as processes of recognition. In that his identification of "other" boys is developed from the perspective of the "footballer" group, it reenacts a unidirectional axis of recognition by naming "other" boys within and by the fixing of a constellation of types as extant in school contexts in which the hegemonic form or perspective determines names and values. By working from the dominant perspective, reenacting a single and unidirectional axis of recognition, and by working to categorize or typologize, Martino's theory and research technique reduce the complex negotiations within circuits of recognition to the sense that can be made of them within a typological framework.

Further, the description of "a public hegemonic form of masculinity" as the subject to the verb *places*, which takes the object *certain boys*, is—while adequately abstract for the genre of writing—misleading in that such phrasing cements the account of masculinities at a structural level. It assumes that masculinity is a "thing" and that this abstract thing acts in/on the world. But, surely, the "placing" of certain (nonhegemonic) boys happens precisely through the kinds of verbal abuse that Martino describes. These forms of abuse are performative and are enacted within circuits of recognition. Within circuits of recognition there is a complex set of agencies and complicities that make possible the authenticating of "other" positions and the shoring up of the "center." A superstructural account of masculinity as *acting on*, such as implied by Martino's phrasing, provides a structural account of power but avoids the more complex question of how power operates in and across moments of recognition. This not only overrides the visibility of the violence of naming but also obfuscates the double movement required to establish the normative—a double movement whereby the other is simultaneously brought into being and "managed" so as not to cause further trouble—named, shamed, and tamed. This authenticating double movement is made possible on the basis of one axis of recognition, a *re-cognizing* axis of recognition *as*....

As mentioned at the beginning of this essay, Martino suggests that his data "may be useful in thinking about entry points and thresholds for engaging hegemonic boys in 'getting boys—or indeed men—to recognise the injustice they have experienced themselves ... enabling them to empathise with other people's experiences of injustice, and to recognise the ways in which they have themselves participated in perpetuating injustice'" (2000, 110, quoting McLean 1995, 23).

Martino's imperative assumes the existence of masculinities and the taken-for-granted relationship between (what are understood to be) male bodies and masculinity. A critique of this relation and that it is an artifact of citation/iteration rather than essential would open consideration of the interdependencies through which we all come to an understanding and (an uneven and undemocratic) valuing of our positions within gender. By charting a gender reality in which masculinity is performed by male bodies, and in order to maintain this version of the intelligible, Martino has tidied up the "mess," making a place for the dispersed and incoherent. This has pedagogical implications that will be discussed herein when I make suggestions as to an alternative educational ethic. For now, it might be useful and provocative to note that Martino's work reveals a researcher's complicity in the differentiation (and differing values) of forms of masculinity. Grouping and naming (key methods and interpretive frames in the discourse of masculinities) arrest and make knowable what is *in its iterative unfolding* a much messier and dispersed constellation of bodies and gender alignments. Power, rather than just being superstructural, also operates within circuits of recognition that (re)work constellations. Finding types of boys and naming them and then educating on the basis of groupings and their supposed value misses the enormous potential for observing and disrupting the circuits of recognition in which power organizes orders of gender through bodily and semiotic violence.

While not advocating for the continued abuse and violence directed at others, the alternative of avoiding or attempting to remove the shame at work in circuits of recognition and proffering identity options has something "preposterous" about it (Sedgwick 2003, 62). The removal of shame, built into pedagogies of tolerance and social justice, seeks to reinforce ideals of autonomy and coherence, it affirms the possibility of coherence for an individual subject and assumes a space of autonomy outside of both the negative and positive dimensions of recognition essential to the ongoing relational formation of identity. I would take up Eve Kosofsky Sedgwick's critique to suggest that the negative as well as positive affects/effects of "othering" within circuits of recognition are "integral to and residual in the processes by which identity is formed" (2003, 63). I would also suggest that avoiding the negative aspects of these processes perpetuates the more foundational and troublesome myths of autonomy and coherence that underscore perspectives on identity formation. Keeping these myths unquestioned means, also, that opportunities for being undone, for the ethical opportunity of becoming incoherent, are not only avoided but are deemed to be problematic as signs of weakness. It would seem that, in its melancholic turn from the threat of the loss of gender/body alignments, the discourse of masculinities performs not only sublating movements but also reinforces these myths of coherence and autonomy.

* * *

I am intrigued and provoked by Connell's dismissal of Judith Butler's work on gender: "Butler ...., the main proponent of the 'performative' account of gender, is strikingly unable to account for work, child care, institutional life, violence, resistance (except as individual choice), and material inequality. These are not trivial aspects of gender" (Connell 2000, 20). In what is more complaint than critique, Connell seems to be suggesting that larger structures of social organization are the places in and through which both adequate analysis and change might take place, and we can trace this structuralist mode of analysis to Martino's analysis of "masculinity" as operating *on* the material world. But what of the day-to-day, moment-by-moment iterations of otherness on which not only the formation of types of masculinity depend, but on which the formation of a self-evidence between male bodies and masculinity depends for its "realness"? The dismissal (and limited reading—Connell stops at 1990) of Butler falls in line with a much longer-term dismissal by Connell of poststructuralist work. Alan Peterson (2003) argues that there is a limitation in the way Connell's framework deals with power and that the framework encodes forms of gender essentialism. This happens within the discourse of masculinities because structural analyses of power provide some but only limited accounts of how power is enacted and offer limited scope for interventions that will adequately disrupt the organization of gender. The drive to identify different types of masculinity and to educate on the basis of these enacts oppositions of margin and center, and does not embrace the kinds of ambiguity that boys "who act like girls" make manifest.

The transmutation of Gramsci's hegemonic/counterhegemonic relationship into a proliferating binary enacted through the designation of hegemonic/nonhegemonic boys reties a "knot" Sedgwick describes as "recalcitrant" in identity politics (2003, 64). Like Sedgwick, I would argue that one is always stuck if one has to take a position/declare a place in a typology, to be recognized *as* ..., because this strategy lends itself to declarations of autonomous selfhood and the pretense of a (defensive) coherence. Following Butler's ethical inquiries (2001, 2004b), I would contend that one way out of the impasse would be to destabilize the separateness and coherence of "forms" of masculinity and, indeed, masculinities' separateness and coherence from femininity. Instead of working within essentialist assumptions and toward forms of coherence, I would contend that we should look for *"the possibilities of a transforming praxis which turns all humans into beings without a presupposition"* (Düttmann 2000, 102). This contrary theoretical suggestion depends on an interpretation of the discourse of masculinities as a melancholic turn that shores up the place and status of masculinity. A transforming praxis might stem from a queerer melancholy (in contrast to a reproductive, defensive one) provided by gender nonconformity that, if left even momentarily unforeclosed, might keep unstable and unreal the "taken-for-granteds" on which masculinity depends.

Connell's intervention and its subsequent use by Martino in the way that it deploys the notion of hegemonic masculinity and generates the grounds for the proliferation of types of masculinity leaves the idealized link between male bodies and masculinity intact. Through the proliferation of masculinities, what remains unquestioned is the necessary relationship between male bodies and (one form or other of) masculinity. This effects a *containment* in the guise of a *differentiation*. The discourse of masculinities refuses a loss, incorporating the (potentially) lost into its own self by way of its framework and methods. What might be lost is the self-evident link between male bodies (and the "fact" that the male body is real) and masculinity. The discourse of masculinities enacts the double movement of melancholy by both refusing to lose this ideal of a gender/body alignment and, as a way of avoiding the grief of the loss, incorporating this ideal into its self. This constitutes a disavowed and self-affirming loss for the discourse of masculinities. In this way, the discourse can be interpreted as a less reflexive, more reproductive and defensive melancholia and as an outcome of an unspeakable or unrepresentable loss of an ideal. Into the "ego" of this discourse is taken/incorporated an idea—the taken-for-granted existence of masculinity and the correlation of male bodies with forms of masculinity.

*   *   *

Butler usefully contends that "life histories are histories of becoming, and categories can sometimes act to freeze that process of becoming" (Butler 2004a, 80). Though Connell warns about the use of typologies of masculinity (1995: 76), there has been, since the introduction of his framework, a tendency toward the proliferation of categories (types of masculinities) within the discourse of masculinities such as that manifest in the work of Martino. Kathy Davis (1997) suggests that Connell's frame controls rather than embraces the ambiguities inherent in the production of masculinity. Davis's suggestion and Butler's remarks about categories can be extended to suggest a need for greater reflexivity on the part of researchers involved in the investigation, analysis, and critique of gender. The kind of framing and categorizing researchers do is a process of freezing, even if, as Connell would argue, the construction of gender is a dynamic process (1995, 81–86). Further, given the authority of research in the field of education, and particularly the impact and authority of Connell-influenced research in gender education, it is critical that research be seen and see itself reflexively as a pedagogical discourse—that is, as a discourse that regulates the production and distribution of knowledge.

The conceptual intervention in this essay is offered because for any critical democratic project we are called to subject our own categories to scrutiny. The production of research findings determines how gender is understood, imagined, and pedagogized through the processes of research and in school settings. In other words, "having or bearing 'truth' and 'reality' [the privilege of those that gather data and provide interpretation] is an enormously powerful prerogative in the social world" because "knowledge and power ... work together to establish a set of subtle and explicit criteria for thinking the world" (Connell 1995, 27). Because as researchers we are in the business of producing knowledge as power, Butler provokes us to surrender our claim to knowledge and be "undone" as knowers. For Connell, Martino, and others who use structural analyses in research about masculinities, this means avowing and perhaps surrendering, then grieving the loss of the facticity of the (male) body.

To stimulate the avowal and grieving for this ideal, the sissy boy's becoming has been a key part of my thinking in this essay. His performance of gender nonconformity draws attention to the process by which circuits of recognition produce what can and can't be known—what is intelligible in the field of gender. The moments when boys are declared "other" because of the uncomfortable/discomforting quality of a feminized/feminizing performance involve complex relations (declarer, declared, witness) that shore up the reality (naturalness, essentialism) of gender. The moments of recognition in and through which the sissy boy takes and/or is given a place within the school *as* a sissy boy identify the foreclosing and disruptive tension produced by a less-than-successful turn or incorporation of the ideals of masculinity. The ordering of gender demands that the sissy boy be named, shamed, and tamed because he is a *queerer* melancholic who shamelessly voices that which should be lost—"inappropriate" gender/body alignments. His performance and his declaration can unsuture the pretense of gender cohesion.

Following Butler's suggestion of ethical possibilities, the shameless voicing of the sissy boy can be seen as a call for those involved in circuits of recognition to awaken to the precariousness of the other. In discussing how an awakeness to the precariousness of the other makes an ethical demand on the *I*, Butler cautions that "this cannot be an awakeness to ... my own life, and then an extrapolation from an understanding of my own precariousness to an understanding of another's precarious life. It has to be an understanding of the precariousness of the Other" (2004b, 134). It is only by being awake to the precariousness of the other that we can be called out of narcissism, drawn from a concern for our own needs and our own vulnerabilities. Keeping in mind that narcissism is a mode characterized by taking the self as object of love and desire *and* by a sense of egocentric megalomania, I read Butler as suggesting that not only are we drawn into the sociality and relationality of the very possibility of our being when we are awake to the "other"s' precariousness, but that we must also, as we're drawn from narcissism, surrender any pretense to the possession of our own power or will. Butler explains that being drawn from narcissism means being called into discourse (2004b, 138). A call into discourse signals the social semiotic constitution of our selves—that is, that we, as an *I*, are made possible by and are therefore dependent on discourse. The dependence we have on discourse for the constitution of our very being means that we each are made possible by the other. So, if there is no other, there is no discourse and there would be no *I*. Ethics is enlivened in acknowledging this dependency because being awake to the relational and discursively mediated constitution of ourselves means that we cannot pretend to either self-coherence or to autonomy, suggesting that we can never determine or control how we are addressed and made possible within discourse. Our constitution in and through the semiotic labor of address is at the heart of our humanness and key to a humanity aware of and careful of address and its potential for violence.

When Marco is addressed by his teammate as a "fucking sissy" he is declared other. But, in being declared other, he is declared other *to something*—the more "authentic" form of masculinity. His being declared makes possible the constitution of this more "authentic" form of masculinity. The circuit of recognition enacted at this moment is a necessity of a gender norm that seeks to ensure that male bodies and masculinity (of one kind or another) are aligned. However, neither Marco nor his schoolmate can fully determine how they are addressed. The schoolmate attempts to ensure the unassurable by preempting and foreclosing the fluidity and incoherence of his own body and his "gender" by addressing Marco as "other"—as a "fucking sissy." He pretends autonomy and self-coherence through an act of linguistic/semiotic violence. He is doing the labor required to sustain the realness of masculinity.

Martino's suggested pedagogical intervention, whereby young men are encouraged to use technologies of self to reflect on their role in the vilification of nonhegemonic boys, cements the axis of recognition as one that extends from self to other, from *I* to *non-I*. This builds into pedagogy an awakeness to one's own life and in suggesting, as Connell does, that social justice should stem from empathy with the pain produced for others, this pedagogy understands the other's precariousness on "my" terms. This is presumptuous, to be sure. But, as Butler's ethical suggestion implies, in that this pedagogical strategy suggests a coherent and autonomous place from which to empathize it propels a narcissistic assurance of coherence and autonomy and avoids the ethical demand of being undone by the other's precariousness. Because it ensures a place from which to empathize and self-problematize, this kind of pedagogy runs the risk that the very possibility of a "normal" or "authentic" form of masculinity might actually be made more real. In line with Marco's schoolmate's masculinity-authenticating labor in this circuit of recognition, the teacher's snicker bears witness to the declaration and signals complicity with the possibility of "real" masculinity and further signals the "realness" of the male body. The circuit of recognition, then, awakens and, once again, affirms the facticity of the male body and its natural and unproblematic relationship to one or another form of masculinity.

Pedagogical discourse and educational imperatives stemming from the discourse of masculinities focus on separateness or distinctions and produce a differentiated coherence out of the hegemonic/non-hegemonic binary. This works with one axis of recognition—*I* to *non-I*, from the hegemonic to the nonhegemonic or other through particular methodologies and into educational imperatives. A single axis of recognition most crucially obfuscates the need for declarers, those declared, and witnesses to accept shared responsibility in the violence of naming, and makes researchers complicit with such a process. Alternatively, to quote from Butler, "suspending the demand for self-identity or, more particularly, for complete coherence, [might] counter a certain ethical violence that demands that we manifest and maintain self-identity at all times and require others to do the same" (2001, 27).

*   *   *

In the world of school education in Australia, there is a tension between the coherence demanded by institutionalized school-based education and its target-setting, outcomes-measuring demands on the one hand and the impossibility of making gender cohere on the other. An acknowledgment of this tension and an acknowledgment of the multiple and conflicting investments made through circuits of recognition may provide an ethics for use in education that focuses on the emergence of "improvisational possibility within a field of constraints" (Butler 2004c, 15) made possible by *queerer melancholic* negotiations and built on an alertness to the precariousness of all of us within the terms of gender.

Like Butler, I identify an ethical query at the moment of the declaration of the gendered other, the "fucking sissy." When all those in circuits of recognition encounter the gender-nonconforming boy, Butler would ask, "[H]ow might we encounter the difference that calls our grids of intelligibility into question without trying to foreclose the challenge that the difference delivers? What might it mean to learn to live in the anxiety of that challenge, to feel the surety of one's epistemological and ontological anchor go, but to be willing, in the name of the human, to allow the human to become something other that what it is traditionally assumed to be?" (Butler 2004c, 35) Butler further articulates the collective precariousness of such an ethical demand by explaining that "it implies becoming part of a process the outcome of which no one subject can surely predict" (39). In other words, it demands that one face one's own incoherence and the incoherence of others. To enact such an ethics, "one must enter into a collective work in which one's own status as a subject must, for democratic reasons, become disoriented, exposed to what it does not know" (36). Because it *re*-renacts the essentialist link between the male body and masculinity, the discourse of masculinities enacts a melancholic turn, refusing the loss of gender/body alignments. Working *at the moments* when sense is made of gender—that is, in the instance of circuits of recognition when the intelligible is performatively produced from the unintelligible—might counter the ethical violence inherent in demanding that we manifest and maintain coherence.

One final comment is due here. At the symposium I made a remark, when I concluded the presentation of this essay, that there emerges from the above ethics of a nonpresumptive recognition, open to the precariousness of the other, the possibility of a *pedagogy of incoherence*. I am not arguing that we should be without hope in the work of gender education. But, I would argue that we should be without the hope of coherence because without the hope of coherence, of being recognized *as …*, a different kind of hope emerges—the hope that our precariousness, our incoherence might make an ethical demand on all within circuits of recognition. Butler commented at the time that such a pedagogy might provide for moments or phases of incoherence rather than Düttmann's idealized *"transforming praxis that turns all humans into beings without a presupposition"* that underscores my proposal. I would like, in accepting the critique, to suggest that this essay provokes the idea that, in educational contexts and in response to the circuits of recognition that (re)iterate gender norms and fictions of coherence, we might productively counter the normative reworking of gender and the ethical violence of demands for coherence if we entertain, even momentarily, our own journeys into Butler's "collective work in which one's own status as a subject must become disoriented." What if, instead of attention being paid to the proliferation of types of men and boys, attention was paid to circuits of recognition in their iterative unfolding, and to the tensions experienced by and investments made by those involved?

NOTES

I would like to thank Murray Couch, Cristyn Davies, Greg Noble, Linnell Secomb, and the reviewers for their feedback and criticism on drafts of this essay.

1. This anecdote draws on many recounted experiences both from my own research and the published research from those such as Martino. It is designed here to stimulate discussion of the processes of recognition via declaration, and is intended to resonate rather than represent in some positivist, reductive sense.
2. The violence of gender signaled by "throwing like a girl" is famously recounted in Young (2005).
3. Elsewhere (McInnes 1997) I have used Judith Butler's work on performativity to explore the tension enlivened by declarations of otherness and the opening and closing of disruptive potential at such moments, arguing—very much in line with Butler—that it is to the opening and closing of such tensions that critical energy should be directed because it is here where the taken-for-granted-ness of social categories and social values is most insidiously enacted.
4. *Anerkennung* (recognition) signifies the process of acknowledging; *Erkenntnis* (re-cognition) signifies identifying something *as* something.
5. In "Toward a new sociology of masculinity" Carrigan, Connell, and Lee (1985) make what appears to be the initial introduction of Connell's framework. However, the key text taken up in educational contexts is Connell's 1995 book *Masculinities*. This text, his own more recent summations/reflections on the masculinities framework (Connell 2000, 2002), and Martino's use of Connell's work will be central to my analysis. I am not trying to represent the entire field of masculinity research and conduct a thorough analysis and critique of all of the research and theorizing done about masculinities in the last ten or fifteen years; a genealogy of this scale is beyond the scope of my project. A provocative, contextualizing account of research on men and masculinities can be found in Peterson (2003).
6. *Melancholy* is distinguished from *mourning* by Freud (1917) on the basis that in mourning the lost object is known and grieved, and in melancholy the lost object is unacknowledged and therefore ungrievable.
7. Of course, there is more to be considered about *fucking sissy* as a declaration. The sexualized effect of the highly charged negative affect of such declarations in circuits of recognition appears to both enact violence *and* an erotics.

Becoming Sissy: A Response to David McInnes

CRISTYN DAVIES

University of Western Sydney

David McInnes's conceptual intervention has prompted in me distant recollections. I was called a "sissy" as a child, although I can't remember who did the naming, and what exactly it was that I did, or didn't do, in my "becoming sissy." I do remember that I didn't want to be one, and that my being a sissy came with another instruction: "Don't be such a girl!" Looking back, I understand that my "becoming girl" involved a lot of hard work, and being the conscientious type (another kind of performance that no doubt worked in tandem with my "becoming girl") I suspect that I'd worked overtime. There was a "too-muchness" to my becoming girl that meant I was in imminent danger of "becoming a sissy"—a kind of being, it seems, that no one really wants to see in little boys *or* girls.

My then best friend played at being a tomboy.[1] I'm not sure whether this was a position that she'd taken up, or been obliged to take up by virtue of her interaction with me. From all other accounts I've heard, this was a kind of being through which she was at her best. She was happy to play in the mud, and could climb trees with the agility of a cat, and once, when she was compelled to wear my Communion dress for an occasion *she* didn't believe in, she'd scaled a fence in her back yard to throw sticks and stones at the boys on the other side who were teasing her. She might not have intended to break their bones, but she was sure going to do everything she could to deter their ill intentions. A few years later, I was forbidden to spend time with her.[2] Apparently she was a "bad influence" on me: too often in trouble, unruly, and flirting with boys in ways that weren't appropriate for *nice* girls. Of course, I was devastated by the prohibition against seeing her. Perhaps it was the generative effects of prohibition that encouraged something about this particular childhood interaction—its narrative—to stick.[3]

I won't discuss here my complicated relation to any kind of butch/ femme continuum. But I will say that, more recently, I've been called a "faggot." I don't know who did the naming—that is, I don't know *their* names. The two young men who drove past in the hotted-up red car weren't my friends, so I was sure that they weren't playing the dangerous game, or performing the political strategy, of *resignification.*[4] The young men laughed and the car went on around the bend. As the cry "faggot!" rang out I was in no doubt that this new name was addressed to me. I was being hailed in an all-too-familiar way, although the exact nature of the address was a revelation. Part of that familiarity was about the empty road: there was no one in front of, or behind, me for several hundred meters. There was no one else's body to take the weight of the word. The force of the delivery of that name, and the frame of expletives around it, had physically pushed me toward the path's edge, and I stood in confusion for a moment. Judith Butler was right: "To be injured by speech was to suffer a loss of context, that is not to know where you are" (1997a, 4). The discursive disorientation I experienced was embodied in my physical reaction, putting into question exactly what my place really was, performing my concern that, in Butler's words, "such a place may be no place" (4). Sweat trickled down the back of my neck—sweat that I wanted to feel was not panic related, but was instead a product of my walking swiftly down the street, a result of the routine of exercise and nothing else.

*   *   *

One of the powerful effects of Butler's contribution to thought is her remarkable ability to enter the space of contradiction, of incoherence, to engage the subject's opacity to herself, and to illuminate these spaces in discourse as viable, necessary, and potentially transformative. For Butler, "a theory of subject-formation that acknowledges the limits of self-knowledge can work in the service of a conception of ethics, and indeed, of responsibility" (2001, 22). David McInnes's invitation to enact a "pedagogy of incoherence" is, in part, a request for researchers to keep the meanings attached to gender lively. Informed by Butler's theory of performativity figured through the lens of melancholia, and Alexander Düttmann's suggestion that "language is a constellation" (2000, 1), McInnes argues, if "research seeks to generate the names for the constellation it may well render less visible the dynamic and iterative emergence of the constellation of body/gender alignments silencing the disruptive potential, enacting complicity with the naming/sublating movement of re-cognition" (2005, 5).

McInnes subjects the discourse of masculinities to the kind of intellectual rigor advocated by Butler when she acknowledges the politically efficacious function of identity politics while simultaneously recognizing that identity categories are also "instruments of regulatory regimes" (1993b, 308).[5] Confessing that she is "permanently troubled" by identity categories, Butler attends to the role of sexual identity categories, specifically the sign *lesbian*—suggesting that "it is precisely the pleasure produced by the instability of those categories which sustains the various erotic practices that make [her] a candidate for the category to begin with" (1993c, 308). Similarly, McInnes is keen to "keep the future uses" of masculinity as a "sign" dynamic so as not to foreclose future possibilities (Butler 1991, 311).

One of the difficulties McInnes confronts in undoing already established critiques of masculinity in boys and men is a shift from structuralist to poststructuralist accounts of exactly how masculinity might be played out. Poststructuralism may be understood as a philosophic response to the assumed scientific position of structuralism—a paradigm par excellence in the social sciences—and as a movement concerned with decentering structures and offering a critique of a presumptive metaphysics while simultaneously extending the critique offered in structuralism of the humanist subject. R. W. Connell's dismissal of Butler's critique of gender suggests commitment to a structuralist framework with a dubious relation to the rationalism and realism inherent in positivist analyses (Connell 2000, 20).[6] Challenging the positivism, rationalism, and realism inferred in structuralism, poststructuralist analyses of gender critique the problematic construction of political identities through binary opposition—a framework in which there must always be an "other." Structuralism's ahistorical synchronic analysis of structures provoked renewed interest in diachronic analyses in a poststructuralist critique concerned with *critical* history. Connell's reading of Butler's theory of gender performativity as not accounting for structural and institutional inequalities of any kind is less a rejection of Butler per se than an indication of the skepticism directed toward deconstructive and genealogical accounts of gender that don't take as their object the *real*—whatever that unstable signifier has come to mean.

Connell's work is acclaimed for its recognition of multiple masculinities, and for demonstrating ways of reading "gender relations among men" by naming categories of masculinity such as hegemonic masculinity, subordinate masculinity, complicit masculinity, and marginalized masculinity (1995).[7] Within this framework, Connell defends this naming of types of masculinity, suggesting that "masculinity that occupies the hegemonic position in a given pattern of gender relations, [is] a position [that is] always contestable" (1995, 76). Despite Connell's disclaimer, this act of grouping and naming simulates and continues the kind of discursive work already practiced on the playground in order to *re-cognize* each other in Düttmann's sense of the word—that is, to identify something *as* something, or to make *it* intelligible through discourses that confer power, or alternatively, that take power away from the subject.[8] Subsequently, this method of categorizing types of masculinity has been taken up by much of the scholarship that examines masculinity (particularly in the discipline of education)—one of the effects being that masculinity is often mapped and remapped onto the male body (even if its embodiment and performance is problematized)—shoring up the precarious relation between masculinity and the male body.[9] This theoretical framework limits, if not discards, the potentialities of understanding how masculinity might be figured by female bodies—thus reinforcing binary thinking and also fixing masculinity to male bodies.

McInnes describes Connell's naming of types of masculinity as a "process of freezing."[10] Butler also uses this metaphor to describe the potential effects of naming: "A name tends to fix, to freeze, to delimit, to render substantial, indeed, it appears to recall metaphysics of substance, of discrete and singular kinds of beings; a name is not the same as an undifferentiated temporal process or the complete convergence of relations that go under the rubric of 'a situation'" (1997b, 37).

The process of "fixing" or "freezing" suggests a prior fluidity, and would seem to promise an intelligible social future, one in which the subject is made recognizable through normative discursive regimes. A name can act metonymically—that is, a name acts as a kind of substitution, or shorthand, for more subtle and pervasive relations that we might understand as the workings of power. Extending Michel Foucault's analysis of power, Butler concedes that "the name carries within itself the movement of a history that it arrests" (1997b, 36). Being named is a necessary condition for becoming a subject, but what that name signifies, its historicity, continues to constitute the ways in which that subject is read through relations of power by himself, and also constitutes the way the subject is read by others.

So, what does it mean to name types or categories of masculinity? Inquiring into "female masculinity," Judith Halberstam investigates the operation of Eve Kosofsky Sedgwick's term "nonce taxonomies"—that is, "categories that we use daily to make sense of our worlds but that work so well that we actually fail to recognize them (Halberstam 1998, 14). Halberstam's project is to denaturalize discourses of masculinity, demonstrating its performative dimension, and to create a discursive space in which masculinity can be read in relation to the female body. Her account of masculinity is qualified with the term *female*, signaling the unmarked assumption that masculinity is the domain of men. Like Butler, McInnes, and Sedgwick, Halberstam is concerned with revealing as fictional the *essential* relation between male bodies and masculinity. She also unpacks the discursive move toward "masculinities" in Paul Smith's work, pointing out that dominant masculinity becomes the site "to begin deconstructing masculinity" (Halberstam 1998, 16). She is concerned with problematizing Smith's motivation for keeping his critique of masculinity at the site of the male body in which he claims that "it is the equation of maleness plus masculinity that adds up to social legitimacy" (Halberstam 1998, 16). Smith's critique is in danger of reiterating the relation between masculinity and "maleness" he might seek to undo. Unlike McInnes, Halberstam believes "the recognition of a host of masculinities makes sense," but she is concerned that Smith's analysis not only shores up the relation between masculinity and the male body, with its focus on hegemonic masculinity in men, but that it also makes female masculinity inconsequential (1998, 16). McInnes and Halberstam both isolate the dangers of approaching the question of masculinity by focusing on "hegemonic masculinity" in men and working outward from there. However, unlike Halberstam, McInnes questions the liberalism inherent in a proliferating masculinity. Surely this kind of approach to critiquing masculinity continues to work within the binary structure that it seeks to undo?

Connell also acknowledges "masculine women or masculinity in women's lives," suggesting that "masculinity *refers to* male bodies … but is not determined by male biology" (2000, 29; emphasis original). While Connell is careful to explicate how this system of referral might take place with attention to hegemonic and nonhegemonic (rather than counterhegemonic) performances of masculinity in men, this analysis, not unlike Smith's, is at risk of shoring up the system of referral Connell would otherwise seek to agitate. What does it mean to displace this system of referral—a system that operates within a heterosexist discourse by envisaging masculinity outside of the male body? "If we proliferate the possibilities on the margin without disrupting the center," Butler asks, then have we "unwittingly preserved the distinction between margin and center rather than contributed to a more fatal displacement of heterocentrism?" (1998, 227). Butler's recent analysis of categorization at the site of gender suggests a double movement at work in which "a life for which no categories of recognition exist is not a livable life," while she also acknowledges that "life for which those categories constitute unlivable constraint is not an acceptable option" (2004c, 8). Butler warns against "legislating for all lives what is livable only for some," and while Connell's research certainly doesn't hold the constitutive power of legislation, this kind of structuralist critique of masculinity easily lends itself to the liberal humanism still at work in school curriculum and policy (Butler 2004c, 8).

Significantly, Connell has addressed the criticism not only of the discourse of "masculinities," but also the generation of types of masculinity by suggesting, whether "the outcomes are stable or unstable, mostly fluid or mostly fixed, is surely an empirical question, not one to be settled in advance by theory" (2000, 22–23). This claim implies a separation between empiricism and theory rather than a more complex set of relations in which *matter* is not "prior to discourse"; instead, Butler suggests, "matter is fully sedimented with discourses on sex and sexuality that prefigure and constrain" the very empirical evidence a structuralist account of gender and sexuality might seek to secure (1993a, 29). Surely a relation between theory and practice is a reciprocal exchange in which these domains are not so separate—are they not, in fact, inextricably bound to and by each other in ways that make the other viable? Isn't the field of empiricism situated in the theoretical—so much so, in fact, that to affect a divide between theory and empiricism would be a redundant move? Isn't it unproductive to situate theory and practice on either side of a curious divide? Not surprisingly, this kind of thinking has encouraged theory—that now overdetermined and yet permanently ambiguous category historically associated with rationality—to be thought of as masculine. And subsequently, so, too, has practice been associated with the *natural* (this description also a discursive construction), which is often figured as feminine.[11]

What is concerning about the discourse of masculinities as a happy pluralism, and the subsequent generation of types of masculinity under this rubric, is a focus by some researchers on the male body as the site where masculinity continues to be discursively generated. As Halberstam has noted, this phenomenon means that "the suppression of female masculinities allows for male masculinity to stand unchallenged as the bearer of gender stability and gender deviance" (1998, 41). It is the category of gender that should be taken as the object of analysis, and revealed as a fiction (albeit a prevailing one) that gains its very power through an endemic reiteration. Butler's critique demonstrates that the categories of both *sex* and *gender* are discursive constructions that work together at the site of subjectification, along with other categorical naming that marks the other such as: *race, class,* and *sexuality* (1993a, 14).[12] Addressing the question of proliferating categories within the domain of binary thinking, Butler most recently examines the category *gender,* suggesting, one "tendency within gender studies has been to assume that the alternative to the binary system of gender is a multiplication of genders. Such an approach invariably provokes the question: how many genders can there be, and what will they be called?" (2004a, 43).

Careful in her recent work to argue that gender does not just refer to the masculine and the feminine, Butler asserts that gender is the "apparatus" through which these categories are produced, alongside the biological and the performative (2004c, 42). Suggesting that gender might be the site in which femininity and masculinity are "deconstructed" and denaturalized," Butler keeps meanings attached to gender lively so as not reinstate normative understandings in which the masculine and the feminine are synonymous with the term *gender* (2004c, 42). Like much of Butler's thinking, her most recent theorizing about gender is demonstrated through critique that reads regulation and its relation to the process of normalization, not just as constraint but also as a productive site of resistance (2004c, 55). Wherever there is a site of constraint, Butler isolates the productive potential, or field of agency, that suggests a dynamic and viable future.

* * *

McInnes's inquiry engages Butler's notion that "a theory of the subject should take into account the full ambivalence of the conditions of its operation" (1997b, 15). Part of this ambivalence is registered in McInnes's work at the site of the *category* as both regulating device and also, the scene of recognition. It is for this reason that he situates the category *sissy boy* precariously in his essay herein, noting, "I am not suggesting that *sissy boys,* or 'boys who act like girls' is a stable category; I am focusing on the iterative process of recognition/naming that constitutes gendered "others."

The term *sissy boy* acts as both slur and the possible site of resignification in which boys who engage their gender practice differently will continue, in McInnes's words, "working the tensions of gender recognition and destabiliz[ing] the formation of ordered masculinity and femininity" (2005; 2007). Writing from a therapist's perspective, Ken Corbett isolates the difficulties inherent in naming, in not being named, and how these processes contribute to fundamental discursive and conceptual frameworks. "Homosexual boyhood as a conceptual category does not exist," he writes. "The existence of homosexual boys has until now either been silenced or stigmatized. Bullies identify sissies. Psychiatrists identify sissy-boy syndromes. There has been virtually no effort to speak of the boyhood experience of homosexuals other than to characterize their youth as a disordered and/or nonconforming realm from which it is hoped they will break free. The fate of these boys is contemplated with the kind of hushed charity that obscures antipathy" (1999, 112). Caught between complete erasure and the troubling discourse of psychiatry that pathologizes gender nonconformity—sissies and tomboys—Corbett also speaks of "girly-boys." We might also want to ask here of the fate of "boyish" girls, of their relationship to tomboys, of their childhood, and their gendered future. Recognizing that his patients are "beset by contradiction and paradox," Corbett argues that "queer people can feel unnamed within a gender matrix that is founded on certain ideals of heterosexual masculinity and femininity" and that "the category problem reasserts itself with regard to the relationship between gender and sexuality" (1999, 112–13). Interested in processes of recognition, McInnes responds (if inadvertently) to Corbett's assertion that "within the sissy-boy discourse, gender is as gender was; virtually no effort has been made to critically theorize gender" (1999, 110). Significantly, McInnes locates this ordering of gender in the *proper* order of the school, suggesting that performances of gender that deviate from what are perceived as normative practices may threaten the order of the institution more widely. We might want to ask here, as Butler does in her critique of Jessica Benjamin's work on recognition, "At what psychic price does normative gender become established?" (2004c, 144).

McInnes's reworking of the category *sissy boy* led me to think about the case of Christopher Tsakalos, a thirteen-year-old Australian school student who was compelled to leave Cranebrook High, in Sydney's western suburb of Penrith, after repeatedly being called "faggot" and "poofter" by large numbers of the student body. These terms of address were followed by threats to Tsakalos's life and the promise of continuing homophobic violence from some students if he didn't leave the school (McMullen, 1997). I will briefly examine the public rhetoric in media circulation about this case, and make reference, also, to my own earlier narrative. Both instances have left me wondering whether *faggot* is the new *sissy boy*, a naming wrought by that theoretical leap where sexuality is used to police gender.

Schools are spaces in which much behavior is highly regulated. Surveillance is the sine qua non of a daily life in which teachers survey students, students survey teachers, the general public surveys students, and students are encouraged to survey each other. This latter transaction is built into an institutional structure within which "prefects" and "monitors" are endowed with the rhetorical and hierarchical status of privilege for conforming (frequently signified by a badge carrying the school emblem and the word *prefect*, so linguistically close to *perfect*), and ensuring others also conform to the established regulations of the school. "The panoptic schema," Foucault argues, "without disappearing as such or losing any of its properties, was destined to spread throughout the social body, its vocation was to become a generalized function" (Foucault 1977, 125). It makes sense that gender, race, class, and sexuality are the metasubjects of this regulation, perhaps more prominently so in the microcosm of the school than in most other spheres. In this sphere of heightened regulation, there is also behavior that is left *unmarked*—that is, some incidents that unfold on the school playground are left unregulated because such actions fall outside of the bounds of recognition or intelligibility despite recourse to "the law."

So distressing was his leaving of Cranebrook High School that Chris Tsakalos and his mother got the attention of various media. The ensuing controversy led to a shake-up in the New South Wales education system with regard to addressing homophobia in schools. One of these media interviews took place on *Sixty Minutes*—a ubiquitously framed current-affairs program.[13] The title of the segment was "Pride and Prejudice"—an unsubtle pun on Jane Austen's now canonical satire of heterosexual romance in which the author offers a commentary on the exchange of women in Georgian society. Despite Austen's playful and irreverent tone, her heroine, Elizabeth Bennet, secures—or *is secured by*—a "successful" marriage. This rhetorical framing device sets the tone of the interview between reporter Jeff McMullen and Chris and Vicky Tsakalos—a tale in which pride and prejudice are figured differently, but narrative resolution in both tales is equally sought after.

Although it's clear that *Sixty Minutes* intended the segment as an
exposé of the operation of homophobic violence in schools, and particularly the failure to recognize it *as* violence, the interview is characterized, and the narrative generated, by that now familiar analytic
move: the binary opposition. Sedgwick's nuanced analysis of the closet
as a pivotal metaphor for understanding the discursive operation of
homosexuality understands binarism as *"peculiarly* densely charged
with lasting potentials for powerful manipulation—through precisely
the mechanisms of self-contradictory definition or, more succinctly,
the double bind" (Sedgwick, 1990, 10; emphasis original). Sedgwick
situates the homosexual/heterosexual divide within the wider context
of equally unstable normative definitions responding to different "sets
of contiguities and often at a different rate" (11). Not unlike Butler,
Sedgwick critiques the discursive construction of incoherence as one
that some theoretical paradigms desire to shore up, writing, that she
"will suggest instead that contests for discursive power can be speci-
fied as competitions for the material or rhetorical leverage required to
set the terms of, and to profit in some way from, the operations of such
an incoherence of definition" (11).

Sedgwick's argument suggests that definition, or to return to Butler's example, *being named*, is more profitable in the marketplace—both
literally and rhetorically. Despite the entry of queer theory—a site that
allows for, if not advocates, the incoherence of the subject's relation
to gender and sexuality—the prominent discourses circulating about
sexuality within schools (and also the discourses adopted by much of
the resources to teach against homophobia) are still figured through
binary thinking and liberal humanism.[14] Subjects are expected to
know themselves and be easily knowable. "As children move through
adolescence into adulthood," Susan Talburt argues, "society expects
that they will acquire knowledge of self and other (the world and their
place in it will become intelligible to them) and that maturing youth
will become intelligible to others, knowable as such and such" (2004,
17). Bronwyn Davies suggests that this desire to be knowable and
knowing, and for coherence, is habituated through processes of learning language in which children "learn to constitute themselves and
others as unitary beings, as capable of what is recognized as coherent
thought, as gendered, and as one who is in particular kinds of relations to others" (2003, 1). Within the current school system, difference must be coherently marked so that one can enter discourse as an
intelligibly marked other.

Responding to Chris Tsakalos's victimization on the playground,
McMullen continues to mark him as "other" by invoking competing

sets of power relations inspired by a discourse of sexuality that affects a homosexual/heterosexual divide. Positioned as suburban other—a narrative that is characterized as contrary to the supposedly more desirable inner-city gay urban experience—Chris's newly found sexuality requires an equally new landscape in which increased capital is figured as purchasing the fiction of *safe space*.[15] Immersed in an urban landscape, McMullen's commentary implies that Chris is allowed to *be himself* rather than a subject in a new system of signifiers where *being gay* requires a differently competent kind of performance. Outside the grounds of Cranebrook High School, Chris's new urban environment demonstrates a trade-off between the dubious protection offered by the school gates and the discursive space in which *coming out* is synonymous with *being out* on the street—preferably on the few blocks between Sydney's inner-western suburbs Erskineville and Newtown (recently gentrified locations that attract a queer crowd) or, alternatively, Sydney's inner-eastern Oxford Street in Darlinghurst—a more boutique-oriented inner-city strip offering a limited assortment of queer nightlife options.

The reporter positions Chris as a subject who must know his sexuality, but it also disavows the possibility of such knowledge by suggesting—in a paternalistic characterization of youth—that the subject is too young to know himself:

Jeff McMullen: How old were you when you started to feel that you were different to other boys?

Chris Tsalakos: About seven. [*Chris's mother Vicki Tsakalos gives a look of surprise to her son.*]

Jeff McMullen: That young?

Chris Tsalakos: Yeah, that I knew I was different.... But I just couldn't accept who I am, because I didn't know what I was.

Jeff McMullen: Vicki, do you think that at Chris's tender age that he really has the critical judgment to know who he is?

Vicki Tsalakos: I know he's thirteen, and it's really hard for anyone, even at times for me, to accept that he's gay, and that he knows that he's gay. But, it's just something that a mother knows. (McMullen 1997)

Offering a critique of the prevailing discourses of youth, and youth's relation to sexuality, Kerry Robinson suggests that "children are perceived to be socially constructed as the dependent, immature and the powerless 'other' in relation to the independent, mature, powerful and critically thinking adult"—a discourse that is played out in this exchange by the reporter (2002, 417). Throughout the interview,

Chris's gender nonconformity, or his departure from established social scripts that attempt to determine "appropriate" gender embodiment, is catapulted into the discourse of sexuality—specifically homosexuality. His being different is *felt* in the body first, and later *named*—a naming by the other, not by Chris. It is only after repeatedly being called *faggot* and *poofter*, as well as being physically assaulted, that Chris intervenes in this process of recognition by *coming out* as gay. After all, what kind of choice does he have other than resignification when the discourse of sexuality is so much more powerful at policing differences in gender embodiment than claiming, "Don't you realize that my performance of gender is marginalized masculinity, but as for my sexual orientation, well, who knows?" Unlike *marginalized masculinity*, the term *gay* now encapsulates the discourse of pride—its historicity does the discursive work of turning the shame of being called *faggot* (a term open to resignification only in some coteries, and probably not the school playground) into a positive way of being. This excerpt of the interview also reveals gay male sexuality as something that can be known by motherhood, or perhaps the femininity implicit in motherhood, where knowing is felt in the body first and uttered, or named later.

Chris's male body as a generative site for the production of masculinity is lost, and instead he speaks shamelessly of what is supposed to be silently lost and repudiated. Nowhere in the interview is sexual desire mentioned, but sexuality operates as the discursive tool used to regulate gender[16]:

Jeff McMullen: Do you think that he's brought on some of the problems through his own flamboyance?

School Principal: Um, he may have, he may have.

Jeff McMullen: So, do you think he needed to tone it down to fit in here?

School Principal: Everybody has to work on their interpersonal skills: Chris, you, me, everybody. It's part of the learning process in a school context.

[*Cut to Derek Williams, then president of the now defunct Gay and Lesbian Teachers and Students Association*]

Derek Williams: Just from talking to the boy and seeing what he's like, I think you'd have to be completely thick not to see that the boy is homosexual. I mean, it just stands out a mile. He's a stereotypical effeminate gay boy, and why can't ... he's a lovely kid. I mean, why can't he be allowed to survive in the school system?

Jeff McMullen: Having marched in the Mardi Gras on this issue, is there any turning back from being gay?

Chris Tsalakos: No, I'm proud of it. I'm going to be gay and stay gay.

Jeff McMullen: What if you are mistaken, what if at the moment at thirteen you don't really know?

Chris Tsalakos: I know who I am. I know it. I know that I am gay, because I just know. (McMullen 1997)

It isn't just the school principal who falls into the discursive trap of a voluntarism in which a subject selects his choice of gender performance, and that this choice could well work to invite trouble. Williams also takes Chris's gender nonconformity to be synonymous with homosexuality. Not unlike the rhetoric that has circulated about women who have been (sexually) assaulted, the rhetoric here suggests that Chris's very flamboyance meant that he was somehow "asking for it," with "it" standing in here for the regulatory force of violence that seeks to put a subject in his place—a no place, a nowhere. Providing a critique of sexual harassment, particularly as it operates in the school environment, Robinson argues that such behavior "is a critical expression of the converging power regimes of gender and heterosexist oppression" and that "not only does it maintain hierarchical heterosexual gendered relationships, but is [also] a powerful means of reinforcing culturally dominant relations of gender across intersections of class, "race," ethnicity, sexual orientation and so on" (2005, 22–23). While Chris's "flamboyance" is positioned as the *cause* of his problems—that is, his being harassed by other students—this interview also stages powerful, and unexamined, performances of class and racial difference. Disturbingly, the school's principal echoes the regulatory force of gender normativity under the guise of acquiring appropriate pedagogic subjectivity in the school as a way of policing gender and shoring up, in this case, the relation between masculinity and the male body.

Chris is required to give a knowing account of himself in the face of the other—reporter McMullen—while this other mobilizes competing discourses (of youth and youth's precarious and unmentionable relation to sexual development), ensuring that Chris's narrative will contain fissures and ruptures, and break down by virtue of its claim to knowledge. If, as Butler suggests, "the 'I' is the moment of failure in every narrative effort to give an account of oneself" (2001, 37), then this interview sets up and stages the subject as always already disoriented from himself, as well as invoking and maintaining liberal discourses in which the subject is autonomous and unified. Escape from shame leaves no room for error or for an incoherent subject. There is, too, the ominous presence of the law and its relation not only to sexual desire but also to sexual practice, which is always silently present in this interview. The subject here is thirteen years old, and at the time of this interview (1997), the age of consent for gay men in New South Wales was eighteen years of age.[17] Perhaps desire is left unspoken because desire raises the question of whether one acts on, or practices, one's desire—in which case this subject would be *breaking the law*. He would also be challenging discourses of childhood in which the child is positioned as without sexual desire, and without sexual identity.[18] In the last few lines of the interview, reporter McMullen asks Chris whether there is "any turning back" from being gay, and I'm struck here by the literal and metaphorical implications of turning, particularly the kind of turning Butler discusses in her analysis of melancholia when she notes that "melancholia thus returns us to the figure of the 'turn' as a founding trope in the discourse of the psyche. In Hegel turning back upon oneself comes to signify the ascetic and skeptical modes of reflexivity that mark the unhappy consciousness; in Nietzsche turning back upon oneself suggests a retracting of what one has said or done. In Althusser, the turn that the pedestrian makes toward the voice of the law is at once reflexive (the moment of becoming a subject whose self-consciousness is mediated by the law) and self subjugating" (1997b, 168).

There is a curiousness here in that Chris marches forward in the annual Sydney Gay and Lesbian Mardi Gras Parade, which started as a demonstration on June 24, 1978; that original event can certainly be figured as one that turned its back on the law in order to challenge prohibitions against homosexuality.[19] But the "turning back" that McMullen suggests is a turning back to see that one was mistaken, that one got it wrong, that one isn't really queer after all. Chris Tsakalos embodies queer melancholia as a site of power, but his position is always precarious, ambivalent, and open to misrecognition.

This returns me to my own narrative—one, if you like, of mistaken identity in which I too was "hailed" as a faggot. Or was this a tale of mistaken identity? I certainly related to the sexual orientation implicit in "becoming faggot," but was perplexed by the potential of being read as male. If, as Butler suggests, "Hegel has given us an ek-static notion of the self, one which is of necessity, outside itself," and that we are "the self over here who considers its reflection over there, but is equally over there, reflected and reflecting" (2004c, 149), then what can we say of these moments when we recognize parts of ourselves in (mis)recognition? Which parts of ourselves are erased, and how do we contend with our "fundamental vulnerability" in processes of recognition? How do we negotiate our ambivalent relationship to the other? Ambivalent about the excitement of passing, and distressed by the implicit misogyny in having lesbian identity erased, I wished I had refused that hailing, and not turned around—a kind of turning that signified, "Yes, that's me, I'm the one you're talking about." Perhaps Monique Wittig has it right when she notes that a lesbian is not a woman (1993, 103–9).

I'd like to suggest that this kind of ambivalence is both the site of power and the site of what Butler might refer to as "a precarious life" (2004a). On the subject of incoherence, Butler suggests that the "point here is not to celebrate a certain notion of incoherence, but only to consider that our incoherence is ineradicable, but non-totalizing, and that it establishes the way in which we are implicated, beholden, derived, constituted by what is beyond us and before us" (2001, 35).

McInnes's "pedagogy of incoherence" takes up Butler's nuanced reworking of the performativity of gender through the lens of melancholia not to celebrate incoherence but to, in Adam Phillips's words, "keep ... definition on the move, which is where it is anyway" (1997a, 159). As Phillips suggests, it "may be more useful to talk about gradations and blurring rather than contours and outlines when we plot our stories about gender" (159).[20] It is Butler's attention to the liveliness of language, the subtle workings of power through the circulation of discourse, and the regulating effects of normative practices that motivate David McInnes's inquiry.

NOTES

I would like to thank David McInnes for providing me with an exciting critique, for thought-provoking conversation, and for collegial support. Special thanks to Peter Bansel, Judith Butler, Bronwyn Davies, Sara Knox, Robert Payne, and Kerry Robinson, each of whom provided me with insight, unparalleled intellectual rigor, and humor. For editorial advice, thanks to Penny Gay, Sara Knox, and, especially, Kerry Robinson.

1. As Judith Halberstam suggests, "Tomboyism tends to be associated with a 'natural' desire for the greater freedoms and mobilities enjoyed by boys.... Tomboyism is punished, however, when it appears to be the

sign of extreme male identification (taking a boy's name or refusing girl clothing of any type) and when it threatens to extend beyond childhood and into adolescence" (1998, 6).

2. Halberstam also asserts, "If adolescence for boys represents a rite of passage (much celebrated in Western literature in the form of the bildungsroman) and an ascension to some version (however attenuated) of social power, for girls, adolescence is a lesson in restraint, punishment and repression" (1986, 6).

3. As Judith Butler suggests, "The prohibition does not seek to obliterate prohibited desire; on the contrary, probation seeks to reproduce prohibited desire and becomes intensified through the renunciations in effects" (1997b, 56).

4. Butler notes, "The revaluation of such terms as 'queer' suggest that speech can be 'returned' to its speaker in a different form, that it can be cited against its originary purposes, and perform a reversal of effects" (1997a, 14). However, she also notes that not all acts of resignification succeed in their application

5. This essay was first published in the 1998 anthology *Inside/Out: Lesbian Theories, Gay Theories*, and was in part a provocative response to the anthology's title. As her abstract states, Butler "explores the ways in which the assumption of a lesbian identity can serve not only to affirm but also to constrain, legislate, determine or specify one's identity in ways that support the categories of homophobic and heterosexist thought."

6. Connell notes that "the main proponent of a 'performative' account of gender, is strikingly unable to account for work, childcare, institutional life, violence, resistance (except as individual choice) and material inequality. These are not trivial aspects of gender" (2000, 20). See also McInnes 2005, 11.

7. See Connell (1995, chapter 3: "The Social Organization of Masculinity").

8. McInnes cites Alexander Düttmann, noting, "*Anerkennung* (recognition) signifies the process of acknowledging; *Erkenntnis* (re-cognition) signifies identifying something *as* something."

9. See Kenway (1996); and Martino (1999).

10. See Connell (1995, especially chapter 3, "The Social Organization of Masculinity.") See also McInnes (2005.

11. For more on this issue, see Davies (2005a).

12. Judith Butler originally contended that "in this sense, gender is not a performance that a prior subject elects to do, but *gender is performative* in the sense that it constitutes as an effect the very subject it appears to express" (1993c, 314).

13. This should not be confused with the American television news program of the same name.

14. See McInnes and Davies (2006), which analyzes some of the resources used to teach about homophobia that attempt to naturalize homosexual identity in order to enable assimilation. These resources make claims

such as "homosexuality is normal and natural" and "homosexuals are just like you and me," etc. Such processes continue to mark the subject as different claiming to be accepting or tolerant of difference while encouraging sameness or processes of assimilation.

15. In the *Sixty Minutes* segment there is an establishing shot in inner-city Erskineville, outside the now defunct Sydney Gay and Lesbian Mardi Gras workshop space. Chris Tsakalos stands in a back alley, chatting animatedly with an older man who imparts his own knowledge of the upcoming parade. Chris considers this new information, wearing his school uniform while diligently painting flowers on his own poster for the parade. See also Rasmussen (2004).

16. Butler has argued that "the implicit regulation of gender takes place through the explicit regulation of sexuality" (2004c, 53).

17. The Crimes Amendment (Sexual Offenses) Bill of 2003 equalized age of consent for all persons, regardless of gender or sexual orientation, to sixteen years of age.

18. See Robinson (2002); and Gittins (1998).

19. In New South Wales, homosexuality was a crime until the Crimes (Amendment) Act was passed in 1984. This legislation makes no distinction between public and private homosexual acts.

20. Phillips references Douglas (1966).

Conversation with Judith Butler III

Judith Butler: Thank you both for the enormously interesting papers and response, and I look forward to hearing what other people have to say about these issues. I thank David first of all for what I take to be quite an original formulation, which is the effort to assess a typologization of masculinity that assumes an alliance between masculinity and male bodies as a form of melancholia that takes hold at the level of methodology. That's extremely important, because I think we tend to think of melancholia either as a dimension of a psyche or as a cultural phenomenon. But to see it actually operating as a presupposition of a methodological procedure that takes for granted that particular alignment between masculinity and male bodies is, I think, quite innovative, and I thank you for it. I think it's a really important move.

You know, I confess, I don't think Connell has ever read me and I don't think I've ever read him. I'm not sure why that is, but it's probably more interesting to think about the field of gender studies as containing within it certain kinds of ruptures or discontinuities, fields that do not actually overlap very often or very well. One thing I would say on the topic, and then I'm going to leave it because there are more important issues here, is that whoever *Butler* is, Butler does not need to be doing X for X to be doable, and for X to be doable in the spirit of Butler's theory of doing. It is important to distinguish between Butler the person and Butler as something that might be used to do something else, something that Butler has not and could not have done.

The maps of contemporary knowledge are complex, and so it seems crucial that I *not* try and be an expert in every conversation taking place in the field of gender studies. I would never say that such inquiries are unimportant or ought not to be done, and I would never even say that you can do work on gender without caring about such subjects. I am simply saying that our contributions are, of necessity, partial and provisional, and none of us operates at the center of any field, occupying a position that could see all aspects of the field perfectly and perspicaciously. The theoretical contributions that I make from my little corner of the world are there to be taken up or not by those who work in some relation to those fields, and maybe that appropriation will work and maybe not. There's a volume, for instance, coming out in England on my work and education, a volume to which Bronwyn has made a contribution. This is a project that is very interesting for me because, you know, the real question there is what people who are in education say to me or instigate in the theory that makes it work for them. What revisions to the theory happen by virtue of its so-called application or appropriation elsewhere? I actually depend on that appropriation, expropriation. I depend on it because then I don't have to do it, and the limiting of the sovereign *I* is a great relief for this less sovereign *I*. It's a funny expectation of theory that X does not deal with Y, therefore ... X deems Y to be worthless. Maybe X has yet to deal with Y. Maybe X plans to deal with Y when X has done the appropriate preparation. In any case, these formulations put too much emphasis on the subject, and try to discern political and theoretical implications from conjectured motives—a bad method in any case!

Theory and even interdisciplinary work has to happen in collaborative networks where people don't necessarily even know each other but are committed to the aims of the collaboration. And my sense is that there's a wonderful kind of supplementing of one's own perspective that happens in such collaborative contexts. That's more interesting to me, quite frankly; it gives me something new, rather than the moment in which I'm simply thumbing through my old texts trying to figure out what I might have meant, and whether what I now say actually is consistent with what I have said. I do not like doing that, and usually refuse to do it. I suspect it is finally an anti-intellectual activity.

So now I'd like to return to the question of methodological melancholia, which seems to be a very significant innovation. Typology is also something that has to be thought about—what it performs, what it facilitates, and what it forecloses. David talks about typologies of a sort that Connell provides, those depending on an iteration of otherness, and I'd like to know more about that. Do we think that there's an effacement of the iteration of otherness that produces the ground upon which typologies are formed? How does that work, and how might the kind of critical questioning of typologization proceed if we accept the idea that there's a certain effacement that forms its ground? I was also quite taken by the notion that Cristyn put forth, that perhaps typologizations can be understood as a continuation of the naming practices on the playground, that we could see methodological typologies on a social continuum of certain kinds of name-calling practices. Of course, we need the idea of a continuum rather than an assertion of identity, since I don't think we want to say that typologies are so much hate speech. On the other hand, we might ask what relation to otherness typologies sustain or refuse such that they can be understood—at least on some kind of continuum—with more overt forms of hate speech.

I have one remark to make about melancholia that then could lead us to the question of *sissy boys* and *faggot girls*, which seem to be central to both presentations. In [Sigmund] Freud's elaboration of melancholia there is, at least in the early essay "Mourning and Melancholia," a way of talking about melancholia as a disavowed grief or an inability to grieve. It is a loss that has taken place, but that cannot be named, and cannot be acknowledged. What was lost? When, and where? Melancholia marks a disorientation in time and space with respect to the question of loss. There have been whole books, like [Alexander and Margarete] Mitscherlichs's *The Inability to Mourn* [1984], that focus on disavowal or refusal as the constitutive act of melancholia. And at the end of Freud's essay there's also an insistence that aggression resides in melancholia—he talks about the situation in which one has been quarreling with someone who then dies, or who is lost or gone, and then the unresolved psychic question for the one left behind becomes, How is this quarrel supposed to continue? There is a desire to have the quarrel continue, doubtless because, at a psychic level, there is still a desire to make one's point and win the fight. But the quarrel is also a way of keeping the other alive: an aggressive resuscitation of the one who is gone. There's anger at the other for having died or left rather than remaining available to be killed or vanquished, and because the reality of the other is missing, the quarrel continues intrapsychically as a quarrel with oneself. The voice of the other becomes sheltered in the ego, and the ego expands to accommodate that shelter for the other's voice. But what emerges is a confusion about whose voice is whose, since now they both emanate from a quarter of the ego, if we can speak that way—we are forced into figuration by these matters, no doubt. That quarrel is, of course, compounded because the other is gone, and the self-beratement that takes place in melancholia can be a very aggressive form of self-attack, one that puts the melancholic at risk of suicide. Melanie Klein writes two essays that I think are quite important in this regard—"A Contribution to the Psychogenesis of Manic-Depressive States" [1935] and "Mourning and Its Relation to Manic-Depressive States" [1940]. In these texts, she takes up this aspect of melancholia and theorizes a kind of possibility of self-aggression on the basis of this Freudian analysis. I don't think we have to take either Freud or Klein as doxa, but the notion of self-attack is important because it carries the aggression in melancholia. When, then, we consider the masculine debasement of the sissy boy as a kind of melancholic refusal, we can discern the sorrow intermixed with the rage. At work is a refusal that claims, I never was one, I never wanted one, I never could have been one— beneath which one hears, I was! I did!—and that forms a certain defensive masculinity on an inordinately fragile basis. Since, as we know, un-worked-out grief can make for serious war, we have to read the aggression or attack, even violence, in that refusal, and that would be something we would have to take into account when we consider name-calling and its cousin, normalizing typologies. The debasing speech act toward the sissy boy does not simply indicate that the name-caller wishes to disavow any possible relation to the one he debases. It may well also be a certain display of an attack on that part of the self that could have been, that once was barely, that remains a possibility, that others could have seen or did see, a self-attack that becomes externalized in a kind of naming practice directed toward another. Perhaps one way of linking melancholy to the question of playground name-calling is to think about certain naming practices as the externalization of aggression, an aggression that could also be understood in the service of a self-attack on that sissy part of the self that never existed, never could, never will— but may well have, and might still.

It may be important to think about this way of externalizing melancholic aggression to a naming practice in order to distinguish it from other kinds of naming practices, because that's only one kind. That's the hateful naming practice, but there might be other kinds that are actually more about hailing, bringing into community or self constitution, even resignifications of *faggot* in loving ways that call upon, refuse, or rework the hateful dimensions of the interpellation into something affirmative.

David McInnes: Self-aggression is also available as a kind of critical resource, for want of a better way of putting it, toward those formations of masculinity, so there's a kind of ambivalent and unstable relationship for the sissy boy that in one of the things I wrote about before was in my relationship to footballers, about a kind of an undermined—an undermined kind of desire, so there's a kind of compulsion toward a metaphorized compulsion toward footballers' thighs, at the same time as there's an anger and a disappointment that men just aren't what you thought they were going to be as masculine.

Judith Butler: That's great. What you're pointing out is that other dimension of melancholia, which is ambivalence, and how an ambivalent structure can be held at the same time. You know, it could be the idealization of the thigh, the disappointment that the thigh is not thighness in its platonic sense, and then a rage against the ideal precisely because of the disappointment that follows from it. There is an interesting turning of rage that happens in both of your discussions that involves its critical capacity. It's probably, for me, untheorized, but I think that the critical dimension of that kind of rage is quite important. I don't know if you are familiar with Ken Corbett, who works on this issue of the sissy boy. He's a psychoanalyst in New York who's written a fair amount on sissy boys and it's wonderful work.[1]

One question I have—given the fact that we have sissy boys and, apparently, we have Cristyn as an early sissy as well—is whether *sissy* floats, as it were, among genders, whether sissy does something to boyness. Does sissy qualify the boy—is it a qualifying adjective? Or is that a kind of boy—a typology, and so a noun? Or is it a negation of boyness? Does sissy act upon boyness, does it have to be an adjective that is added to the noun precisely because it is never fully a symbol of either? It's not exactly a noun phrase, because that would be a grammatical tension. *Sissy boy*, as in *not boy boy*—a negation of boyness that nevertheless qualifies boyness, at which point the adjective and the noun are in a slight quarrel. And if Cristyn can be one, which is complicated but surely possible, then it would seem that being a girl does not disqualify one from being named a sissy; there are girls who are not sissies but what *sissy* does is intensify girlness. And I would imagine that when she's called a sissy or when she's called *too much* of a girl, that in both cases we're seeing something about how girlness can be amplified or intensified beyond a stable, mundane meaning. Again, sissy is adjectival in a way that negates boyness and amplifies girlness, but it doesn't belong to the noun; rather, it acts upon it in some way. I want to suggest that this might be a point of departure for thinking about an operational gendering that is not fully assimilated into the noun. Even though saying *You're a sissy* designates it grammatically as a noun, the phrase also acts upon the noun. So maybe we need to think of it as a performative or as an action of some kind that alternately qualifies and intensifies, aggrandizes, and diminishes.

I would suggest, too, that maybe the sissy boy is a figure that has to be understood both as part of the internal complexity of a psyche and as constantly disavowed, displaced, and externalized. And I think we need to link disavowal and externalization more strongly than perhaps I have done in the past, because the sissy boy is already a kind of figure—what is *not* me, or *cannot* be me—and so becomes forcibly externalized and placed outside of oneself. It's not just a way of describing somebody's flamboyance, but a way of relocating externally a part of that self's disavowed psyche, housing or incorporating it externally so that it's literally not assimilated into the *I* who one is. So, again, it's not a phrase that can be substituted for by a purely descriptive operation—Oh, there's that boy in his flamboyant dress. What I say when I say *sissy boy* is also some part of myself, which in the saying and in the naming externalizes what I disavow, and even aggressively maintains that part as external for the purposes of maintaining its externality to who I am. If that border between what is part of me and what is outside me becomes too porous, violence can result.

Let me raise a couple of other questions here. There's a question of whether we need to be skeptical of all names, whether names are generally the problem. Sometimes I do feel that names are the problem, but other times I feel they aren't and so something of my own ambivalence is doubtless at work in my discussion of this problem. The difference between *Undoing Gender* and *Gender Trouble* probably has to do with my sense that a livable life does require recognition of some kind and that there are occasions in which names do sustain us, that there's a sustaining function of the name. Call me my name, do not cease to call me my name, do not forget my name, this is the name by which I wish to be called—these are important moments, even as simultaneously I do worry that they can freeze mobility, become reified along the way. How, though, do we understand the young boy who declares publicly, I'm gay, I know it. Is he stabilizing what is dispersing? Is his self-naming practice a moment of freezing what is otherwise mobile? Or does it serve a different function? I don't have an answer, and I do not know the body. The way Cristyn describes it is that he's called first a faggot by others, or he's called gay, or people say he's gay, and he is spoken about in that way. In any of these circumstances, there's an interpellation or an address from the outside and then, only after, a taking up of the name for himself—I am gay.

Cristyn Davies: He's called *poofter* and *faggot* and then he resignifies it by ...

Judith Butler: He signifies it as gay. There's a way in which he shifts decades. He brings the speech up through a couple of decades. It is a pedagogical moment; it's an instructive moment. As in, *You fool, this is what we're called now.* [*Laughter.*]

But my question is, if we can actually pull the self-naming apart from its relationship with having been named or its response to having been named. When he calls himself something, is he positioning himself in relationship to those

who would demean him, and so, through the name, countering the demeaning term and expressing a capacity for self-
definition that would otherwise be deprived to him? Is he
expressing a felt desire? I don't know. It could be that the
desire is also instilled through the name. If it's expressing a
felt desire, it might also be stabilizing desire. It could also
be, at least according to the analysis you give us, a relationship to the mother's desire, because she's out there saying,
That's what he is, that's what he wants to be. But is she making room for him, or is she producing her gay son, who will
never have another woman besides her? I don't know. You
know, I'm just asking. We don't want to idealize this scene
of self-definition too quickly, because many things could be
happening in this scene in which a boy comes out to his
mom and his mom responds, Yes, you're gay. Is he fulfilling
her desire? At the same time, he's laying claim to knowing
who he is now and what he will be in the future: it's kind
of an in-your-face, My being gay is not going to change!
Okay, maybe one could stand for oneself through time, but
perhaps one standing for oneself through time is also a way
of saying, I'm going to resist the force of those of you who
would have me be otherwise.

So it is here that I wonder what happens to the question of desire in that particular fight. Does one even know
one's desire anymore when one's in that fight? Or is one's
desire simply to stay in the fight and to refuse the interpellation that will degrade one? Does one even have a moment in
which one could have a fantasy or a dream that strays from
the declared identity in question? That's a question of what
one wants, and I don't know where the question of desire
is in that struggle, where the space is for the reflection on
desire, for the imagining of desire. The language becomes so
highly politicized.

There are just two final points on this—one about the
spatial conditions of being addressed and defining oneself,
and another on turning—turning back, turning away from
the scene of address. In the two scenes brought up today, we
encounter a question of how one is addressed on the street
or in the playground. Naming oneself and being named by
another, on the street or in the playground: each indexes
possibilities of constraint, possibilities of punishment, of
escape, of no escape, of there being witnesses, or there not

being witnesses. We have to consider the social parameters of those spatial environments when we try to figure out what naming does and does not do. It may be doing something other than stabilizing a dispersion; it also may actively be positioning oneself in relationship to a spatial and a social world—an entire matrix of obligatory heterosexuality, for instance—that is implied without being explicitly named by the act of naming.

Regarding the question of turning, when one is called a name, and one turns around in response to that hailing, could the turning around itself constitute a kind of refusal? If by calling you that name they intended to make it impossible for you to turn back and show your face, does actually turning to show your face refuse the force of the call? If the call is meant to efface you, and you show your face, then the call has failed to work, and it fails precisely at the moment in which you turn around to face the call. Similarly, we can imagine contexts in which the refusal to hear or heed the call is itself a refusal, and the one who calls is left alone with his own echo as you move on and away. I don't know.

Cristyn Davies: I don't know, either.

Judith Butler: In saying yes, in turning back and facing those who call you that name—what if you had said yes and then they'd seen? Would the *yes* have been a refusal of the force of interpellation, which was meant to keep you from being able to say anything at all, which was supposed to be able to silence you and efface you? In this sense, facing and saying may be quite the opposite of refusing, refusing the turn. It does seem to me that when Chris [Tsakalos] turns back and says, Yes I am and I know and I will stay [gay], and, By the way, this is the right term, you fool, there is a refusal in the turning back and facing, and we might even say that he is, as Sheridan remarked yesterday, constituted in the turning.

It's not that he turns, but that in the turning the self is constituted or performed. But rather than regard the self either as appropriately or inappropriately designated by the name, the self is constituted not only by the name, but in the bodily relation to the name, the turning. If one asserts that mobility, if one turns, then one has not been fully paralyzed or branded by the name. And if one turns toward the name, it may be that someone has something to say to the name and to the one who utters it. He turns back, he faces, he names himself—is this an acceptance of the interpella-tion, a refusal of the interpellation, or a seizing of the scene of interpellation?

Cristyn Davies: It's all those things, isn't it?

Judith Butler: Maybe. But the fact that he offers a different name when he's called is very interesting. It says to me much more that the young boy we are discussing seizes the power of naming in that scene and insists on seizing the power of naming. This is why it might be that Chris could become something else, a different name, at another time, since what he's become is somebody who names himself, and this identity, we might conjecture, may be more fundamental, even more radical, than being gay. I don't have an answer. But I thank you both for enormously rich discussions.

NOTE

1. See Corbett (1991, 2001).

CHAPTER 4

Words That Matter: Reading the Performativity of Humanity through Butler and Blanchot

LINNELL SECOMB

University of Sydney

INTRODUCTION

Edward Said, responding to the canon wars within the humanities, calls for a new humanism that is cosmopolitan and learns from the past while also being "attuned to the emergent voices and currents of the present, many of them exilic, extraterritorial, and unhoused"

(2004, 11). Rejecting both traditionalists who want to preserve a predominantly European and male literary canon as well as poststructuralists' critiques of the Euro-phallocentric humanist grand narratives of enlightenment and reason, Said defends a "different kind of humanism" (2004, 11). For Said, language is central to the renewal of humanism, and humanism is "a technique of trouble" (2004, 77), a process of critique, questioning, and resistance that involves interrogating texts, words, and discourses so as to reveal silences, exclusions, and mythologies. Only through language, Said contends, can the "obstruction[s] of language" be diagnosed (2004, 29).

While Said's representation of poststructuralism ignores poststructuralism's concern with rethinking or rearticulating the concept of the human through the critique of the limitations of existing humanism, his insistence on the centrality of language is nevertheless germane. Poststructuralism, too, conceives language as central, with various theorists elaborating its performative productions, the articulation of language/knowledge/power, and the effects of representation and discourse.

Though this paper does not attempt to engage directly with the debate about humanism, it is nevertheless situated within the context of a concern about varying conceptions of the human and nonhuman. It approaches this question by investigating recent debates about asylum seekers, analyzing the Australian government's linguistic constructions and pronouncements as well as the resistant words of refugees. However, it begins via a detour that rehearses the now familiar history of the development, from J. L. Austin to Jacques Derrida and Judith Butler, of theories of linguistic and somatic performativity. It prolongs this digression in order to elaborate Maurice Blanchot's theory of language, hoping that this will further elucidate aspects of Butler's theory of performativity as well as providing tools for the delayed engagement with refugee discourses.

This essay attempts to trouble the predominant discourses about refugees by utilizing aspects of Butler's and Blanchot's theories of language, each of which are themselves, rearticulated through their juxtaposition.

CONSTATIVE, PERFORMATIVE, AND ITERATIVE

Austin's distinction between constatives (descriptive statements) and performatives (utterances that enact an event or occurrence) introduces a wedge that begins to shatter the construction of language as representational. While for Austin most language is constative—that is, it merely describes the world—he also proposes that some utterances bring about a new situation by performing an act. Austin illustrates this with the example of marriage, where saying "I do" in the right circumstances transforms the speaker into a wife or husband. Other examples include naming a ship, pronouncing a sentence of guilt or innocence, and making a promise, all of which bring about an event rather than simply describing an event.

However, the distinction between constative and performative quickly becomes complex and unstable. Jonathan Culler points out that many speech acts turn out to be explicit performatives—for example, acts involving promising, ordering, and declaring—and that, in addition, even apparently straightforward constative statements may be implicit performatives. Culler explains, for example, that the statement, "The cat is on the mat" is an affirmation—"I affirm that the cat is on the mat"—indicating that apparently descriptive statements may also be performative acts of asserting or affirming a situation or event. Similarly (foreshadowing here the later discussion of Butler's example), the statements "It's a girl" or "It's a boy" upon a child's birth may turn out to be a pronouncement affirming, pronouncing, and inaugurating gender identity. What this suggests is a complex relation between constative statements and performative utterances insofar as constatives may also perform actions such as the action of stating, affirming, and describing (Culler 2000, 505).

In "Signature Event Context," Derrida critiques the traditional philosophical conception of language that elaborates "a theory of the sign as representation of the idea which itself represented the object perceived" (1988, 6). Derrida finds Austin's theory useful in overturning this traditional conception, for the operation of the performative indicates that speech is not limited to the communication of thought content and does not necessarily describe or represent a perceived object. Nevertheless, in order to demonstrate the radical effects of Austin's theory, Derrida elaborates the consequences that Austin himself had attempted to delimit as exceptions. Austin, for example, insists that for performatives to be felicitous the speaker has to intend the outcome of the utterance. He therefore distinguishes "serious" utterances such as "I do" in a marriage ceremony from quotations of this utterance in the context of theater, poetry, or joking where there is no intention to marry. Derrida insists, however, that all utterances are quotations, citation, or iterations and that this cannot be used to distinguish serious and nonserious utterances.

Indeed, Derrida suggests that performatives garner their effect not from the intention of the speaker but from the citationality of the utterance. The utterance only has its consequence because it is recognized as reproducing a social and linguistic convention. Derrida therefore asks, "Could a performative utterance succeed if its formulation did not repeat a 'coded' or iterable utterance, or in other words, if the formula I pronounce in order to open a meeting, launch a ship or a marriage were not identifiable as conforming with an iterable model, if it were not then identifiable in some way as a 'citation'?" (1988, 18).

The intentional consciousness of the speaker is further destabilized by the difference that accompanies each citation or repetition of an utterance. Each quotation introduces a difference, producing a dissemination or a residue that escapes any unity of meaning. The "infelicities" of the performative utterance, and the parasitic abnormal quotations of ordinary performatives, that Austin attempts to set aside themselves demonstrate this excess and difference introduced in iteration. Derrida insists, "The iteration structuring [the utterance] a priori introduces into it a dehiscence and a cleft which are essential" (1988, 18).

Culler draws on this analysis to suggest that "both the political and literary act depend on a complex, paradoxical combination of the performative and constative" (1997, 100). Culler explains, for example, that political claims often consist of (constative) statements about situations in which it is through the making of the statement that the situation (performatively) comes into existence. He provides an example of this paradoxical combination of constative and performative in the U.S. Declaration of Independence, in which a central sentence reads, "We therefore ... do solemnly publish and declare that these United colonies are and of right ought to be free and independent states" (Declaration of Independence, quoted in Culler 2000, 510). This appears to be a constative description of the already existing unity of the States but it is also a performative act that brings into existence the United States of America (see also Derrida 1986).

LINGUISTIC AND SOMATIC PERFORMATIVITY

Judith Butler develops further the performative effect of language and discourse. In *Gender Trouble* and *Bodies That Matter* Butler extends the limited linguistic origin of Austin's performative by applying this concept to constructions of gendered identity and subjectivity more generally. Butler suggests that gender is not an essence of the self but an action or a performance that inaugurates the self. I become a woman, for example, through my performances of femininity and/or I may resist this seemingly natural identity through my performance of tomboy or a butch persona. Gender is, for Butler, a doing or a performative enactment rather than the expression of an inner essence or being. This suggests that there is no "doer behind the deed" (1990a, 142): identity does not preexist its enactment but is produced through this performative doing.

Perhaps it is this claim that has contributed most to the reductive interpretation that for Butler "the object is nothing but the language by which it is constructed" (Butler and Connolly, 2000, para 19). However, to suggest that there is no doer before acting is not to suggest that there is no substance or materiality before performativity. Indeed, movements, gestures, and performativity necessitate a body that acts. Butler's point is not that there is no body here but that there is no pregiven identity emerging from that body and that subjectivity arises through the performativity of that body.

For Butler, the pronouncements "It's a girl" or "It's a boy" at the moment of birth are not constative descriptions but interpellations that in naming the gender prescribe, define, and construct the infant's gender identity. This performative labeling initiates a process of "girling" or "boying" through which each is compelled to preformatively conform to her or his gender assignment (Butler, 1993a, 232). While Culler had revealed the performative aspect of a constative statement by suggesting that the statement is always an affirmation or assertion, Butler extends the force of the performative arguing that such statements, cumulatively, inaugurate and create gender identities. This productive extension of the performative reveals further the materializing force of speech. The utterance "It's a girl" is more than just an assertion; it is a pronouncement that brings gendered life into existence.

Butler adopts and adapts Austin's performative to demonstrate its effects on the production of gender, but she also extends the concept of the performative by revealing the embodied performativity that inaugurates gendered subjectivity. While two different aspects of performativity are evident here—performative utterances ("It's a girl") that produce effects rather than describe existing situations, and performative bodily enactments that through repetition produce identities—these are not necessarily distinct or separable. Rather, Butler has extended Austin's limited application to suggest that not only do words produce effects, but embodied actions and practices also produce objects and events. Understanding language as performative rather than constative challenges a representational view of language as descriptive and reveals the productive effects of language. Similarly, understanding the actions of subjects as performative dispels an essentialist view of a preexisting identity that is expressed through actions and reveals instead the production of the subject through repeated performativity.

While Derrida has extended Austin's account of the performative by suggesting that its productive force arises not from the intentions of the speaker but from the repeated chorusing of the utterance, Butler extends Austin's account in another direction: not just words, but also actions, are performative in the required sense. Both words and embodied actions bring about an event or identity rather than simply expressing or describing a preexisting situation or essence.

Butler's achievement in extending linguistic performativity by inventing the new concept of somatic performativity has been insufficiently acknowledged. Gilles Deleuze and Félix Guattari suggest that the invention of new concepts defines the work of philosophy (1994, 15–34). Concepts help explain previously obscure problems. René Descartes *cogito*, Derrida's *différance*, and Simone de Beauvoir's *second sex*, for example, all help to explain aspects of experience (though clearly these concepts may be superseded by later analyses). Similarly, Butler's *somatic performativity* shifts our understanding, beginning to illuminate the complex relations among body, action, and language.

Not only does Butler extend the Austinian linguistic performative by postulating a corporeal performativity that brings into existence the gender it enacts, but in addition, and more radically still, she questions the preexistence of a natural biological sex onto which a gender is said to be mapped or inscribed. Butler asks, in *Gender Trouble*, "[I]s 'the body' itself shaped by political forces with strategic interests in keeping the body bounded and constituted by the markers of sex?" (1990a, 129) thereby suggesting that the physical body, too, is molded and constructed. Butler elaborates this possibility further in *Bodies That Matter* by proposing that matter, and the physical body itself, be understood as "*a process of materialization that stabilizes over time to produce the effects of boundary, fixity, and surface that we call matter*" (1993a, 9; emphasis in the original).

Butler insists that this is not a form of idealism that would deny the existence of the material world, but instead an explanation of how we encounter that world: "To claim that discourse is formative is not to claim that it originates, causes, or exhaustively composes that which it concedes; rather, it is to claim that there is no reference to a pure body which is not at the same time a further formation of that body.... In philosophical terms, the constative claim is always to some degree performative" (1993a, 10–11). What this suggests is that sex is not the preexisting natural, biological foundation on which social gender is constructed, but that sex, too, is an effect of a performative linguistics that pronounces it to be natural and prediscursive. Butler does not deny the existence of matter but demonstrates its performative productions.

Butler encapsulates the complex intertwining of language and materiality, suggesting, "Language and materiality are fully embedded in each other, chiasmic in their interdependency, but never fully collapsed into one another.... Always, already implicated in each other, always already exceeding each other, language and materiality are never fully identical or fully different" (1993a, 69). She returns to this image of an intertwining or chiasmic relation between language and materiality in subsequent texts. In an interview with William Connolly she argues that "to focus on linguistic practice here and non-linguistic practice there, and to claim that both are important is still not to focus on the relation between them.... We are ... caught in a chiasmic relation, one in which the terms to be related partake of one another, but do not collapse into one another" (Butler and Connolly, 2000, para 20).

In responding to Rosi Bradotti's critique of her work, Butler reiterates this point: "The relation between [speech acts and bodily acts] is complicated, and I called it a "chiasmus" in *Bodies That Matter*. There is always a dimension of bodily life that cannot be fully represented even as it works as the condition and activating condition of language" (Butler, 2000, 198–99). Recalling Maurice Merleau-Ponty's concept of chiasm—the experience of simultaneously touching and being touched in a handshake (1995, 142); the "reciprocal insertion and intertwining of one in the other" (1995, 138)—Butler pushes us to think beyond both materialist and constructionist positions, wishing for a more complex and subtle articulation of the word-world relation.

SUBVERSIVE SPEECH

While Butler argues in *Gender Trouble* and *Bodies That Matter* that language as performative inaugurates the subject and the subject's connection with the world, indicating that words have material effects, she nonetheless in *Excitable Speech* cautions against a too easy and reductive collapse of speech and action (1997a, 22–23). In this reflection on hate speech and censorship she argues that these forms of legal regulation ignore the infelicities of speech acts; misidentify the causes of injury; repeat injurious terms in censoring them; and are applied inconsistently creating conservative outcomes in which sexuality is censored while racist speech, equated with freedom of speech, is claimed to be protected by the Constitution (23, 37, 39–40).

Butler suggests that the performative effects of speech have been used to justify the legal regulation of hate speech which is said to be a verbal assault equivalent to a physical injury (4), and to support censorship of pornography which is seen as acting on women and constituting them as an inferior class (21). Butler counters these applications of performative speech theory, arguing that performative interpellations do not literally produce physical bodies but create social existences: hate speech is not a literal physical assault, but is *like* an assault (4–5). Moreover, she argues that to describe pornography as performative conflates representation and conduct (23). Finally, Butler argues that this conflation of speech and action and the attribution of a "magical" efficacy to speech ignore the iterative and citational aspect of the performative that is frequently ineffective and infelicitous (23). Moreover, the insistence on the totalizing efficacy of hate speech and pornography leaves no room for a critical performative response (21) and denies agency to the addressee positioning her or him as a passive victim (41).

While Butler fully acknowledges the performative effects of language, she nonetheless insists that words are complex entities that may simultaneously subjugate and injure while also inaugurating the subject. Moreover, language is endlessly reiterated and rearticulated, enabling resignification, and acquires its efficacy not through the single utterance of a lone speaker but through repeated citations by a chorus of speakers. To censor speech using hate speech legislation ignores the potency of resignification by a subject inaugurated and produced by both positive and negative acts of naming.

Butler is not here reneging on her earlier account of the importance of performativity, but is instead, in the face of a reductive and conservative application of performative linguistics, elaborating the nuances of the theory. Against a deterministic account, which insists on a necessary relation between the utterance and the effect, Butler focuses on the radical indeterminacy of the speech act. As a result of iteration and citation the signifying effects of words are open to transformations proliferating the effects of utterances. This is already apparent in *Gender Trouble* and *Bodies That Matter*: while gender is produced through linguistic and somatic performativity tending to produce normative identities, nonetheless variation, incoherencies, and failures enable the possibility of altogether other outcomes: drag kings and queens, butch and femme personas, tomboys, sapphists, trannies, leather men, bears, inverts, queers, and so on. Not only are identity subversions possible but, additionally, the injurious effects of insults such as "queer" can be reversed and adopted as a sign of resistance: "We're here, we're queer, so get used to it."

The radical duality of performative interpellations—creating and delimiting the subject—indicates that words, embedded in histories and structures of transforming meaning, make possible the subject's "linguistic survival as well as, potentially, that subject's linguistic death" (Butler, 1997a, 28). Blanchot also elaborates this dual aspect of language—giving death and life—though somewhat differently. For Blanchot, language negates the world, replacing it with the concept, though through the materiality of words language also gestures toward the ineffable being of the world.

SUBLATION OR CHIASM

While Butler does not, to my knowledge, refer directly to Blanchot, his work on language and literature has influenced the domain of poststructural linguistics that is central to Butler's exploration of somatic and linguistic performativity. Derrida draws extensively on Blanchot's writings, and many commentators feel, as Ullrich Hasse and William Large put it, that "Blanchot is the most important precursor to what is called deconstruction and it is difficult to find an idea in Derrida's work that is not also present in the writings of Blanchot" (2001, 131). Butler's theory of language is situated within the context of Blanchot's earlier analyses. While certain resemblances are therefore evident, there are also divergences that clarify the significance and specificity of Butler's formulations.

Rejecting a representational or informational theory of language, Blanchot suggests that language negates the object by replacing it with a concept or thought. Blanchot, like Culler, uses the school-primer example of the cat to clarify. As soon as we named this animal, it "ceased to be a uniquely real cat and became an idea as well" (1981, 42). In naming the cat I replace the materiality of this moggy—its actually existing shape, colors, short- or longhaired furriness, and resonating purring—with the concept of the cat—including, perhaps, the ubiquitous mat on which it sat. For Blanchot, this conceptual cat destroys the cat in its material existence. If it does not actually annihilate the material creature it does, at the very least, portend the negation, the future death and nonexistence of the animal. The concept lives on untarnished and perfect even after the cat in its materiality has long ago expended all of its "nine lives."

This account mirrors the poststructuralist formulation in which the word (signifier) represents the concept (signified) and meaning emerges from the relation between signifieds. The material cat does not determine the meaning of the conceptual cat, which instead garners its significance from its relation to, and distinction from, similar terms: *animal, creature, dog, lion, pet,* and so on. The material cat exists but is annihilated or abolished in the sense that it does not determine the meaning of the word or the content of the concept *cat.*

While Blanchot does not use the example of the declaration of gender at the moment of birth to further illustrate his argument, he does refer repeatedly to the concept of *woman*. To speak of an object, to name a subject, gives us control over it, Blanchot suggests, and he explains using the idea of *woman*: "when we speak, we gain control over things with satisfying ease. I say, 'This woman,' and she is immediately available to me, I push her away, I bring her close, she is everything I want her to be, she becomes the place in which the most surprising sorts of transformations occur and actions unfold" (1981, 41). In naming this person *woman* I suppress her living, breathing actuality: "A word may give me its meaning, but first it suppresses it. For me to be able to say, 'This woman' I must somehow take her flesh and blood reality away from her, cause her to be absent, annihilate her" (42).

Blanchot is not claiming that any physical act of annihilation, any physical destruction or injury, has taken place. Like Butler, who insists that abusive linguistic acts are not equivalent to physical assaults, Blanchot concedes that no act of murder or killing has occurred. "Of course my language does not kill anyone" he writes (1981, 42). Nevertheless, he also insists that an "ideal negation" has been enacted: "And yet: when I say 'This woman,' real death has been announced and is already present in my language; my language means that this person, who is here right now, can be detached from herself, removed from her existence and her presence and suddenly plunged into a nothingness in which there is no existence or presence; my language essentially signifies the possibility of this destruction.... Therefore it is accurate to say that when I speak: death speaks in me" (42–43).

Blanchot's thesis is that in naming the object we replace it, in its materiality, with a concept. Once this naming takes place we perceive the world through these concepts, thus obliterating, for us, the object in its materiality. He writes that "man was condemned not to be able to approach anything or experience anything except through the meaning he had to create" (42).

Blanchot's analysis augments Butler's theories of linguistic and somatic performativity. Like Butler, who suggests that the pronouncement "It's a girl" inaugurates girling producing femininity, Blanchot suggests that the use of the word *woman* enables the shaping, molding, and construction of the concept *woman*. The pronouncement "It's a girl" not only inaugurates a process of "girling" through which femininity is produced, but also obliterates the infant in her physical existence allowing a perception of her only through this concept of *girlness*. The performative effects of language, we may conclude, are made possible only through the necessarily negating operation of language: through the inevitable replacement of the object with the concept. Butler's further insight (as we have seen) is to reveal how the creation of the concept (*girl/woman*) then results in a rematerializing effect through which the negated infant or woman rematerializes herself, "becoming woman" through a reiterated embodied performance of the concept *woman*.

However, Blanchot, too, achieves a rematerializing effect though he achieves this along a differing trajectory. There are two distinct steps in Blanchot's conception of the relation between language and materiality. In the first step he separates language from the world, suggesting that words occlude the objects to which they ostensibly refer. In the second step he argues that words are, nevertheless, imbued with the materiality that they have apparently annulled.

Blanchot not only proposes that words occlude material objects, replacing them with concepts, but also contends that language itself, words themselves, exhibit a certain materiality. Language not only negates the world; it also substitutes words for the nonexistence it has brought about. These words, as Blanchot writes, are "a completely determined and objective reality" (1981, 44). Words do not simply convey meanings—convey, for example, the idea of the woman in her absence and even in her presence. Rather, words have their own materiality in their "rhythm, weight, mass, shape" (46). But more than this, words are imbued with a prelinguistic existence, with "the profound work of the elements" (53), with sensuous materialities, so that they express within them the ineffable and unrepresentable being of the world. Words, Blanchot writes, evoke "vague, indeterminate, elusive existences in which nothing appears, the heart of depth without appearance" (49).

This materiality of language is further elucidated in the work of Giorgio Agamben, Alexander Garcia Düttmann, and Martin Heidegger. Agamben, like Blanchot, insists on the materiality of language beyond its restricted function as communication, description, or representation. In his aphorism "The Idea of Matter" Agamben speaks of the "woody substance of language," suggesting that those of us who have not experienced this "matter of words" are "prisoners of representation" (1995, 37).

Martin Heidegger reveals a further aspect of this woodiness of words when he speaks in *On the Way to Language* of the relation between saying and being. He writes that "Saying and Being, word and thing, belong to each other in a veiled way, a way that has hardly been thought ..." (1982, 155). Heidegger seems to be suggesting that etymologically, saying and being are related, and that they mean the "presencing of beings" or the "showing, [which] lets beings appear" (155). Words do not so much negate the object as let the object appear. "[A] thing may be only where the word is granted," Heidegger concludes (1982, 150).

One interpretation that may be drawn from these reflections on language suggests the convoluted double-aspect of language. Language occludes the real world, but also at the same time and indissociably reveals the being of the world. The word, from one angle, represses and replaces the object, but from another angle it reveals the being of the object. And it is through the materiality of words, or the woodiness of words, that this saying as showing is possible.

These thoughts on language suggest that word and thing cannot be separated. As Düttmann makes clear in his introduction to Agamben's *Idea of Prose*, the sensible or material and the intelligible or conceptual cannot be conceived as an opposition but are gathered together through the milieu of language (1995, 19). The material object is not "some sensible thing presupposed by language and knowledge" (Agamben, 1995, 123). Idea and thing are not opposed, rather: "... the thing no longer separated from its intelligibility, but in the midst of it, is the idea, is the thing itself" (Agamben, 1995, 123).

Blanchot insists on the materiality of the written word, pointing to the precedence of "the paper on which one writes, the trail of ink, the book" and affirming that "happily language is a thing: it is a written thing, a bit of bark, a sliver of rock, a fragment of clay in which the reality of the earth continues to exist" (1981, 46). Through this materiality, Blanchot suggests, the object that has been occluded by its naming reemerges and is preserved in the word; "whatever [language] designates is abolished; but whatever is abolished is also sustained, and the thing has found a refuge (in the being which is the word)" (48).

Similarly, Butler invokes the materiality of utterances that are "the vocalization of sound," "material sputterings" (1993a, 69) produced by the body, by vocal cords, tongue, teeth, and mouth so that, writes Butler, "Language emerges from the body constituting an emission of sorts" (2004c, 198). Yet Butler simultaneously insists on the ideational aspect of words, suggesting that speech is inaugurated by the "psychic effort to reinstall and recapture a lost maternal body" (1993a, 69). This conception of language, both material and ideational, enables Butler's complex theory of somatic and linguistic performativity. Words and bodies are distinct, for Butler, but so closely enmeshed that each imbues the other producing effects and affects. The word *girl* introduces *girling*, resulting in *becoming woman*. Through the iterations and fallible citations of *girling* this performativity of femininity may introduce other personas creating femmes, princesses, queens, queers, and even, finally, tomboys and butches. In this process body and word are both performatives, entwining, interacting, and producing proliferating personas, identities, and meanings—normative and otherwise.

While Blanchot's conception of language as a materiality that suppresses and preserves the world provides a useful frame for understanding Butler's open-ended somatic and linguistic performativity, there are finally significant differences that ought not be overlooked. Blanchot's theory sublates and preserves the world, maintaining an unchanging if ineffable being within the materiality of language. Butler subverts this dialectical formulation, introducing the displacements, disseminations, and difference that iterative performativity produces. While for Blanchot the being of the world reemerges and finds refuge in the materiality of the word, for Butler word and world are a chiasmic entwining, creating an oscillation that disseminates difference. For Blanchot, language preserves the being of the world; for Butler, language endlessly produces and reproduces a proliferating world, which in turn stutteringly vocalizes ceaselessly evolving words and speech.

Performing Humanity

Frantz Fanon, resisting the racism that denied his humanity, wrote in *Black Skin White Masks*, "I wanted to be a man, nothing but a man" (1982, 113). Sojourner Truth similarly insisted "'Ar'n't I a woman?'" (quoted in Gilbert 1991, 134). This insistence on humanity, in the face of a dehumanizing racism, calls for a rethinking of the critiques of humanism. The benevolent pretensions of humanism have been exposed by critiques that reveal that humanism is founded on a masculine, Eurocentric Enlightenment tradition that valorizes reason and mind over emotion and body and thereby excludes the seemingly more carnal and passional woman and racial other. Some have argued, however, that we ought not therefore abandon humanism but instead create a more encompassing humanism. Sarah Kofman reads Robert Antelme's *The Human Race* as a call for a new humanism that rejects both the fascist abjection of camp detainees as subhuman as well as a reverse negation by which the Nazi Schutzstaffel (SS) would be constituted as animal. In a double gesture, Antelme insists on the commonality of all in the human race but also on difference and incommensurability within this unity (Antelme 1998; Kofman 1998). Said, too, attempts to reanimate humanism, insisting, like Antelme, on the significance of language in the reformulation of humanism. For Antelme, language functions as a tool of resistance against the dehumanizing strategies of the SS and is the "last thing in common" among the SS, the World War II detainee, and the world outside the concentration camps; for Said, humanism involves "a detailed, patient scrutiny of and lifelong attentiveness to the words and rhetorics by which language is used by human beings who exist in history" (2004, 61). If language is central to the construction of the human, then the task of decoding words and of analyzing the performative effects of language will be central in understanding the varying formulations of the human, humane, and humanitarian—and of the inhuman.

Australian prime minister John Howard is a master of word games. When accused of racism and of playing the "race card" during the 2001 election campaign, which was dominated by debates about asylum seekers from Afghanistan, Iran, and Iraq who were entering Australia on boats sailing from Indonesia, Howard was indignant, saying that the allegations were inaccurate and "'politically offensive'" (quoted in Marr and Wilkinson 2003, 280). He asserted that he was not manipulating racist sentiments; as he claimed, "'I don't find any racism in the Australian public ... I don't find, as I move around the community, people expressing racist sentiments about the illegal immigrants at all'" (279).

Not only are Australians not racist in Howard's view, but, for him, Australia is a humane society. In late August 2001 Howard claimed in a radio interview, "'We are a humanitarian country. We don't turn people back into the sea, we don't turn unseaworthy boats which are likely to capsize and the people on them be drowned.... We are faced with this awful dilemma of on the one hand trying to behave like a humanitarian decent country, on the other hand making certain that we don't become just an easy touch for illegal immigrants'" (quoted in Marr and Wilkinson 2003, 47). Within days, however, Howard had instigated policies that did, precisely, force unseaworthy boats to turn back.

Throughout this period, the Australian government also reduced those seeking asylum in Australia to a series of acronyms—SUNCs, UAs, UBAs, and PIIs—and their dangerously unseaworthy boats were called SIEVs. Setting aside the vicious irony of calling boats the government knows to be dangerous SIEVs (but nonetheless refusing to assist), this proliferation of acronyms obscures the tragedy and suffering experienced by those seeking refuge. The naming and categorizing abbreviated by these acronyms continue this dehumanizing effect: *suspected unauthorized non-citizens, unauthorized arrivals, unauthorized boat arrivals, potential illegal immigrants,* and *suspected illegal entry vessels.* The implications of the words *illegal, suspect, unauthorized,* and *noncitizen* facilitate an easy slippage that equates refugees with the denizens, criminals, and even terrorists, obscuring the persecution that prompts desperate attempts to escape danger and find refuge. Indeed, the specter of terrorism was explicitly invoked by Howard, who suggested that "'Australia has no way to be certain terrorists, or people with terrorist links, were not among the asylum seekers trying to enter the country by boat from Indonesia'" (quoted in Marr and Wilkinson 2003, 280–81). While this opinion was countered by the Australian Security and Intelligence Organization, which pointed out that foreign forces have the resources to more expediently gain entry to Australia (Marr and Wilkinson 2003, 281), fear of terrorism continues to haunt the debate about refugees.

In *Precarious Life* Butler explains how, post-9/11, the term *terrorism* has been used to reformulate binary oppositions that distinguish between "us" and "them" so as to revive anachronistic divisions between "East" and "West," and civilization and barbarism (Butler 2004b, 2). The violent events of September 11, 2001, are declared "acts of terror" while the violence of U.S. foreign policy is construed as self-defense. More generally, states such as Israel and Russia label resistance groups as terrorists while state violence is variously justified (Butler 2004b, 4). In the Australian context, the specter of the terrorist was reframed so that even vulnerable and defenseless asylum seekers could be performatively transformed into a violent threat. This enabled the violent and life-threatening actions of the Australian state to be construed as self-defense against the seeming threat posed by those seeking asylum.

The Australian government's ambiguous and contradictory statements are a complex and subtle performative production. The government simultaneously reassures Australians that they are humane and nonracist while also inflaming the very racism that is denied. Howard's utterances about a humane, nonracist Australia performatively produce complacency about Australia's racist past and present, disguising and perpetuating racist attitudes by labeling them nonracist. His depiction of asylum seekers as illegal and aligned with terrorism performatively produces an image of asylum seekers as inhuman—an image reinforced by the erroneous claim that asylum seekers threw their children into the sea in an attempt to force Australia to rescue and bring to shore these endangered lives.

While Howard's performative naming of "illegal immigrants" does not produce illegality, it, together with other performative utterances, creates a category of people perceived as inhumane and inhuman who can then be subjected to treatment that would otherwise be viewed as unethical and unjust. This process of performatively dehumanizing refugees may be clarified using Blanchot's theory of negation. The name *illegal immigrant* negates the asylum seeker so that Australians cannot perceive the suffering, persecution, and legitimate flight of the asylum seeker. Instead of the asylum seeker we perceive only the conceptual illegal immigrant. This conceptual illegal immigrant, like Blanchot's conceptual woman, is manipulable and controllable. The persecuted asylum seeker is negated, replaced by a conceptual threat to "humane" Australia. The illegal immigrant can be imprisoned, or denied entry, whereas the asylum seeker would be given refuge by a humane society: renaming the asylum seeker as *illegal immigrant* enables the "humane" society to ignore its racist inhumanity and to legitimate abusive imprisonment and armed repulsion.

While the asylum seeker is interpellated as an illegal immigrant, other discourses regarding immigration and asylum also proliferate, countering the government's performative utterances and providing a vehicle for resistance. The asylum seeker's identity is not inevitably determined by the government's proclamations, for she may resist the interpellation, asserting instead an alternate discourse about her refugee experience. The anonymous "Cambodia Poem" reverses the Australian government's constructions of humane and inhuman through a constative account that also performatively constructs new images of the human:

> What a sad day!
> 50 immigration men
> 26 people frightened
> 6 children crying ...
> 2 gates opening
> 50 police moving ...
> 26 rejections arrived ...
> 26 refugees starting to cry
> 1 famous lawyer helping to fight
> 100 politicians telling a lie
> 1 law useless
> 1 treading upon human rights
> (Anonymous 2004, 41)

These images of the 26 frightened refugees, rejected and forcibly deported by 50 immigration men, 50 police, and 100 lying politicians expose the hypocritical violations of human rights by the self-proclaimed humane society. The poem reverses Howard's opposition between the humane Australian society and the inhuman terrorist-harboring refugees, for here it is the nation that contravenes human rights and the refugees—crying, despairing, and fearful—who experience and perform human suffering. Through its constative description the poem also performatively produces the humanity of those seeking, and denied, refuge.

Butler's and Blanchot's theories of language both contribute to an analysis of the negations by which asylum seekers are occluded and replaced by performative interpellations that create the category "illegal immigrants" and, via an association with terrorism, construes them as an inhuman threat to the "fair-go" nation. However, Butler's and Blanchot's differing conceptions of the rematerializing interconnections of words and things suggests ultimately differing understandings of the relation between the materiality of the refugee and her representation. For Blanchot, words are imbued with materiality; they have their own sensuousness that expresses the being of the world. Blanchot's theory suggests a dialectical movement by which naming the object negates its materiality—though through a reversal this materiality secretly haunts language revealing the being of the world. This would indicate that the being of the refugee—her ontological existence, including, perhaps, her humanity—would ultimately be revealed in the language that names her.

For Butler, however, the outcome could not be predetermined or stabilized in this way. Butler's account of language suggests a chiasmic relation between words and world—a touching by which words bring about events and identities in part through the movements, actions, and performativity of bodies, and simultaneously the performativity of the body creates identities, categories, and labels: *girl, woman, refugee*. In this account, neither word nor world are stable categories; the relation between the two creates oscillating, ever-transforming identities, objects, and ideas. There is no being of the refugee, the woman, or the human that could finally "show" itself in language. Rather, words and bodies are contested, changeable, mutually constituting, and the performative production of the refugee and of the human cannot rely on a preexisting being but must be constantly defined, redefined, and troubled by the play of performative and iterative languages.

If there is to be a renewed humanism, Butler's theory of language suggests that this could not rely on identifying the essential nature of the human. There would be, for Butler, no preexisting human existence behind the enactment of this identity. Rather, the "human" would be produced through a never-ceasing debate, contestation, and troubling of the demarcations among the human, inhuman, and nonhuman. Through this troubling, words and worlds chiasmically entwine producing an ever-renewing and transforming somatic and linguistic performativity of the human.

Sustaining Language/Existing Threats: Resistance and Rhetoric in Australian Refugee Discourses: A Response to Linnell Secomb

SUSANNE GANNON AND SUE SALTMARSH

University of Western Sydney & Charles Sturt University

If language can sustain the body, it can also threaten its existence.

> —Judith Butler, Excitable Speech.
> **A Politics of the Performative**

In this essay we respond to Linnell Secomb's provocation by examining the ways in which refugee discourses operate to simultaneously sustain and threaten bodies. We take her endpoint, the anonymous

163

"Cambodia Poem," which tells of events that occurred in 1991,[1] as our starting point as we write about events occurring more than a decade later. We trace the "demarcation" of the human via recent practices of mandatory immigration detention, and their contestation.[2] We apply Secomb's reading of linguistic performativity, inspired by the work of Judith Butler (1993a, 1997a), into an analysis of the strategic deployment of language by government in the production of public rhetoric, and its reconfiguration through acts of resistance by refugees, citizens, and activists. We contrast correspondence between bureaucracies with correspondence between private individuals, and we conclude with a consideration of the possibilities of art for producing ethical encounters. In this juxtaposition of "public" and "private" discursive spaces, we also bring Michel de Certeau's (2002) theorization of institutional strategies and the tactics of everyday life into the conversation to help us trace how language figures in establishing—and troubling—the limits of the human in social and civic life. In the first half of this essay we use Certeau's work to consider how the generation of government rhetoric might be understood not merely as speech acts contrived by a collectivity of singular subjects in the service of party politics, but also as performative citations of racist discourses under the guise of Australian nationalism. In the second half of the essay, bringing Sara Ahmed's (2000) notion of the "stranger" into the conversation as well, we consider how in ostensibly more "private" spaces, utterances that circulate in the public domain are "untethered from [their] origins" (Butler 1997a, 93) by refugees, citizens and activists and taken up for "altogether other outcomes," as Secomb puts it. We agree with her that it is important to understand how the outcomes of language can be simultaneously both destructive and creative.

Our analysis in both sections of the essay is also influenced by the examination in *Precarious Life* (Butler 2004b) of the ways in which social and civic life are circumscribed. We wish to highlight the ways in which vulnerability and difference are reconfigured in racist and pejorative terms through the citation and reiteration of strategic practices by which existing discourses circulate. We consider how the performativity of language enables acts of resistance and refusal, so that "the tactics of everyday life" deployed by refugees, citizens, and activists become a means by which intelligibility and viability might be restored and social life transformed. Our work recognizes the relationality through which each of us is dependent upon, vulnerable to, productive of, and implicated in the embodied, lived experience of others. Our discussion maps onto Butler's notion of language as both threatening and sustaining bodies that are "formed within the crucible of social life" (2004b, 26). Secomb reminds us that such analysis should attempt to account for "the complex relations among body, action, and language." What we aim to accomplish is both an examination of refugee discourses as they are produced and circulate in the public domain of government rhetoric, and a troubling of those discourses and their material effects through examination of embodied ethical encounters (Butler 2004b, 43) that arise in everyday life.

EXISTING THREATS: RHETORIC AND REGULATION

Our discussion of existing threats to intelligibility and viability takes place in the context of Australian immigration detention policies in place since 1989 (see McMaster 2001). Don McMaster notes, "The detention component of Australia's immigration policy makes it one of the severest of Western liberal democracies" (2001, 67) and argues that these practices operate both as political acts of deterrence and as acts of discrimination. Following on from this distinction, we argue that existing threats to the intelligibility and viability of refugees and asylum seekers in Australian immigration detention are located not merely in the material conditions of incarceration but also in the interplay between government rhetoric and regulation, which together function as performative technologies of citationality and relationality. Our interest in this section of the essay is twofold: first, we are interested in understanding how the regulatory practices of forcible indefinite detention can be understood in terms that exceed the limits of corporeal isolation and social exclusion, to operate as citations and reiterations of previous acts of detention and incarceration through which racist discourses of Australian nationalism are in part constituted; second, we consider how the citation and reiteration of racist discourses takes place through the tacit manipulation of representation in the public sphere, emphasizing how these practices function to problematize and foreclose the human relationality articulated through individual and public resistances to refugee discourses.

The regulatory dimensions of refugee discourses in contemporary Australia, particularly those associated with mandatory indefinite detention of refugees and asylum seekers, are understood here as modes of abjection, which Nikolas Rose (1999), following Butler (1993a), refers to as "a matter of the energies, the practices, the works of division that act upon persons and collectivities such that some ways of being, some forms of existence are cast into a zone of shame, disgrace or debasement, rendered beyond the limits of the liveable, denied the warrant of tolerability, accorded purely a negative value" (1999, 253).

While cast, in political parlance, as a necessary means of policing Australia's borders in the interest of protecting national security, the incarceration of refugees and asylum seekers has a more immediate function of rendering those incarcerated as abject others against whom a preferred version of national identity is defined. Such practices, we would argue, are not merely political responses to an immediate "crisis" mobilized around global questions of "terrorism," but are instead citations of a racialized legacy of exclusionary practices that pervade Australia's sociopolitical history. Thus, we see the disproportionate presence of refugees and asylum seekers from the Middle East and Asia currently held in immigration detention in terms of what Angela Davis refers to as "the structural persistence of racism" (1998, 62), in which tensions around the unauthorized arrival of racialized, abject others within Australian territory—and the potential risks to national security, economic stability, and social cohesion that they supposedly represent—euphemistically displace/replace the question of racism as a central topic of public debate.

In this way, the "energies, the practices, the works of division" that explicitly operate to threaten the bodies and lives of refugees and asylum seekers in immigration detention, and to constitute those held in immigration detention in abject terms, are underscored by—and project into the future—the specter of racialized nationalism, of which whiteness is the defining feature. Thus Australia's history as a "white nation" (see Hage 1998, 2003) continues to haunt, through innumerable citations, both the present and future of refugee discourses. The legacy of racialized internment, violence, social exclusion, and structural disadvantage in Australia is extensive, and includes some massacres of Indigenous people from the earliest days of the colony (see Cuneen 2001); the genocide of Aboriginal Tasmanians (see Ryan 1996); the "white Australia" policy, introduced in the new Federation of 1901 as the first Act of Parliament; the Stolen Generations of Aboriginal children forcibly removed from families and communities (see Human Rights and Equal Opportunity Commission 1997); the disproportionate incarceration and deaths in custody of Aboriginal people (see Human Rights and Equal Opportunity Commission 1996); the internment, during World War II, of Australian migrant citizens (see Bonutto 1994; Peters 2003); the mandatory detention, since 1989, of "boat people" arriving in Australia predominantly from Asia (see McMaster 2001); and, more recently, the "children overboard" affair and the Tampa crisis (see Giannacopoulos 2005; Perera 2002), of which Suvendrini Perera writes,

> The wider questions surrounding the Tampa may belong to the twenty-first century: the tensions between globalizing and nationalist forces; the Australian government's attempts to draw a line in the sea against the incursions of international law; its desire somehow to take control of a world where the borderless flow of information, goods and finances also inevitably involves the movement of people across borders. But these contemporary concerns clearly are also being played out in a recognizably colonial and highly racialized register. The phobias and hatreds that emerged in Australian public life in the spring of 2001 open the door to a much older storehouse of images, narratives and representations. (Perera 2002, 14)

While Australia's racialized discrimination against refugees and asylum seekers maps onto global discourses that exceed the local context, the racist legacy of Australia's colonial past and assimilationist cultural politics (see Perera and Pugliese 1997) is continually invoked through contemporary refugee discourses as a normative dimension of social and civic life. Citation, as Certeau reminds us, "appears to be the ultimate weapon for making people believe" (2002, 188), and the citation of racist discourses with a long and pervasive history in Australian civic life is a powerful means of reinscribing racialized privilege as a discursive norm.

As Butler observes in her discussion of the citationality of the performative, "If a performative provisionally succeeds ... then it is not because an intention successfully governs the action of speech, but only because that action echoes prior actions, and *accumulates the force of authority through the repetition of a prior and authoritative set of practices*" (Butler 1997b, 51; emphasis in the original). Thus, we understand the regulatory—and indeed, the rhetorical—means by which refugees and asylum seekers in Australia are constituted in pejorative terms as performative of the cumulative force of racism's discursive legacy.

While we are mindful that intentionality has no ultimate determining or governing force over the consequences of racist speech and conduct, we would argue that intentionality—to the extent that its operations are known/knowable—remains a crucial site for analysis. In particular, racist discourses merit interrogation, not merely in terms of their genealogical derivations or their normative circulation in social life, but also as the effects of complex mechanisms of production by which official, preferred versions of events and issues are produced and made available for public consumption. As Butler argues in *Precarious Life*, "politics—and power—work in part through regulating what can appear, what can be heard" (2004b, 147), and it is to these regulatory practices, both tacit and overt, that our analysis now turns.

The manipulation by government of representation in the public sphere is central to what Nicholas Jones refers to as "the vastly expanded interface between politicians and journalists" (2001, 6), an interface that is increasingly reliant on politically appointed public-relations professionals who produce/manage the representation of political leaders, party policies, and affairs of government. Indeed, the public-relations practices of government have come to signify a key dilemma of contemporary life, which is whether, and how, and to what extent the fictions that circulate as "truths" in the contested terrain between public and private are able to gain currency sufficiently to substantively reconfigure the symbolic, material, and relational dimensions of social life. How is it, we might ask, that—despite widespread recognition that not only media, but also government manipulation of information prior to its entry into the public domain persistently obfuscates the details of public affairs—the language and imagery produced for public consumption continue to acquire the status of fact, reality, or truth? And how is it that, having acquired the status of the "real," these fictions become an effective means by which to reconstitute the terms and material conditions of social and civic life—to sway public sentiment, to reform policy, and override legislation, to influence judiciary and other social systems, to redraw national and international borders, and to initiate military attacks that endanger and destroy lives, families, histories, and cultures?

We find Butler's work in *Precarious Life* (2004b) concerning the legal and bureaucratic processes surrounding practices of indefinite detention particularly useful in highlighting how, for example, the discursive constitution of detainees as dangerous is both sanctioned and reiterated through the suspension of law and the appropriation of sovereign power into the apparatus of governmentality. The state-sanctioned suspension of the rule of law and the subsequent devolution of sovereign power to bureaucrats and government officials, Butler argues, invests government bureaucrats, rather than elected leaders or members of the judiciary, with "extraordinary power over life and death" (2004b, 59). Thus, the bureaucratic machinery of government becomes the site at which there is "a ghostly and forceful resurgence of sovereignty in the midst of governmentality" (59). She presents a compelling argument, too, concerning how official acts of speech operate, through the media, in terms that exceed the parameters of state discourse, so that "[t]hese official statements are also media performances, a form of state speech that establishes a domain of official utterance distinct from legal discourse" (80). In this way, Butler argues, notions of which lives are intelligible and which are not, and which deaths are grievable and which are not, circulate and gain currency in the social sphere. Our interest here, however, is not only the intersection of state and media discourses through which certain fictions acquire the status of "truths," but also the deliberate "games of truth" (Foucault, 2002) through which the "spin doctoring" practices of government make explicit attempts to manipulate the performative use of language in the public sphere. The following example, taken from 2004 correspondence between the Australian Press Council (APC) and the Department of Immigration and Multicultural and Indigenous Affairs (DIMIA), demonstrates the operation of institutional "strategies" (Certeau 2002) concerned with the delineation and maintenance of "proper" spaces from which the structures of power operate. According to Certeau, a strategy is understood as "the calculation (or manipulation) of power relationships that becomes possible as soon as a subject with will and power (a business, an army, a city, a scientific institution) can be isolated. It postulates a place that can be delimited as its own and serve as the base from which relations with an exteriority composed of targets or threats (customers or competitors, enemies, the country surrounding the city, objectives and objects of research, etc.) can be managed" (2002, 36).

Through an analysis of the correspondence between the APC and the DIMIA, we consider how the performativity of language figures as a crucial site of contestation in the strategic practices of government. Such institutional strategies are understood beyond political attempts to manipulate public sentiment by influencing (or attempting to influence) the representational practices of the media, and are seen instead as attempts to prescribe a place of power that far exceeds that which is being continually carved out within the rhetorical and material practices of political, military, and juridical discourses. Thus, the site of language and meaning becomes the new territory of a colonizing endeavor.

In June 2004 the APC, Australia's self-regulating body for the print media, published an adjudication following receipt of complaints about terminology used by the *Sydney Morning Herald* to describe asylum seekers. The APC subsequently issued a reporting guideline concerning the use of the term *illegal immigrants* to refer to asylum seekers, cautioning the press to be careful in the use of such terms. Guideline 262 reads:

Status of Unauthorized Arrivals

The Australian Press Council has received complaints about
the terminology that is applied, and ought to be applied, to
those arriving in Australia who do not have normal immigrant
credentials. Technically in Commonwealth immigration legislation they are referred to as "unlawful non-citizens". However, they are often referred to as "illegal immigrants" or even
"illegals".

The problem with the use of terms such as "illegal refugee"
and "illegal asylum seeker" is that they are often inaccurate
and may be derogatory.

The Council cautions the press to be careful in the use of such
unqualified terms in reports and headlines. (Australian Press
Council 2004b)

This guideline illustrates how language use is contested in the
public sphere, such that "[t]he terrain of representation, of language,
imagery and narrative … emerges as a crucial point for contesting the
disconnection and separation of refugees and asylum seekers from
wider society" (Perera 2002, 20). Here the dialogue among citizens,
the print media, and the APC takes place in the contested terrain of
refugee discourses, with participants in the dialogue engaged in a
struggle over intelligibility—and, in particular, how the language by
which intelligibility is constituted might be challenged, (re-)defined,
(re-)produced, unraveled, "unmoored from its racist origins" (Butler
1997b, 93) in order to be thought, spoken, and written otherwise.
The APC carefully invokes the rhetoric of immigration legislation
(rather than, for instance, the language of social-justice principles and
international human rights conventions favored in many activist discourses) to frame this particular guideline, illustrating how both pro-
ducers and consumers of media texts attempt to query and ameliorate
the representation of refugees and asylum seekers in terms that might
foreclose—through the powerful discourses of criminality and citizenship—their intelligibility and viability.

In the same month, a letter was issued by DIMIA's director of public affairs to the chairman of the APC (with a copy also sent to the
Sydney Morning Herald) in response to the APC adjudication and
guideline. The following excerpts from the DIMIA letter provide an
important example of institutional strategies deployed by government

to manipulate language use in the public domain, albeit by means that are unlikely to be widely known to the general public:

> I am writing to you in regard to Australian Press Council Guideline No 262 and Adjudication number 1242.
>
> Your advice to the media, specifically your adjudication in relation to a complaint against the Sydney Morning Herald, on "the terminology that is applied, and ought to be applied, to those arriving in Australia who do not have normal immigrant credentials" does not reflect reality.
>
> You wrote: "In this instance, the paper acknowledged that 'illegal immigrants' was an incorrect description of the asylum seekers and conceded that it should have used its preferred term 'asylum seekers'".
>
> The presumption relied on in the complaint and on which the adjudication appears to be based is false. It is not true that an asylum seeker cannot be an illegal entrant or indeed be an illegal immigrant. Nor is it pejorative to use the correct terms to describe an illegal entrant or illegal immigrant. (Department of Immigration and Multicultural and Indigenous Affairs 2004)

The declaration that the APC's advice to the media "does not reflect reality" is the first of a number of "truth claims" designed to frame and narrate "the real" from a position of power and of authoritative "knowing" on behalf of the state. The social sphere is thus circumscribed by attempts to manipulate both what can be spoken/written for circulation in the public domain, and through the explicit designation of certain terms and their use as "real" (and thus legitimate) and others as failing to "reflect reality" (and thus illegitimate). In this way, the public sphere, as Butler points out, "is constituted in part by what can appear, and the regulation of the sphere of appearance is one way to establish what will count as reality, and what will not" (Butler 2004, xx).

The power to narrate the terms and conditions of the social, however, lies not just in the authority to manipulate language, frame public debate, or withhold and/or selectively release information (though as Brindle 1999; Barns 2005; Turner 2002; and others have pointed out, these are certainly practices commonly deployed in attempts to manipulate public perception). Notably, the power to narrate is also inscribed in Western scientific rationalities that afford primacy to those individuals and institutions that speak on behalf of the "real." According to Certeau, "Narrations about what's-going-on constitute our orthodoxy. Debates about figures are our theological wars. The combatants no longer bear the arms of any offensive or defensive idea. They move forward camouflaged as facts, data, and events. They present themselves as messengers from a 'reality.' Their uniform takes on the color of the economic and social ground they move into. When they advance, the terrain itself seems to advance. But in fact they fabricate the terrain, simulate it, use it as a mask, accredit themselves by it, and thus create the scene of their law. (2002, 185–86)

The fabricated terrain unfolding in the DIMIA letter is, we would suggest, the place of power from which the state seeks to foreclose public dissent not only in relation to immigration detention but also—and notably—in its attempts to manipulate the performativity of language in the public sphere. The language of "reality" and the accusation of "false" presumptions on the part of the complainants and the APC together function to produce a discursive field in which DIMIA retains sole entitlement to establish and censor the terms of public debate. Already equipped (through both legislative means and through force of violence using police and military action) with power to limit and foreclose dissent, the Australian government seeks to extend its powers of influence by both establishing and forcefully occupying the conceptual terrain from whence critique and dissent emerge. As Butler points out, "[such] power of the state's judicial language to establish and maintain the domain of what will be publicly speakable suggests that the state plays much more than a limiting function in such decisions; in fact, the state actively produces the domain of publically acceptable speech, demarcating the line between the domains of the speakable and the unspeakable, and retaining the power to make and sustain that consequential line of demarcation" (Butler 1997b, 77).

This power to demarcate what can and cannot be spoken is underscored by constituting those who contest the government's language of abjection as themselves abject others within the discursive terms of Australian citizenship. For example, the DIMIA letter goes on to say,

> The sensitivity in some quarters to the use of the words "illegal" or "unlawful" or "unauthorized" to describe asylum seekers arriving without Australia's permission seems to have at its root vigorous attempts by some in the community to mislead the public into believing a myth that all unauthorized arrivals are asylum seekers and that all asylum seekers have a right to

> enter a country of choice without authority and therefore "can never be illegal". This is just not true. The reality is clear in international law and has been made crystal clear by the High Court of Australia.... Accordingly, describing a person as an illegal, unauthorized or unlawful arrival, or their presence as illegal, unlawful or unauthorized is doing no more than using the correct objective descriptions. (Department of Immigration and Multicultural and Indigenous Affairs 2004)

Here the binaries of real/unreal, true/false, and fact/fiction demarcate the terrain in which DIMIA and its representatives occupy a proper, rational space, while those who oppose—the APC, its member organizations, and members of the public who contest and challenge the legitimacy of the official rhetoric deployed in refugee discourses—are relegated to the "improper" place of the false, the unreal, the fictitious. The language used to describe opposition to DIMIA as "vigorous attempts by some in the community to mislead the public into believing a myth" constitutes those who engage in public discussion as individual agitators and deceivers whose interests lie outside the normative terms of citizenship, rather than as active participants in ongoing democratic debate. Such discursive maneuvers raise questions about the crucial role of critique and dissent in social life, and highlight the anti-democratic agenda that attempts to delegitimate those voices that would call decision makers to account. As Butler notes, "To decide what views will count as reasonable within the public domain, however, is to decide what will and will not count as the public sphere of debate.... The foreclosure of critique empties the public domain of debate and democratic contestation itself, so that debate becomes the exchange of views among the like-minded, and criticism, which ought to be central to any democracy, becomes a fugitive and suspect activity" (2004b, xx).

The voices of critics are thus anticipated and foreclosed through the construction within official government rhetoric of untenable and unintelligible subject positions (i.e., as those whose agendas would mislead the public or exploit the circumstances of those in detention), so that "[d]issent is quelled, in part, through threatening the speaking subject with an uninhabitable identification.... Under social conditions that regulate identifications and the sense of viability to this degree, censorship operates implicitly and forcefully" (Butler 2004b, xix–xx). In this instance, DIMIA's attempt to foreclose dissent constitutes individuals pejoratively and threatens the relationality upon which the operation of a media self-regulating body is predicated. In forwarding the letter to the *Sydney Morning Herald*, DIMIA attempts to undermine the credibility of the APC and its member organizations, and to override the APC's adjudication using a rhetorical appeal to the kind of objective rationality which is central to the ethos (if not always to the practices) of journalism.

We see in such strategic manoeuvres existing threats—to the intelligibility and viability of refugees and asylum seekers, as well as to the ongoing existence of democratic freedoms in social and civic life—that have their basis in the citationality and relationality of language rather than solely in regulatory powers such as those deployed in the practices of indefinite detention. We see examples of these rhetorical and regulatory threats in DIMIA's explicit attempts to foreclose debate by, offering "correctives" to supposedly incorrect and misleading "presumptions"; by reciting as "facts" DIMIA's preferred terminologies and descriptions of refugees and asylum seekers within the discursive frames of criminality and (non)citizenship; by deploying bureaucratic processes as mechanisms by which individuals are "deemed" (see Butler 2004b, 58–59) to be (il)legitimate in the terms of refugee discourses, and therefore deemed to be particular types of (dangerous, undesirable, abject) social subjects within the powerful discursive terms of criminality; and by contesting language use in the public sphere through explicit attempts to manipulate members of the press and media self-regulating bodies. In each of these examples, the citation of Australia's racist colonial history and cultural politics is insidiously woven so that the abject other of nationalist discourses remains inscribed in immigration law, in practices of indefinite detention, and in refugee discourses as they are played out in the public sphere. DIMIA's reiteration of such practices notwithstanding, however, increasing numbers of Australians have begun to call for a reconfiguration not only of corporeal detention, but also—and notably—of the discursive constitution of refugees and asylum seekers in both the private and public spheres, so that Australians might begin to enter into what Butler refers to as an "ethical encounter" (2004b, 43) with those currently held in immigration detention.

Sustaining Language: Resistance and Relationality

In this section we examine textual encounters in which refugees and citizens have taken up language as a tactic, where everyday life has opened alternative citational spaces to those colonized by government rhetoric, social spaces where language becomes a technology for sustaining bodies. The Howard government has worked hard to ensure that "personalizing" and "humanizing" details of asylum seekers are absent from public discourse. Here we explore attempts to rehumanize and repersonalize refugees in ostensibly more "private" and local discursive spaces. In private letters and local theaters utterances that circulate in the public domain have been, as Butler has put it in another context, "untethered from [their] origins" (Butler 1997a, 93) and resited/ recited by refugees and citizens. Certeau suggests that while "[p]ower is bound by its very visibility," a degree of tactical "trickery is possible for the weak" (Certeau 2002, 37). Thus, the performativity of language in these social spaces enables acts of resistance that sustain rather than threaten the corporeal and ethical viability of the refugee subject.

In our desire to explore rehumanizing tactics and sustainable language, we do not wish to evoke the figure of the refugee as a "fetish" in our own rhetorical work. Like Secomb's work, Sara Ahmed's discussion of the fetish in postcoloniality is also indebted to the work of Maurice Blanchot. The conceptual shift toward the "other"—whether we call that figure *illegal immigrant* or *refugee*—is always already an abstraction, untethered from the particularity of individual human lives (Ahmed 2000, 143). This is what Secomb calls the strategy of "negation" through which human subjects are made into categories rather than individuals, and consequently become "manipulable and controllable." Ahmed also describes how the stranger—in this case the refugee—risks becoming "a commodity fetish that is circulated and exchanged in order to define the borders and boundaries of given communities" (150). In Australian resistance to government policy, the figure of the refugee has been evoked to define communities of people who take up certain activist practices and, by implication, to place those who don't outside those activist communities. Although communities might be seen to have porous boundaries and fluid membership, they solidify in particular, embodied spatial moments. Television footage from 2003 and 2004 of Easter pilgrimages to Baxter and Woomera immigration detention centers (IDCs) portrayed a particular, embodied activist community, those who were there in the desert pushing at the wire, defining these activists against people outside that community and protest event. More "ordinary" people—those watching the television news rather than featuring in it—were constituted as not only other to the refugees inside the wire, but also as other to the sort of people who protested, those who took an oppositional stance against these practices. In contrast to these very public—and

sometimes alienating—demonstrations of refusal of government rhetoric on refugees, other actions took place in more subterranean, per-
sonalized, and everyday spaces. We wish here to consider the textual
encounters that took place in these spaces and to both invoke and
problematize an oppositional rhetoric of resistance.

We begin with the letter-writing campaign of Rural Australians
for Refugees (RAR). Between 2001 and 2005 RAR linked over two
thousand Australians to approximately four thousand detainees in
onshore and offshore detention centers. The campaign grew through
word of mouth, and correspondence often began with an initial letter sent into a void with just a number,[3] an IDC address, and a name.
Excluded from human intelligibility in the public domain, the private
spaces of these letters became sites within which refugees could perform themselves as human, and where language—English specifically,
a second or third language for most refugees—was the means of that
performance. In those private spaces—individual letters back and forth
between individual citizens and noncitizens—refugees wrote themselves into existence again as human, as did the Australian citizens
who inscribed themselves as other to their government.

Most of these letters are not available for public consumption in the
ways that television footage or correspondence between DIMIA and
APC are available.[4] We ask you here to imagine, instead, some scenar-
ios. Imagine, for example, that a young Afghan woman in detention
writes back to a letter she has received from the outside. She writes from
a place where she is just a number in the bureaucracy of the detention
center, but through the act of writing back to her unseen audience of
one, she becomes a first-time mother with fears and aspirations for her
baby, who has never known life outside detention. The letter recipient,
on the outside, is transformed momentarily from not just a citizen of
this country that denies humanity so profoundly to others but also
becomes a mother, a grandmother, an aunt who finds a space and language to write about female commonality, babies, families, hope, and
love. Imagine this woman, sitting thousands of miles from the young
woman she has never met, who is on her veranda reading the letter that
has come just that morning over vast deserts or huge oceans, holding
the paper that has been in the hands of the woman kept apart from
her. Through this imaginary journey, the citizen also reenters the category of the human, through the event of the letter and the potential
reciprocity of the correspondence. The letters provoke her into strange
journeys for "nappy rash" ointments, talcum powder, baby clothes.
They send her searching for information about Eid-al-Adha, and what
gift might be appropriate for a festival she had never heard of in her

small Australian town. The letters elicit from her language that holds out hope and the promise of some other future. Through the letters, the conceptual refugee becomes a particular individual person with a unique name and embodied material particularity. Every letter says "I am" to its recipient, rehumanizing the participants in ways that the operations of immigration policy otherwise forbid and demonstrating the chiasmus of constative and performative utterances that Secomb traces in her essay. The letter is a speech act that is simultaneously *illocutionary*, being "itself the deed that it effects" (Butler 1997a, 3), and *perlocutionary*, invoking subsequent actions, demonstrating that the distinction is "tricky and not always stable" (44). The correspondence "exceeds itself in past and future directions, [is] an effect of prior and future invocations that constitute and escape the instance of utterance" (3).

The letter-writing exchanges crossed the wires of every IDC and linked Australian citizens in every region to men, women, and children in detention. This subterranean and private activism—the tens of thousands of letters—represents what Butler calls "the struggle for recognition" in which "each partner in the exchange recognizes not only that the other needs and deserves recognition, but also that each, in a different way, is compelled by the same need, the same requirement" (2004b, 44). The exchange of the letters "dislocates us from our ... subject positions" (2004b, 44) whether they are constituted by the conditions of detention, for the refugees, or by the privilege of citizenship. The manager of the RAR letter-writing campaign warned prospective writers, "Coping with their stories might be difficult.... Remember it is their situation, not yours, and there is no point in your collapsing under their burden..." (Rural Australians for Refugees 2005).

Letter writing entails a certain risk to the complacent subject, a vulnerability to the other that is the prerequisite of "an ethical encounter" (Butler 2004b, 43). Through the letters and the relationality entailed in the correspondence the writers are already becoming something new. As they write themselves into existence in their letters each person aims to "to solicit a becoming, to instigate a transformation, to petition the future always in relation to the Other" (44).

Although not public texts, and though each is a private performative act, together the letters form a long, slow wave of repeated citations across the continent that have helped to resignify *refugee* in terms other than "queue jumper" and "illegal immigrant." Against the "gating" of asylum seekers that government use of language performs, the letters open the possibility for Australian citizens to "perceive the suffering, persecution, and legitimate flight of the asylum seeker" (Secomb, this volume). Rather than considering each letter as a discrete and separate speech act, we might read them together as "a ritual chain of resignifications whose origin and end remain unfixed and unfixable" (Butler 1997a, 14). Each act of letter writing enters what Butler calls "a certain nexus of temporal horizons ... an iterability that exceeds the moment it occasions" (1997a, 14). The letters themselves are material things. As Secomb's work with Blanchot reminds us, "the paper ... the trail of ink" may be limited by language but can also be "a refuge" from its tendency to obliterate materiality. The letters, written by hand, read held in the hand, bearing stamps affixed with human saliva, bear witness to the irreducible corporeality of the subjects who write.

The RAR letters remain, however, anonymous—private in their particular effects and in their details of particular lives. Although anonymity, as the "Cambodia Poem" demonstrates, can be a powerful place from which to claim a speaking position, erasure of the personal, of persons in their embodied specificity, their unique geographies and histories, it is a strategy that the Australian government has used to great effect. The second text that we examine in our search for sustaining language is an instance in which private discourse—a particular personal life—has migrated into the public domain, into the space of the theater. Theater has always been a tactic in social life in the sense that Certeau suggests in that a theater script is written with an eye to its "anticipated relocation, the thought of another site" (Colebrook 2001, 547). The writing of a script necessarily entails "a metaphorical shift that takes this present object as the sign of something other than itself" (547). Shahin Shafaei is an award-winning Iranian playwright and actor whose work is banned in his own country, and who spent twenty-two months in the Curtin IDC up until 2002. Since his release he has performed in several theatrical events that have shaped another discursive wave of dissent across Australia. His story is one of the stories told in the play *Through the Wire* (Horin 2004), which toured on mainstage and regional theaters nationally, with Shahin Shafaei acting the role of himself in the performance of a version of his own story of escape and detention. The play tells the stories of four refugees, and their friendships with four Australian citizens. As the *Central Western Gazette* reports from rural New South Wales, "Iranian refugee Shahin Shafaei brought the human face of the Australian Government's refugee policy to the people of Orange last night" (Harris 2005), but the review does not mention that there are seven other cast members. In this review, Shafaei, the only refugee actor in the cast, becomes "the human face" of refugee policy, the face in the Levinasian sense that

Butler uses in *Precarious Life*. The face is "a condition for human-ization," though it also operates in the media, in some instances, to dehumanize (Butler 2004b, 141). Certain faces are "marshalled in the service of war, as if [Osama] bin Laden's face were the face of ter-ror itself, as if [Yasser] Arafat were the face of deception, as if [Sad-dam] Hussein's face were the face of contemporary tyranny" (141). For the readers of the *Central Western Gazette*, Shahin Shafaei's face is "marshalled" in the service of compassion, as the human face of the government's refugee policies, as one of the faces that citizens can-not see when people are imprisoned in remote locations, cameras are forbidden, and chartered flights deport people in the middle of the night. More than compassion, Shafaei's face provides the possibility of recognition, and through the performance of refugee lives, embod-ied and sustaining language evokes (at least the possibility of) ethical encounters with those others from whom we have been kept.

Prior to *Through the Wire* and after his release, Shafaei presented over 250 performances of his monologue *Refugitive* (Shafaei 2004) in small venues throughout the country to well over ten thousand Aus-tralians, in another discursive wave of dissent. The text retells extraor-dinary elements of everyday life throughout the time he was in Curtin detention center, from bureaucratic effacement to hunger strikes and lip sewing. The play serves Shafaei as a space in which "to give an account of himself" as a refugee but, as Butler reminds us, "speech works pri-marily not to convey information (including the information about my life) but as the conduit for a desire, and as a rhetorical structure that seeks to alter or act upon the interlocutory scene itself" (Butler 2001, 31). In psychoanalytical terms, as Butler points out, there is a certain transference that takes place when we bear witness to the narrative of another (32). This transference, enacted in this play through the per-formance and witnessing of trauma in detention, is part of the work of what we have called in this essay *sustaining language*.

In contrast to the naming practices of the spin doctors, which have attempted to forbid the name *refugee* to refugees, Shafaei claims the name for himself. In the play's title *Refugitive*, he couples together *refuge* (a place of shelter, protection, safety from pursuit, danger, or trouble) with *fugitive* (a person who flees danger or an enemy, who searches for refuge—a *refugee*). The fugitive is estranged from home but not yet in sight of any safe place, in a liminal zone, a mobile body untethered from any secure geography or temporality. In Western popular culture, "the fugitive" is a lost man, always on the run. In *Refugitive*, in contrast, the character "The Man"—like Shafaei for the first ten months of his detention (see Morgan 2004)—is contained, detained, isolated in "a small room with a mattress in one corner" in an Australian IDC. The longed-for refuge at the end of a difficult journey is, in reality, a place of imprisonment and denial. In the last section of the play, Shafaei as The Man evokes the figure of his title: "I need a pen, I should write something before the end, something for someone, someone will hear this, this escape ... these fugitives ... maybe later it will become a film ... fugitive ... Refugitive ..." (Shafaei 2004, 17). The escape will come not from the release of his body from detention, but through language. It is writing that will escape, writing that makes something else possible—other bodies in another time and place reading and performing his story; a film The Man imagines as his witness.

Shafaei performs *Refugitive* with just a blanket, a mattress, and his body. It is a one-man play with a single setting and multiple shifts of character. Shafaei, anchoring the performance with his portrayal of The Man, moves seamlessly among characters as he forms his body and his voice into those of the DIMIA Manager and others as they appear in his cell. His slippage among characters, bodies, and modes of language, disorders binaries that separate "us" from "other." In taking all these subject positions into his body, the actor Shafaei disrupts their constitutive force. The text reinscribes, through parody, the language of the government and of international human rights:

> DIMIA Manager: You people are not welcome in Australia, I am saying this on behalf of all Australian people.
>
> The Man: But we are refugees!
>
> DIMIA Manager: From now on don't forget that you are queue jumpers, illegal immigrants ... would you please pass me my Australian Oxford dictionary edited by Howard University, ... there we are, you are boat people.
>
> The Man: But according to the convention we have the right to seek asylum in Australia, and Australia has already signed the convention?
>
> DIMIA Manager: Unfortunately we don't have that dictionary, that convention one here. (Shafaei 2004, 12)

The play takes up the hate speech of government rhetoric: *queue jumpers, illegal immigrants, boat people, you people*. Shafaei, "the one to whom it is addressed," takes up this hate speech and turns it into "the occasion of a speaking back and a speaking through" (Butler 1997a, 93). The utterance is "untethered from its origins" even though the character at that moment is supposedly a DIMIA officer, enacted through the body of a refugee. The "locus of authority in relation to the utterance" (Butler 1997a, 94) has been shifted to The Man, the refugee. As Butler argues, "it is precisely the expropriability of the dominant, 'authorized' discourse that constitutes one potential site of its subversive resignification" (1997a, 157). The Man inscribes himself within discourses of human rights—as refugee, seeker of asylum—and invokes Australia's obligation under international law. In contrast, in his first move the DIMIA Manager takes up, and undoes, a discourse of hospitality that pertains to civic and social life with "You people are not welcome here." His response is a bureaucratic one and he defers to textual authority—the "Australian Oxford dictionary edited by Howard University"—but this is a circular, self-referential authority, like that of the media spin doctors discussed in the first part of this essay.

The Man talks repeatedly about language—about writing in particular—as his salvation. As the IDC has not been the refuge he desired, his longing for language will be his refuge. Just as the thousands of letters in the RAR campaign slipped through the wire and over the walls, so The Man sees in writing the possibility of exceeding the boundaries of his detention. For Shafaei himself, writing was both the activity that had him banned in Iran and the activity that engendered hope during his incarceration in Australia (see Shafaei 2005), as is evidenced by his character: "I wish I had a pen here, that dangerous tool, for the people who escape from reality, in my homeland or even here" (Shafaei 2004, 16).

The imperative for The Man must be to bear witness, and to claim language in such a way that it subverts the DIMIA Manager's claim to speak on behalf of all Australians will be contradicted by the surge of these truths. But as the play and his hunger strike progress he becomes too ill to write and he still does not have a pen: "I know that I am at the end of the way. I see myself very close to the lights ... but I can't finish before writing my.... I should speak my last words, maybe to the wind, to carry them to the first brave pen to write, to write the truths ... please, please ..." (Shafaei 2004, 18).

Speaking is not sufficient for his last words—it is writing that inscribes truths, writing that circulates beyond spatial and temporal limitations. Through writing—through "the first brave pen to write"—witnessing becomes possible. The materiality of the written word becomes a refuge in which, as Secomb has described, "the object that had been occluded by its naming reemerges and is preserved."

Through the letters, and in the play, writing is the performative speech act that takes up language to sustain, rather than threaten, the existence of the refugee subject.

Earlier we claimed that the encounter with the particularity of Shafaei's experience—his face, his body, his words—in the space of the theater provides the possibility for recognition, for an ethical encounter with (an)other, but we must also problematize this appealing storyline. Ahmed argues that insisting on particularity does not guarantee that we can "grasp" any truth of a person. Particularity is not "simply on the body or the face of this other" (2000, 144). There is no neat equation in this encounter, nor is there symmetry. Rather than "reifying the very moment of the face to face," Ahmed suggests that we complicate the notion by focusing on the "temporal and spatial dislocations that are implicated in the very possibility of being faced by this other" (144). Focusing on particular modes of encounter rather than particular others opens up an encounter, means that we inevitably "fail to grasp it" in a "temporal movement" that stretches forward "from the now to the not yet" (145) and back through all the already beens that haunt it. Butler points out how the erasure of history—such as the "prehistory" of 9/11—undergirds acts of material and symbolic violence perpetrated by governments (2004b, 6). In Australia, *Refugitive*—the man, the play, and the performance—reinscribes a certain historical trajectory to the moment of encounter. Shafaei does not leave the past behind in order to make a new life, but ceaselessly reiterates the past. The hundreds of performances in small towns and suburban halls can be read together as another "ritual chain of resignifications" (Butler 1997a, 14). The details shared in the letters create trajectories that stretch forward into imagined futures, and backward to stories of flight, fear, and danger. Each textual encounter—in the letters and performances—interacts with the others contributing to "the condensation of an iterability that exceeds the moment it occasions" (Butler 1997a, 14). Through all these texts, "others make moral claims on us, address moral demands to us, ones that we do not ask for, ones that we are not free to refuse" (Butler 2004b, 131). The face of Shafaei, The Man on the stage, the precarious "human face" of refugee policies represents a "series of displacements ... a scene of agonized vocalization ... [ending] with a figure for what cannot be named, an utterance that is not, strictly speaking, linguistic" (Butler 2004b, 133). The face of the other, notes Butler, "comes to me from outside" and the relationality that it impels "is also the situation of discourse" (2004b, 138). The address of the face makes an ethical claim that is prior to and beyond language.

Nevertheless, in the performances of refugee lives in letters and in theater, access to language is crucial. As Butler stresses, "those who gain representation, especially self-representation, have a better chance of being humanized, and those who have no chance to represent themselves run a greater risk of being treated as less than human, regarded as less than human, or indeed, not regarded at all" (2004b, 141). There are countless others without the currency of the English of the letter writers and of Shafaei, who has a masters degree in English literature from the University of Tehran, who have not been able to tell their trauma. Shafaei is articulate and media friendly. For others in detention who did not have these resources, the alternative was "a situation of desperation" (Shafaei 2005). Shafaei, privileged and articulate in comparison to his friends, writes and performs that desperation in *Refugitive*, in the gap between himself and them: "Not many of them can speak, even, so they can't express themselves … in that situation where they… cannot make any decision, at least this [hunger strike] is the last decision that they can make about themselves because you feel that powerless. And they want to show that they are still alive" (Shafaei 2005).

In the play, resisting their demonization in media and government rhetoric, Shafaei recites the courage of individuals who went on hunger strikes and who sewed their lips together. In an ethical response to those others as well as his own life, Shafaei's performances of *Refugitive* and the utterances on refugees and redeployment of hate speech within it operate citationally as they circulate and reiterate the humanity of these others in detention for the thousands of Australians who saw the play. The claims they make on us are prior to and beyond language. Ahmed suggests that an ethical communication must hold both proximity and distance together, so that "one gets close enough to others to be touched by that which cannot simply be got across" (2000, 157). In this "testimonial aporia" ethics is less about speaking than about *"the conditions of possibility of hearing"* (157; emphasis in the original). There is an address made in each living room and each veranda where a letter is read, in each theater where *Refugitive* is performed and, as Butler argues, any such address—in an ethical encounter—necessitates a response. "To respond to this address seems an important obligation during these times," she writes. "This obligation is…about a mode of response that follows upon having been addressed, a comportment toward the Other only after the Other has made a demand upon me, accused me of a failing, or asked me to assume a responsibility" (2004b, 129).

This "comportment toward the other" is not driven by the will of the subject to act in accordance with rational discourses of international human rights or of social justice. More significantly, it is driven by a certain disintegration of that willful discrete subject. The border between self and other is destabilized, the gap between self and other is breached in that moment of recognition. Language arrives, in such an ethics, "as an address we do not will and by which we are ... captured" (Butler 2004b, 139). In the words of Levinas, the ethical encounter "is a rupture of being" (quoted in Butler 2004b, 132).

In the first part of this essay we talked about the refugee as abjected by the deadly language games of bureaucratic spin doctoring, as cast out into "a zone of shame, disgrace or debasement" (Rose 1999, 253), but abjection is more ambiguous and complex. Grosz says the abject is not readily classifiable "for it is necessarily ambiguous, undecidably inside and outside (like the skin of milk), dead and alive (like the corpse), autonomous and engulfing (like infection and pollution). It disturbs identity, system, and order, respecting no definite positions, rules, boundaries or limits" (Grosz 1989, 74).

When we are complicit with, or actively engage in, the abjection of those named as "dangerous" and as other, we lose the possibility of becoming ethical subjects ourselves. We cannot hear, we are not captured, our complacency is neither ruptured nor disturbed, we refuse to be addressed, and consequently, "something about our own existence proves precarious" (Butler 2004b, 130). In the moment of address we are mutually constituted as human and called into existence as moral beings. The moment of address calls us forth, impels us, and "in some way we come to exist, as it were, in the moment of being addressed" (130). In the second part of this essay we considered how various textual encounters bring us to moments of address—of recognition—replete with ethical potential. As Secomb has stressed, "neither word nor world are stable categories ... words and bodies are contested, changeable [and] mutually constituting." And where language sustains rather than threatens lives, it ruptures our being, provokes the dissolution of inside/outside, self/other; disturbs identity; disrespects positions; and makes demands of us that we cannot avert or avoid.

CONCLUSION

In this essay we have welcomed Secomb's provocation and followed her lead in attempting to analyze the simultaneously creative and destructive outcomes of utterances in refugee discourses. Though language threatens bodies, we find, it can also sustain them. In the first part of this essay we examined a 2004 dispute between DIMIA and the APC over how language might be used to "deem" refugees as (il)legitimate in the print media. We detailed how government spin doctoring attempted to foreclose debate through the recitation as "facts" of discourses of criminality and (non)citizenship that abject refugees and asylum seekers and exclude them from the category of the human. Mandatory detention and overt hate speech toward asylum seekers had circulated widely for a number of years prior to this dispute, and the claims of DIMIA in their argument with the APC rested on the citationality of discourses of hatred and abjection that had been in circulation for some time, that are themselves citations of racisms that are definitive in Australian colonial history and national identity. The power of language to threaten the existence of the human has been perhaps most stark, as Secomb reminds us, in the "suspected illegal entry vessel" Siev X tragedy. Despite the drowning of 354 asylum seekers when this vessel capsized between Australia and Indonesia in late October 2001, the toxic effects of hate speech invoking criminality, endemic racism, and media censorship ensured that these lives were not grievable to the Australian public. The rhetorical effects of government hate speech in defining and proscribing the viability of human subjects cannot be underestimated. We were interested in the first part of this essay in tracing how government lies were established and maintained through overt and covert manipulation of the media not merely by government but by the invisible and insidious industry of professional spin doctors and public-relations consultants employed by them.

Butler notes that "the body is alternately sustained and threatened through modes of address" (1997a, 5). In the second part of this essay we traced manifestations of sustainable language in correspondence between private individuals, and in art through theater. As Butler argues, "Language sustains the body not by bringing it into being or feeding it in a literal way; rather, it is by being interpellated within the terms of language that a certain social existence of the body first becomes possible" (5). In the textual encounters that we examine, in the reception and production of these texts, language brings bodies into a relationality that has the potential to reinscribe both asylum seekers and Australian citizens as viable and ethical human lives. Refugees, in particular, are made intelligible through performative speech acts, particularly through writing. Both the practices of threatening and sustaining language gain their effects through the citationality of language rather than through regulation or through individual acts that remain tethered to sovereign subjects. It is in reiteration and replication that language acquires social force and inscribes social subjects. It is the "chorus of speakers," Secomb points out, that carries the citational force of language rather than "the single utterance of the lone speaker." It is in the relationality of language that we can find language with the potential to sustain social subjects. A space opens up—in "strange encounters" with others (Ahmed 2000)—that requires us to abandon our sovereign subject positions and to enter into an ethical communication with the other that is mutually constitutive and transformative and engenders "an alternative sense of agency and ultimately, of responsibility" (Butler 1997a, 15). Yet this encounter is precarious. The ability to mourn cannot be predicated on the familiar (Butler 2004b, 38), yet it must overcome the indifference and the fear that prevails in contemporary political discourse. Our encounters with refugees in texts and in person dislodge us each from our sedimented subject positions; they "solicit a becoming ... instigate a transformation ... petition the future" (Butler 2004b, 44). Recognition of the other entails recognition of our mutual particularity and vulnerability, recognition that the other is enfolded within us and we are enfolded within each of these others. These are the preconditions for sustainable language. Loss, mourning, and love all become possible in its embrace.

NOTES

1. The *Southerly* editorial introduction to "Cambodia Poem" (Anonymous, 2004) explains the deportation that the poem desribes as follows: "The 21 May 1991 saw the transferring of the 'Pinde Bay' people from Villawood to Darwin."
2. Indefinite incarceration of asylum seekers in IDCs in remote mainland sites (Baxter, Curtin, Wimmera) and offshore locations (Christmas Island, Manus Island, and Nauru) has been the key plank of recent immigration policy in the federal government of Prime Minister Howard. In early 2005, media revelations of the wrongful detention of Australian resident Cornelia Rau and wrongful deportation of citizen Vivian Alvarez Solon led to the scathing Palmer Report (Palmer 2005), which has provoked changes to policy and to the "culture" of DIMIA, though not the replacement of the responsible minister, Senator Amanda Vanstone.
3. Letters to an IDC resident had to be addressed to the official number by which the refugee was known in order to be delivered.
4. See Burnside (2003) for an instance in which extracts from letters from another campaign were published.

Conversation with Judith Butler IV

Judith Butler: It seems to me that when Blanchot refers to *this woman*, that it's the *this* that's terribly important there. We could read *woman* as a concept problematically wielded, but I think that what concerns Blanchot here is the problem of singularity that the *this* introduces. The *this* emerges for him time and again as a problem. How do we see this woman? Of course, it's [Émile] Benveniste, and even [G. W. F.] Hegel before Benveniste, who says that the *this* which is supposed to assert singularity can be used indifferently to refer to any number of *thises* and so turns out to be substitutable at the same time that it's singularizing. I think that it is this question of what is singular and what is substitutable that emerges when Blanchot writes of the desire for *this woman*. When I say, I love this woman, I try to designate the specificity through a demonstrative pronoun to establish the singularity, but that very singularity becomes confounded by its substitutability.

There is another part of the presentation that challenges me. I should confess here that part of the problem of my work, since the inception of the theory of performativity, has been that I use language as this active, productive, constituting medium and resource, and it has been hard for me to think about the question of what calls on language from beyond language or impressionability, even how the world impresses itself upon us. In a way, the *this* designates precisely that which calls upon language from the outside, that to which language is called upon to respond. After

187

all, we don't just construct the world unilaterally, but are impinged upon by something that is outside of us. And this is why it has been both important and difficult to turn to the work of Jean Laplanche, who has a theory of a primary impingement in psychoanalytic terms, or that of Emmanuel Lévinas, for whom the address of the other, the face of the other, impinges upon us and produces a kind of passivity or responsiveness even prior to any constituting act.

Some one of you found my little piece on Bracha Lichtenberg's "Eurydice" (Butler 2004a). I can't remember who did, but I was surprised. I just thought it was in some little corner of the world where few people would read it. But primary impingement is also something that I have come to understand from Lichtenberg's work. She's a visual artist and a feminist theorist who works with Blanchot, among others, but also works with the memory—traces of the Holocaust or the Shoah. She has tried to figure out how survivors communicate memories of the camps to their children in ways that register at a certain psychic level for that next generation. The children are in some sense impinged upon by the trauma of their parents; it is inherited, it is relayed, and this kind of memory—or, rather, trauma—which is not quite one's own, and not quite another's, forms an opaque bond among the generations. Lichtenberg studies that primary impressionability and how language and visual media register that at some level. I have found all of these ideas quite compelling and challenging, and so have wanted to think through such questions of passivity, of impressionability, in part, to be sure, as a result of my conversations with her, and my engagement with her prose and drawing.

I think when Blanchot does these extraordinary things like writing, "a written thing, a bit of bark" (1995, 328), he makes it into almost an apposition: a written thing, a bit of bark. He lets them stand next to each other with just that comma between them. So is he saying that a written thing can be a bit of bark, or when I write "a bit of bark" that *that* is the bit of bark? There is some way in which, yes, language is preserving something of the bit of bark at the same time it is not quite the same as the bit of bark. Blanchot is not a constructivist. There is a way in which materiality is registered and in some sense preserved in language.

Linnell Secomb: I guess what I'm trying to think through in that attempt to look at what's going on in the discourse around asylum seekers is, that, you know, one way to think about it is drawing on your work on performativity that it could just say, Well, there's this kind of construction of the refugee as an illegal immigrant or whatever, but that doesn't constrain, that doesn't fix the identity of the refugee. That because of, you know, iteration and slippages and … there's the possibility of a resistant positioning … so that's one way to do it. But I guess why I was interested in Blanchot is that I'm wondering whether it's not just about slippage in language; I'm wondering if there's also—a kind of materiality, an unknowable materiality in the world that kind of confronts what we do with language. That doesn't determine, you know, determine what we are or who we are or whatever, but actually that won't let language alone.

Judith Butler: Yes.

Linnell Secomb: You know, so that it's not just about slippage in language but actually language is constantly being, you know, in some kind of weird way …

Judith Butler: Called upon …

Linnell Secomb: Yeah, yeah, so that this trying to respond, trying to think about the position of the asylum seekers, is not just about saying, Well, you know, through slippages you can construct another identity, but actually that the materiality of the world, the materiality of the body, the materiality of experience, you know, forces itself upon language somehow or other. You know, that's what I want to try and do.

Judith Butler: I think it would be great to do. It would be very interesting to consider the efforts to come up with names for managing, containing, controlling this event—whether it's the language of illegality or abnormality—as efforts to contain something that is also making its claim on language. None of those naming efforts actually settle the problem of the material demand that is insistently made upon language. Of course, then, trying to develop a language for what that material demand is will be an infinite regress but that's probably okay, as long as you can see that these active efforts to construct and produce through the name are thwarted or forced into endless repetition through a material demand that's not entirely capturable in language, or is even resistant to it in some sense.

One of the things that happens, of course, when we undertake a discourse analysis of government speech, is that we end up focusing on the productive dimensions of language: what it's doing, how it contains, how it constructs, how it maintains and strategizes. As a result, we emphasize the deliberate activities of government media operations, and we focus on their intentions and strategies. Then we come to think that what is actively done in language forms the sole focus of our approach to language, but I think this is probably errant. We have to be able as well to consider what escapes linguistic representation, what cannot be said or uttered, and what is foreclosed from speakability.

Moreover, even when we try to discern the intentions of policy makers, we have to consider that the language they use is not always the language they have made. So, then we have to ask in what crucible of language such intentions are formed, and, are the workings of the crucible, strictly speaking, without intention? It seems to me that even as one uses a certain discourse to effect certain ends intentionally, one is also used by the history of that discourse, its formative practices, its ways of foreclosing the field of what can be intended or said. Even in [Jacques] Derrida's "Signature Event Context," which many take to be the definitive denunciation of intention, he says quite clearly that intentions *do* exist, that's not the problem; it's just that intention is not the ground of discourse, it's not the foundation of discourse. So the difference we find in Derrida, over and against [J. L.] Austin, is that Derrida asks us how we are to locate intention within the field of discourse, which is not the same as doing away with it altogether. And then, of course, there's another question about why it is that we have come to expect that there could be resolution at the level of nomenclature. If we decide what name asylum seekers are to be called, have we resolved the issue? How has nomenclature become politicized? What's happening there? Are we really just arguing about which name to use, or is there some dense displacement of political struggle at the site of the struggle over nomenclature? I don't know quite how to answer that.

I do, though, have a few remarks to offer about the term *asylum seeker*, but I think I'll just hold on to that for a moment because I wanted to respond to Susanne's discussion. I'm wondering if we might return to that interesting apposition of Blanchot's—a bit of bark, a written thing. Could we say, for instance, a written thing, a bit of humanity? Is there a way in which the letter might also function as a kind of preservation or registration of a materiality that's not fully captured by the letter? There is something in the letter that escapes the letter, and it can be bark, it can be humanity.

I would also like very much to see and will be on alert for this theater piece by Shahin Shafaei that you address. The notion of *refugitive* is interesting as an effort at resignification, since the word functions at several levels. Of course, when Shafaei calls his theater piece *Refugitive* and uses language as he does, it seems he's claiming and subverting the language that hates him. I wonder how that use of language and its resignification could be related to government speech and its strategy and intentions. Are they both taking up language that's already available and doing something else with it for different reasons, and could we say that they're both involved in resignifying strategies even over and against one another? I don't know how one would stage that but I think it would be worthwhile to try to think about.

Fiona Jenkins: I wonder about what we do with discourse analysis. Say we read those statements by DIMIA about how we should probably talk about illegal immigrants or asylum seekers, or whatever the correct term is; it seems to me a risk of discourse analysis that it stays at a level where we say, Look, this is crazy, look, this is comic in a way. I mean, on the one hand, there's a sense in which I want to say something positive about that, which is that wherever we find these ridiculous formulations, wherever we find impossible positions being produced, it's not only a sign that the authority is kind of working in a productive, coercive way, it's also a point of vulnerability, it's a point that's troubled, it's a point that we find comic and that's perhaps a very important, popular way in which these absurd government uses of language come into question; but on the other hand, it also stops short in a certain way of engaging with the seriousness of that discourse in its capacity, for example, to play a juridical role— you know, This is what the High Court said, and therefore all sorts of real consequences follow from that and it isn't funny anymore. I guess I'm asking anybody who wants to answer, I mean, is there a limit of discourse analysis there, or does discourse analysis have to take up the problem of juridical location and address how to open that authority, that political authority, that juridical authority to effective contestation, not a contestation that can be recontained as simply comic?

Sue Saltmarsh: I think one of the really interesting things that raises, I suppose, is the extent to which both representational practices and our collective activities in unpacking those, where they stop and at what point those things call democracy into question, participatory democracy. And I've written a—I've a got an answer to that—except that I see that as a question that reemerges again and again, that it seems to me that practices of governance and the law are becoming increasingly practices of representation rather than participatory engagement. Also, this is where I wonder about our complicity in terms of our consumption of that representation and often a very uncritical consumption, so it's a response.

Judith Butler: I had a couple of thoughts about that notion of the asylum seeker as illegal or not normal, and maybe it relates a little bit to the question that you're asking. I think that there's something of a displacement that happens when, as you say, politics becomes representational in this way, and I was just trying to understand how it's even possible, logically, to have an idea of an asylum seeker who is *illegal*. Because to seek asylum is precisely to seek legal status, and if to seek legal status is itself illegal, if making the petition is held to be illegal, that can only make sense if we take national law to constitute the entire field of relevant law. After all, there are international protocols for seeking asylum, and so when someone seeks asylum, they are not acting illegally. They are, quite explicitly, invoking international law in order to secure asylum within a given national polity. To say that asylum seekers are illegal is to say that international law should be held null and void. And those who make this claim that asylum seeking is illegal are actively producing a conflict between, on the one hand, sovereign national state policy and international law.

It seems to me that in asking for asylum one is invoking the authority of international law and even performatively invoking its potentially binding character on a national sovereign state. For the request to be deemed illegal is actually a way of saying that the protocols established by international law are illegitimate and unbinding, that as a state, we will not recognize them as binding. It's one that's obviously played out in the U.S. in a different way, and that plays out in debates about whether or not Iraq was a sovereign state or had any rights of sovereignty, as well as whether Israel has rights of sovereignty. In Australia, this gets played out through the invocation of a national unity or collectivity of Australians, bound by culture or race, who have to be protected from some imagined onrush of undesirable immigrants. The state makes up stories about children being thrown overboard from boats carrying asylum seekers in order to establish the *barbarisms* lurking offshore; that this story was exposed as a raw fiction allows us to see the state's method of demonizing potentially new immigrants: they're criminal, they're irrational, they're not part of civilization as we know it, and they won't fit in our national identity. Never mind that national identity is simultaneously constructed as racist and malicious in the course of that story. National sentiment gets rallied against these potentially incursive others. But the national sentiment being worked out at the representational level—this is who these people are, let's lie about it, let's make them highly undesirable so that we can show our support for sovereignty over and against the international courts—is a displacement of this larger political issue. I'm not quite sure how to think about the representational issues except that a sovereign state, in order to buck international law, has to be able to produce pretty fierce national sentiment about who is *we* and who is *them*, and that representational strategies are crucial in the structuring and stoking of that affect.

In *The Human Race*, a surviver of Buchenwald, Robert Antelme [1998], writes of the extraordinary challenge to the notion of the human his historical experience in the concentration camps delivered. In those pages, despite the enormous suffering he underwent and witnessed, he still imagines what he calls *the unity of the human*. He is unwilling to divide the human species into different nationalities and different moral orders, even though he understands the temptation to say that Nazis are themselves bestial and inhuman and so outside the order of the human. In the face of their murderousness and cruelty, he says, Yes, this is also part of what it is to be human, even those who commit such acts belong to the unity of the human. Even at the end of that book, which I find astonishing, when he's released from the camp and he's talking with someone from Poland, they share a cigarette back and forth as they lie on their sick beds and they speak German to one another. I was somewhat shocked at this moment. How can you speak German right then, after everything that German has meant in those camps? But Antelme, who was part of the French resistance, finds a commonality with his Polish comrade, precisely in and through the few German words they exchange. I suppose this is Antelme's surprising point—namely, that the human bond can happen in any medium, even the one that has been used to sever that bond. Antelme's conclusion is an absolutely fierce resistance to a nationalist resolution of the Nazi issue: Do not demonize them for being German, do not seek recourse to French nationalism as a way of distancing yourself from the horrors of Nazi atrocities; do not seek to instate new national unities that will guard against the old; reenter that very language, or some other, and find what universality, what humanity exists precisely where you would not expect it. And you can feel the difficulty of such a gesture over and against, say, a Zionism, which would establish Hebrew as a living language, or a French nationalism spawned through Gaullism, that would insist on a national entity to protect minorities for all time. Hannah Arendt clearly knew better on this issue, since for her it is the nation-state that produces and sustains the disenfranchised minorities.

This leads me to reflect that perhaps the criminalization of the asylum seeker is only possible within a lexicon of nationalism. If there is to be a new human, or a unity of a human, it would involve a human exchange that is not restricted to national language or border. And if that very exchange is criminalized, then the human becomes a function of the nation, and produces its own inhumanity. Perhaps nationalism is the unspoken presumption in too many of our debates about the human, but I am wondering whether critique of nationalism might produce new frames for the human, new ways to read, to hear, to see, and so new possibilities for a sensate democracy.

CHAPTER 5

Taking Account of Childhood Excess: "Bringing the Elsewhere Home"

AFFRICA TAYLOR

University of Canberra

Introduction

In this essay I strike up a conversation between Judith Butler's work and my research into the ways in which young children first perform their identities and negotiate their belongings within a pluralist society. In the spirit of "bringing the elsewhere home", I draw upon vastly disparate actors, writers, readers, and contexts to reflect upon the excesses of childhood belonging. I move between Butler's essay "Global Violence, Sexual Politics," which was originally delivered to a queer studies audience in December 2001, only three months after 9/11, as the City University of New York David R. Kessler Lecture in

New York City (and published in 2003a);[1] snatches of her earlier work
on gender (1990a, 1993a); and various musings over the significance
of four-year-olds playing in a sandpit and home corner of a preschool
in suburban Australia.[2]

Taking the nestings of young children's sociocultural identities
within the uneven and contested power relations of the nation as my
point of departure, I set out to explore how queerer imaginings of
belonging, of being in community, of being undone by each other
(Butler 2003a, 200) might be refreshed and renewed by the quirk-
ier aspects of childhood cultural politics. These queerer imaginings
are ones that have some kind of inspirational basis in my readings
of Butler's works over the years. I believe we share a similar desire
to search for new ways of entering community through pushing the
limits around what is already taken as real, to be possible—although I
acknowledge that my own efforts in this regard are more gestural than
groundbreaking. My work is in some part an application of Butler's
ideas to childhood ethnographies, but I would like to think that the
elucidations enabled by such a conversation might in some sense enable
some aspects of children's lives (albeit only my selective representations
of these lives) to speak to us in ways that provoke us to think differently about ourselves as well as about them.

Throughout my own accountings of Australian childhood belongings, I bounce off Butler's guiding question, "Who counts as human?"
(2003a, 199). In applying a selection of Butler's optics to instances of
young children's identity play, I not only break with the orthodoxies
of early childhood thinking (following in the wake of Davies 1989,
2004; Dahlberg, Moss, and Pence 1999; and MacNaughton 2000)
but I also advocate for a series of articulations or translations: between
macropolitics and micropractices; between theory and ethnography;
between national preoccupations and local events; and between adults'
and children's worlds. In fact, if we can think about these articulations
as crossings, as forms of cultural translation or exchanges of intelligi-
bilities, then there are a number of ways in which I attempt to "bring
the elsewhere home" here.

There is also a background to the "to-ing and fro-ing" of this essay
that points to the ways in which my thinking, in a very broad sense,
has been influenced by Butler's writings. It has to do with the ways
in which she continuously and purposefully interweaves her understandings of the political ground of activism and her deconstruction of
the subjects on that ground, to carry off two or more conversations at
once with oneself, to publicly display an engaged internal dialogue that
will neither relinquish the "we" of collective struggle over the full range

of human rights nor persist in a vigilant destabilization of the very categories of "we-ness" that foreclose on what it means to be human. It is like holding on and letting go at the same time.

The dialogue within this essay, its "to-ing and fro-ing," aims to explore the productive potential of translating between disparate macro social processes and micro local events: embattled national cultural politics; border protection in the sandpit; and kids in drag. This is not to establish crude or invariant causal links between these rarely associated processes and events, but to throw some light on our coimplicated political emplacements, or nestings in the world, and, in the process, to cause some unsettling. My efforts to locate children's identity politics within the wider Australian political context are directly inspired by Butler's (2003a) rearticulation of North American sexual politics within the context of aggressive U.S. foreign policy, post-9/11. As I bring together a similar bricolage of unusual elements in this essay, I am also responding to Butler's challenge to "submit ourselves to a process of cultural translation" in order to yield "our most fundamental categories ... to a rupture and a resignification ..." (Butler 2003a, 212–13). Beyond all these attempts at layered translations, however, and against the backdrop of a bleak and violent (inter)national landscape, my overarching desire is to better imagine what an inclusive community that both welcomes and spawns difference might look like.

APPROACHING EARLY CHILDHOOD AS A SITE OF STUDY

It is this desire that brings me to early childhood. I hasten to add that this is not because I am seeking refuge in the kindergarten as a pure and innocent romantic retreat from the "real world." Quite the contrary; I am captivated by what I perceive to be young children's inherent *queerness*, not their innocence, and I see this setting as a highly politicized and political one. In the thick of this "real world" of serious political maneuverings, young children's predilection for wild fantasy and eccentricity makes early childhood a site of riotous possibility and open-ended significations. Fantasy play, as we shall soon see, enables all sorts of strange hybridities and transformations. But early childhood is by no means all about quirky freedom and interesting edges. It has a much more sobering and pedestrian side as a key training ground for conformity and compliance through the introduction of social norms and the encouragement of self-regulating behaviors. Young children embody and enact these contradictions, as they pivot between being hyperregulating and exclusionary on the one hand and radically free border crossers on the other. There is a lot to be learned from their excesses.

One of my main agendas in approaching early childhood as a site of study is to take advantage of the blatant excesses that young children display around "doing" identity, and I will do this by interrogating some of their over-the-top performances as border police as well as boundary crossers of hegemonic social categories. Another agenda is to rethink both the position and the significance of these childhood excesses in relation to being human, or as Butler urges us, to challenge notions of "who counts as human." My refusal to submit to a discrete and hierarchical separation of children's and adults' worlds is a twofold strategy directly connected to this question of who counts as human. First, given my limits as a writing adult focusing upon child/adult coimplication and meaning exchange, and the intergenerational limits that exacerbate those interpretive contingencies of every ethnographic act, I can only gesture toward a blurring of the conventional binary of "knowing adult" and "known-about child." Notwithstanding these constraints, like Butler in her Kessler address I seek to explore what light a minority group's experiences might throw on the overarching violent political predicaments that affect us all (Butler 2003a, 199). Second, by even considering what adults might have to learn from children, I implicitly advocate for a repositioning of children's experiences within the melee of adult-centered discourses of the human.

The best I can offer by way of an appraisal of young children's experiences is an account based on my two year observations of their negotiations of identity and belonging in a culturally diverse Australian early childhood center. From the outset this childhood ethnography has been built upon a number of related premises, including the need for ongoing social transformations through radical participatory democracy; a regard for the early childhood institution as a forum for civil society (see Dahlberg et al. 2000) with an important role to play in this process; and an assumption about the political nature of children's relationships within it. Flowing from such premises I have approached the early childhood center primarily as a site that functions to introduce children to the world of human difference. I see it as a conduit between home (where cultural belonging is established) and the broader community (in which struggles over identity and belonging take place on a daily basis as a part of the ongoing process of nation building, as much as anything else). Despite its important political role and potential as an inclusive community of difference, my view of the pluralist early childhood center is not an entirely rosy one. It still remains a microcosm of our imperfect world, within which certain gender, desiring, raced, ethnically marked and national subject positions already count more and carry more authority than others.

Not all involved would agree with my appraisal. From anecdotal evidence I realize that my perspective goes against the grain of many working and training to work within the field, those who prefer to maintain a belief in childhood innocence, to insist that children are unaware of and unaffected by difference, and to regard early childhood as a utopic enclave, hermetically sealed from the prejudices and undesirable machinations of "the real world out there." However, I remain convinced that most young children are well aware of a wide range of human differences *because they embody them,* and that they also realize that these differences do not all attract and enjoy the same status and authority. In other words, they know that some lives count more than others. I am not entirely alone in this belief. My findings are in keeping with a number of other studies that have found children as young as age three to be aware of race and cultural differences and to have already absorbed the attitudes of others around them to these differences (Adler 2003; Hirschfeld 1996; Holmes 1995; Ramsey 1995; Skattebol 2003; Targowska 2001).[3] And of course there is by now a wealth of well-documented evidence and commentary about preschool children's hyper awareness of gender difference, and their considerable efforts to regulate its performance (see, e.g., Davies 1989; Keddie 2003; MacNaughton 2000; Walkerdine 1999).

Although not the only important subject position, gender figures centrally within the field of early childhood identity politics, and my approach to this field is to a large extent framed by Butler's early work on gender and performativity (1990a, 1993a). As I watch the ways in which these children variously "do girl," "do boy," or, to be more specific, "do white Australian boy," and so on, and think about Butler's question of "how to acknowledge and 'do' the construction one is invariably in" (1990a, 31), I wonder to what extent children are already doing this. Because of the over-the-top nature of much of children's endlessly repetitive "doings," I wonder if they see girlness or boyness as constructions even as they "do" them and still recognize that they are "doing" them. Are these "doings" just about trying to get it right, to be acceptable, to belong, or is there another realm of desire operating here? Can their sometimes radically transformative and hybrid kinds of performances show us something about the possibilities of approaching otherness? Is there any sign of a self/other ethics within their excessive play and if so what are its pedagogical implications?

As I have just mentioned, there seems to be a great amount of effort and energy invested by children in "doing" themselves in the early childhood center, and this does not apply to gender alone. The effort is compounded by the need to carry off and negotiate multiple identities, and through these performances to establish and maintain a space of belonging in their community. I have observed that most unstructured (i.e., adult-free) play time is devoted to working at it. With very few exceptions, the children in my study have been actively engaged in power struggles to either gain or maintain acceptance while playing together. Most confronting is the repertoire of overt *territorial* maneuvers that they employ as they negotiate their spaces of belonging in relation to their own and their peers' multilayered Australian identity positions. In rather uncanny ways, many of these territorial acts—such as the sandpit incident to which I will now turn—mirror those at play in the nation. From my interpretive ethnography of children at play, I offer this first narrative vignette as a reminder of the global political context in which these children are already positioned because of their bodies, which they never let go at the door, and within which they are actively engaged.

Who Counts as Australian?

Lines in the Sandpit

Four-year-old Hakim is playing by himself in the sandpit, making mud pies out of sand and water. At the time of this incident, he had been coming to the center on a regular basis for six months. Along with his family, he arrived in Australia from the Middle East immediately before starting preschool. He often plays alone, but not by choice. He makes daily attempts to join in the games of the other children, particularly aspiring to be accepted by a high-status group of white boys.

Also in the sandpit, playing adjacent to Hakim but quite separately from him, are four-year-old Sam and George. They are key members of the white boys group, which has commanded hegemonic boy status in the center for the last nine months. These two are purposefully digging a garden. It is a collaborative effort, and they are happily interacting with each other. Around their garden they dig a prominent border—a trough that they form with the handle of their spades.

Eventually Hakim requests to join their digging game, but Sam and George shake their heads and turn their backs on him. Hakim crosses over the garden trough border in an attempt to get closer to them and establish eye contact. He asks them again. Once more he is refused, and this time told to go away and to get out of their garden. Hakim becomes noticeably distressed at this stage, and complains that they never let him play with them. By way of explanation, he points to the exposed skin on his arm, saying that they will not play with him because he is brown.

A younger white boy, who does not normally play with any of the others, suddenly runs into the sandpit and crosses over the garden border. Stumbling in the trough, he trips and falls into Sam's and George's garden patch, making a bit of a mess of their neat work. Sam and George ignore him and keep digging.

Hakim, who has been watching this accident, seizes the opportunity and offers to help them fix the damage. Again he is refused, but this time Sam tells Hakim that he cannot play with them because he does not talk like them. A teacher who is watching the boys play intervenes at this point and reminds Sam and George that they sometimes play with Sohan and that he also has brown skin like Hakim. Sam agrees that Sohan does have brown skin, but after reflecting a moment on the difference between the two brown boys, he adds, by way of explanation, "But he talks more like us and he is sort of ... um ... white-brown."

In the aftermath of the Tampa and Children Overboard affairs,[4] and the Australian Howard Government's ongoing introduction of radical "border protection" measures designed to exclude and deter any further unauthorized (and predominately Middle Eastern) asylum seekers (see Brennan 2003; Vanstone 2003), this sandpit incident (recorded in October 2003) reveals four-year-old Sam and George performing their own selectively targeted border protection rites to excess. The incident is an unambiguously racialized struggle over belonging: to the sandpit; to the early childhood center; to the Australian nation. It confirms that at least some children not only recognize skin color as a marker of difference and are aware that it signifies unequal power relations, but are also prepared to exploit this awareness. Not only did the children share an understanding of their border's selective gatekeeping function, but they had no trouble in articulating their respective racialized subject positions in the terms of prevailing Australian discourses of core white and marginal nonwhite ("brown") cultural belongings.

Sam's ability to confer provisional insider ("white-brown") status on Sohan because he "talks more like us" demonstrates further nuanced understandings of this same popular discourse about who qualifies as the "real Australian." As an authorizing white male and an indisputably "real Aussie," Sam gets to decide not only who can "come in" to the sandpit, but also the grounds on which nonwhite others might be regarded as "more" or "less" Australian (Taylor 2005). Again there are resonances here with Howard's remark and election slogan shortly after the Tampa affair: "We, and we only, will decide who comes into our country and on what terms they come" (Howard 2001).

This rather sad sandpit story works well to illustrate how childhood belongings are "nested" within the uneven and contested power relations of the nation (see Anderson and Taylor 2005). This is neither to impose a linear causality on one small incident in a sandpit nor to imply that all racism starts in childhood, but instead to highlight the intermeshing of children's and adults' social worlds and the ways in which national identity struggles are played out across generations and within everyday local contexts.

This vignette also foregrounds the mutually constituting relations (intergenerational as well as transcultural) that take place across the intersecting fields of global, national, and local politics. Working against the parochial protected enclave imaginary, it repositions the early childhood center as an *extraverted* local site—a convergent point of global, national, and local flows (Massey 1993). Indeed, the inherently political and "extraverted" nature of this local site—its transnational convergences and struggles—are embodied in the children themselves.

Although certainly not witnessed in this episode of sandpit play, the extraverted early childhood center has the *potential* to be a site of postnational belongings (Taylor 2005). Because of the current unprecedented levels of transnational flows, the conditions of possibility for promoting early childhood centers as postnational communities of difference have never been greater. Rather than denying the political nature of early childhood, or reducing such conflicts to individual incidents of bad behavior, culturally diverse centers might work to recast these incidents as horizontal rather than hierarchical struggles for national belonging. By working to "unsettle the moral foundation of claims to primary standing" (Anderson 2000, 383) on the part of white Australian children, they might resist engagement with predetermined hierarchical orderings of national rights and privileges, of self-appointed "real Aussie" kids and the rest. This would not only involve reimagining Australian-ness as a horizontal field on which the meaning of "real Australian" is cast open, but also engaging with it, as Butler puts it, through a "a certain agonism and contestation" that "must be in play for politics to become democratic" (2003a, 213).

A postnational interruption to the hegemonic reproduction of the assumed-to-be white Australian nation involves a systematic deconstruction of the conflation of Australian-ness and whiteness within the global circuits of colonialism and immigration (see Anderson and Taylor 2005) and within the micropolitics of everyday lives (for a focus on young children's lives, see Taylor and Richardson 2005a). Although whiteness critique is not the focus of this essay, it necessarily "hovers" within the series of articulations that I offer in taking up Butler's question, "Whose lives count as lives?" (2003a, 199). Unmarked white power remains an ever-present shadow on the world stage, where the sovereignty of the most powerful "first world" nations is increasingly used as a defense for denying the international human rights of displaced "third world" people.

In the Australian context, the unnamed yet authorizing norm of whiteness is never far away. Howard's emphatic mantra "We, and we only will decide" reverberates in my mind as I read Butler's call to make "our claims ... on reality all the more active and vigilant, precisely because the nation-state is being produced again and again along lines of consensus that centralize the heterosexual family, property and national boundaries ..." (2003a, 206). As Butler implies here, a simultaneous shoring up of internal as well as external boundaries is necessary in order to exclude a variety of undesirable others from the imagined as well as the physical space of the nation. For instance, we might reflect upon the ways in which recent moves (in both the United States and Australia) to redefine the legal boundaries of marriage as exclusively heterosexual are concomitant with moves to redefine the legal boundaries of Australian territories to exclude unauthorized asylum seekers (Ellison 2003; see also Taylor and Richardson 2005a). The moral and ontological underpinnings of both material and symbolic exclusions are evident across the spectrum of gender/sexuality and racialized/national identity politics.

I turn now to another recent Australian border protection event, but this time of the internal kind. This one allows us to consider the "who counts" question in terms of the family and begins to shifts the spotlight back onto gender. It bears witness to the moral and ontological imperatives that reconfirm the centrality of the heterosexual family in Australian society and delimits the "rightful" place of young children within it.

Who Counts as a Family?

Looking "through the window" onto a segment of Australian society,[5] the children's television show *Play School* (Australian Broadcasting Corporation 2004) recently depicted a scene of a girl called Brenna enjoying a visit to a fun park, along with her friend Merryn and Brenna's two mothers. This sixty-second vignette triggered a barrage of protests from the nation's political leaders (on both sides of Parliament), who initially claimed that it was an infringement on the rights of parents to gate-keep their children's exposure to same-sex families (*Sydney Morning Herald* 2004a). Despite the ABC's insistence that it was simply representing the diversity of contemporary Australian family life, Australian Communications Minister Darryl Williams, rebuked "his" national broadcaster for not ensuring that issues covered in its children's programs were "appropriate to the age of its audience" ("Gay Play School Backlash" 2004). By this admonition he was implying a dereliction of duty in protecting *children's* rights.

In fact the moral panic (entirely an adult furor, as the child viewers did not even blink) was neither about parents' nor children's rights. It was a fight to maintain the exclusive sovereign rights of the heterosexual family over early childhood. The mere suggestion of giving young children a glimpse of a different kind of knowledge, albeit one that simply pointed to the unremarkably normal activities of nonheterosexual families, was seen as a dangerous threat. If we ever need reminding of the nexus of knowledge and power, this is a great example of it. At the time, the rush to "protect" children from the assumed-to-be-dangerous knowledge that some among their ranks have two mothers, was counterposed by a glaring lack of concern for the children from lesbian and gay families themselves. The valorization of heterosexual lives through devaluing queer ones is a familiar and predictable script, but in this case the paradox of disavowing some children's lives in the name of "protecting children" seems to have gone largely unnoticed.

The efforts of politicians to regulate whose families can and cannot be spoken about on national "children's" television points not only to compulsory heterosexuality as a pivotal arena for reconfirming national consensus but also to the function of state censorship within the nation building process. By attempting to censor which kinds of family stories can and cannot be told, the state is clearly seeking "to make certain kinds of citizens possible and others impossible" (Butler 1997a, 132). Through censorship it seeks to render the subject position of "child of same-sex family" as unspeakable, and hence unintelligible and ultimately discounted. However, as Butler points out in her essay on "Implicit Censorship and Discursive Agency" (in 1997a), this kind of power also has a paradoxical productive effect. "The regulation that *states what it does not want stated* thwarts its own desire, conducting a performative contradiction.... Such regulations introduce the censored speech into public discourse, thereby establishing it as a site of contestation, that is, as the scene of a public utterance that it sought to preempt" (1997a, 130).

Ironically, it is the highly publicized contestation over the airing of the segment, much more so than the rather unremarkable broadcast itself, that has produced the conditions of possibility for thinking differently about families, sexualities, and familial subject positions. Fueled by public debate, it is an *epistemological* challenge that constitutes the crux of this controversy. From the vehemence of adult reactions to even conceiving of such a representation (after all, how many adults are watching *Play School* at 9:30 on a weekday morning?), this family portrait of a happy child with two mothers would appear to be an oxymoron—an aberration that clearly disturbs the moral and ontological bedrock of heterosexual family identity. Most important, it pushes the conceptual boundaries of "real" and "normal" childhood that are so tightly ensconced within the orthodoxies of childhood innocence and hegemonic heterosexual family life.

It is this sacrosanct nexus of the innocent child and the heterosexual family that I wish to pry apart, and it will be my task for the remainder of this essay. To begin this process, I quickly revisit the constitutive relations among sex, gender, desire, and compulsory heterosexuality that Butler so thoroughly worked over in the early 1990s. In particular, I pick up on her insistence that by imposing its own internal causal logic on the relations of sex, gender, and desire, hegemonic heterosexuality is dependent upon maintaining a coherent binary notion of gender (1990; 1993). As an adjunct to this, I propose that the hegemony of the heterosexual family (in its distinctively Western formation) relies upon an originary notion of childhood innocence as well as the accomplishment of a coherently gendered child. According to the hegemonic heterosexual family's own internal and morally inflected logic, it is because the child is always already innocent that it can only be protected by a heterosexual family. Any nonheteronormative family is a danger to the *child because its inherent innocence renders it vulnerable to in-coherent gender identities.*

By developing an eye for the queerness of some children's family play, we can begin to understand the volume and vehemence of protests about *Play School*'s benign lesbian domestic scene on television. If it was simply a matter of children automatically, cohesively, and unambiguously performing their gender identities according to the "natural" order of their biological sex, there would be no grounds for concern. These protests can thus be viewed as a compensatory performance of an invariant "natural" order that does not actually exist, and as a punitive and disciplinary response aimed at reaffirming the exclusive rights of the heterosexual family.

Yet before introducing some of the children that might create such dissonance and attempting to answer some of these questions, I wish to place them in context. To do so means returning to the normative discourses and architectures of the early childhood center, and to home corner in particular, the locus of children's family- and gender-identity play.

NATURALLY STRAIGHT AND INNOCENT?

For those unfamiliar with the highly normative world of early childhood, I will quickly outline the trajectory of the potent and enduring European discourse of childhood innocence to which I have been referring. Often traced back to Jean-Jacques Rousseau's 1762 work *Emile* (see Aries 1962), this is a construct of the Romantic era. Rousseau argued that childhood is a pure and natural state and that it is incumbent upon adults to protect this innocence. When Frierich Wilhelm August Froebel established the first kindergarten (literally, "children's garden")—in Germany some seven decades later, he was heavily influenced by Rousseau's elision of childhood with nature. With more than a few echoes of the prelapsarian Garden of Eden, Froebel's kindergarten classroom was imagined as the extension of the garden. It was designed to be a space in which children, in a state of natural innocence, would continue to explore and investigate the world through free play (Kline 1995).

The legacy of Rousseau's philosophy of natural childhood innocence and Froebel's acquiescent kindergarten design are still clearly in evidence in the contemporary early childhood center. Home corner is one of these interior child spaces designed exclusively for natural free-play exploration. Somewhat ironically, however, it has a decidedly stiff and stilted semiology. In fact, home corner represents a stylized facade of suburban domestic orthodoxy. Impeccably symmetrical, its central welcoming door and framing curtained windows offer a predictable familiarity and an assured sense of order. Inside, the idealized child-sized home is equipped with miniaturized furniture and domestic artifacts—sink, table, bed, baby dolls, telephone—all very conventional and manageable. The dress-up closet stands close by. This is a well-stocked performance space, decked out and ready to support the kind of domestic dramatic play that is considered a normal, natural, and healthy part of child development: a kind of stage on which young children can rehearse future adult roles.

While prevailing discourses dispose the adults to perceive the children as natural and innocent and freely inquiring into the world around them, the architectures and artefacts of home corner are designed to guide this inquiry within a regime of material and symbolic constraints. Whether or not it ultimately succeeds in mediating children's understandings of the adult world in such terms, this sign-laden space is clearly designed to represent an idealized version of domestic life. It implicitly draws upon a spectrum of hegemonic discourses and their associated stereotypes that function to value some lives and ways of living while devaluing others. The semiotic effect of this miniature home, with its decidedly straight, white, and middle-class aesthetic, is to reproduce a universalized ideal of utopian domestic space and normative family relations that are suitable for children to emulate.

As an artifice of homeliness, home corner bears witness to Butler's reminder that "hegemonic heterosexuality is itself a constant and repeated effort to imitate its own idealizations" (1993a, 135). Following the associative logic of its normative signs, one might assume that the domestic and familial play occurring within home corner would be accordingly uncomplicated and straightforward, derivative of happy, natural, and normal heterosexual family life. Accordingly, many children do appear to engage in straightforward heterosexual family play, involving regular mothers and fathers and conforming to the styles and manners deemed appropriate to "normal" development. Many girls "do" mothers, daughters, and wives, according to the norms, and many boys "do" fathers, sons, and husbands within the oppositional set of gender orderings upon which compulsory heterosexuality relies. But whether or not these performances manage to carry off the ideal of heterosexual family life or simply draw attention to the less-than-ideal effects of its own making depends on how you read them.

Some of the more "blokey" white boys would not be seen dead in home corner, for as a domestic space it is already gendered. They openly describe it as a girl's space and stay well away. Refusals and disidentifications such as these are integral aspects of their "real" Aussie boy performances and reinforce (in my eyes as well as perhaps in the eyes of other children) their hegemonic status within the center.

Occasionally some "blokey" boys do make loud and raucous incursions through home corner to momentarily cause upheaval, but rarely stay and play. So for a start, there is a selection process around who will use this space and how they will approach it. Nevertheless, at least half the boys and almost all the girls do play there fairly regularly. Here is one example of girls and boys playing it straight in home corner.

The Family Outing

Harry and Alan are busy modifying and masculinizing home corner. Alan builds a campfire in the middle of the kitchen and barbeques breakfast chops, while Harry fixes the drain in the sink. When breakfast is over and the plumbing done, Harry decides that it is time to go. He carries four small chairs outside and arranges them into the front and back seats of a car. Already in the mood after the campfire breakfast, the boys decide to go camping. Kathy and Ruth arrive at this moment and, overhearing the plans, ask if they can come along, too. The boys are not keen on the prospect of having girls come along. "Only boys go camping. Girls go shopping," Alan asserts, perhaps by way of suggesting an attractive alternative. But the girls protest long and hard at their exclusion and eventually Harry capitulates, but only on condition that the girls agree to pack the car and then sit quietly in the back.

The girls comply. They gather handbags and mobile phones and carry them to the car. The boys collect some books and maps, a basket full of food and some tools. They pack so many things that they eventually declare that there is not enough room to fit two girls, and one will have to stay behind. In solidarity the girls resist this directive and argue a case that both should be allowed to come; neither wants to be left behind. Ruth just gets in and eventually Kathy is allowed to squeeze in, too.

They set off, Harry driving while Alan reads the map. Kathy and Ruth sit quietly in the backseat nursing the baskets of food and tools. Ruth gets out the mobile phone and starts to make a call. "Don't use the phone 'til we get there," shouts Alan. "We haven't fixed it yet!"

Even in this brief family outing scenario, home corner can be seen to be having a disclosing effect *because* of its idealized construction. Rather than functioning as a wholesome site for the dramatization of benign adult relations, in this instance (as in many others observed in this study) home corner has generated traditional and clearly oppositional male and female performances that both spotlight and reproduce unequal gender relations. So as they comply and "play it straight" in home corner—as the boys rehearse their manly privilege and the girls (despite their protests) learn to take a backseat—this staging of the heterosexual family reveals something of the less than ideal aspects of gender relations in the world "as it is today."

The paradox of this performance is heightened because the children have reiterated what they perceive to be normal and natural relations between girls and boys/mothers and fathers within the artifice of the heteronormative domestic idyll. Thus it is that this idealized normative and appropriate space exposes the shortcomings of the world as it is, even as the children seek to get it right by negotiating their positions as "real" girls and "real" boys within it. It demonstrates quite nicely how "parodic repetition of the 'original'" ultimately "reveals the original to be nothing other than a parody of the *idea* of the natural and the original" (Butler 1990a, 31).

Hegemonic gender play such as this is very common and repetitive—to the point of obsession. As we can see from this one short episode, children engaged in such behavior expend much of their energy regulating the norms of oppositional gender roles. These same children will repeat their efforts again and again; it can be quite relentless. And as in the racialized regulatory play in the sandpit—hegemonic play of a different but related kind—it is also highly territorialized (boys in front and girls in back), and these territories need protecting. George and Sam, Harry and Alan all have territories to protect; they have boundaries to maintain in order to keep everyone in their "right" place as insiders and outsiders, dominants and subordinates. They do not have time to drop their guard.

As characteristic heterosexual family play, this episode foregrounds the ways in which a reiteration of the "original" (set of relations, order of things)—in this case, the highly unequal geopolitical gender relations in the family car—becomes the point of fixation. It must be done the "original"—therefore "right"—way or it cannot be done at all. There is a religiosity to this insistence. It is an exhausting task for those children positioned as the key agents of hegemonic gender and whiteness regimes in the center to maintain this kind of compliance and conformity—their own as well as others. From my observations of the different kinds of play, I think that the hegemonic performances are much more demanding, simply *because*, as Butler puts it, they are always "trying to become commensurate with an ideal" (2002a).

But not all children embody hegemonic social positions, and this is reflected in their play. Those boys who do not exhibit hegemonic masculine behaviors and/or are not white are much more likely to cross identity category boundaries. This is obviously the case, for instance, in relation to the "sissy" boys, who seek respite from the "blokey" boys and their regulatory demands by playing with the girls in home corner. But the nonwhite boys like Hakim (who would have loved to join the white and blokey boys) and Sohan (who sometimes is allowed to play with them) are also frequent home corner visitors and not averse to a bit of cooking and cleaning.

Those whose crossings are the most flagrant and the most consistent are of greatest interest to me here—the kids who dress in drag. Their play is most likely to be an enactment and an embodiment of non-normative, and hence "unreal," imaginings. It is this drag play that offers to throw the most light on queerer modes of belonging or, to put it in Butler's terms, to knowing beyond the limits of the "real" (2003a).

Policeman Thelma

Two girls enter home corner and start to rearrange the furniture and small appliances. They work quietly together, first settling their babies and then preparing a meal. This peaceful coexistence is broken when a brash and noisy group of boys burst in and rifle through the closet. The girls leave. Meanwhile the boys are grabbing shirts and caps. Reg snatches his favorite blue frock as well as his police cap. Once attired, they gather around the table to discuss their plans.

"There's robbers out there. We'll have to catch them. Sometimes robbers do speeding. Write it down." Reg takes immediate charge and speaks with authority in a deep booming voice. His two assistants listen obediently and then Reg guides them out the door. He reaches up and pulls his cap down firmly over his brow while clutching a clipboard tightly under his other arm. Just as he is leaving the station/house, the dolls catch his eye, lined up sleeping in a bed beside the door. He pauses to take a closer look. Choosing a doll, he talks to it softly for a moment. Then tucking it under his free arm he goes outside to join the other two boys.

Before long the policemen have started chasing a speeding robber. With a great deal of noise and drama, they catch the offending child. In his gruff voice Reg asks one of his assistants to hold the baby so that he can record the incident on the clipboard. He passes the doll to Gordon, who grimaces, refuses it, and quickly pulls back his hand. The baby drops to the floor. Reg retrieves his baby and comforts it with soothing words. He takes it back into the homely police station and puts it gently back into bed. Looking out through the window he sees a rowdy scuffle developing but he is now reluctant to leave his baby alone. Instead, he takes it to a teacher and asks her to take care of the baby while he returns to work. "I'm a policeman ... and a mother," Reg explains loudly. "My name is Thelma and this is my baby. Can you look after her for me?"

In this play episode, it appears that Reg's rather unpredictable ways of "doing" cops and robbers has created a dilemma for the boys who want to play with him. Although this is Reg's game and he starts off as boss, his rules become increasingly hard for the others to understand and they eventually abandon him. These "real" boys can only enter home corner in a rowdy colonizing pack and can only stay if they can successfully regender it. As Reg's hybrid gender performance intensifies it becomes increasingly unintelligible to his playmates, and ultimately completely destabilizes the binary gender orderings that these "real" boys had worked to establish as the conditional grounds for their participation in the game. Perhaps the combination of his impressively large police cap, his booming deep voice, his heroic mission to catch robbers, are enough to maintain Reg's credibility for a while, despite the frock. But after policeman Thelma becomes a mother on duty, the "real boys" do not reenter the station. They appear to be repelled by Reg's reordering of the norms of play. The remainder of their action-packed game is conducted outside of home corner, away from Reg and in the public arena. Reg's dual desires to become a policeman and a mother, and his insistence of doing them simultaneously while making him increasingly incoherent and thus threatening to the rest of the boys, seem to cause him no problems at all. His competence as a hybrid performer is undermined only by the fact that he does not have enough hands to carry all his props.

Reg's embodiment of his dual fantasy proceeds through a relation to two sets of norms: the norms of male authority (deep voice, assertive manner, leadership initiative, heroism) and the norms of mother (emotional attachment, nurturing manner, soft and soothing voice, attentiveness). Both of his identities are very normative, but they are non-normatively concurrent. It is only the reordering of binary relationships within the one body that makes Reg's performance a transgressive one. It is important to note here that to Reg there is no contradiction, just a few roles to juggle, and no more than any other working parent has to sort out. Reg's embodied double desires and fantasies may have been an unintelligible aberration to the hegemonic boys, but they are a perfect, and regular, fit for him.

In the Royal Stable

Peter, Lily, and Margie are keen to be the first into home corner. They are eager to resume a game they have been playing every day for weeks now. As soon as free play is announced they rush inside and throw open the dress-up closet doors. Peter makes a beeline for his favorite pink wedding dress and announces, as always, that he will be the princess. He dresses quickly, dons his high heels, and teeters to the bathroom to check his accessories in the mirror before the game begins. Margie pulls on her favorite skirt and declares herself to be a princess as well. Lily just drops to the floor and makes neighing sounds. She will be their pony. This game always involves a good chase and the children know the routine well. Lily gallops away, laughing, whinnying, and tossing her head teasingly and expectantly. Margie alerts Peter that their horse has bolted, and Peter gleefully runs after the naughty pony, ceremoniously catches her and leads her back to the royal stable where she is locked up and reprimanded accordingly. Lily the horse appears chastened and compliant. "Naughty pony! No food for you!" the princesses chant. This episode is repeated several times. Each of the children performs a role skillfully and in each reenactment small additions and alterations are made to the script. "You are my best horse-catcher, daughter," Princess Margie says to Peter at one point, with undisguised admiration. Peter nods and smiles back at her.

As usual, Margie eventually tires of being princess. She discards her skirt, but cannot assume her most desirous role until she has completed a ritual transformation. The transformation is elaborate and executed with theatrical flourish. In her final princess act, Margie twirls the wand higher and higher above her head. She reaches up as high as she can go on her toes and then suddenly flutters her fingers from the top to the bottom of her body, as if to absorb the magic from the wand.

The climax of the ritual over, Margie appears to be a little dazed and disoriented. She remains still for some time, eyes glazed, as if reorienting herself to her new but much preferred state of mind and body. Her stilled feet appear to tremble in anticipation of movement. When Margie's spell is complete she blinks slowly and mumbles, "I am a horse."

Stamping one foot, she throws back her head, neighs loudly, and then gallops away from the others to await her customary capture. Princess Peter chases her and yells, "I'll have to rope you so you can't run away anymore!" Margie stops abruptly and allows him to approach her. She asks him teasingly if he would like to ride her. "I'm not sure if I can," the princess replies tentatively, appearing to be a little unsure about this offer. Margie stands calmly and waits for him to make his move. He approaches her slowly and cautiously. Suddenly she rears up and calls out loudly, "No mans [*sic*] will ride me!" This is the cue for Peter and Lily to resume the chase to capture and tame her. Together, they restrain the bad pony and return her to the stable where she is locked up without any displaying any further resistance.

Confined to her stall for a while, Margie changes the script and announces that she is now a good pony. The princesses respond with pleasure, and they reward her with a basketful of fruits and vegetables. She eats until sated and then hangs her horsey head out through the stable window, whinnying softly and contentedly while gazing at some distant horizon.

As complete flights of fancy, these reiterative performances of boy princess and girl horse are both transforming and transformative events. They are fluid performances unfettered by the constraints of gender or species alignments. They offer us an insight into a seamless world in which boundaries, when they are encountered, can be dissolved at will. The slippages among genders, species, and discourses are the salient features of this identity play. In Margie's case, the transformative act itself is a highlight of the performance. She prolongs the workings of the magical spell through which she transforms herself from princess into horse and appears to savor the metamorphic process.

Individual lines of desire intersect to drive the game. Conflict is staged and resolved. When Margie the horse invites mounting, and then rears up and declares, "No mans will ride me!" her innuendo is simultaneously gendered, sexualized, feminist, and species-defiant. There are multiple layers of insubordination evoked by this declarative slippage and yet none of the children is essentialized as oppressed or oppressor. The chase, the capture, the punishment, and the reward are mutually desired and pursued without a trace of coercion. In contrast to the earlier play events, in this one all three children easily accommodate and adapt to each other's changing desires, becomings, and scripts without struggle or detachment. In fact the transmutations— across gender, across species—are not only mutually accommodated in a supportive sense, but are, in fact, the pleasure principle of the game. It is the common pursuit of liberating transformations that actually constitutes these children's engagement with each other.

This mutual engagement in becoming otherwise is the kind of "field of ethical enmeshment with others" (2003a, 205) that Butler describes. As a collective performance of self becoming other, this event manages "to underscore the value of being oneself, of being a porous boundary, given over to others, finding oneself in a trajectory of desire that takes one out of oneself, resituates one irreversibly in the field of others" (205). These identity performances underscore, in the most generous terms, the ways in which identity is never only for oneself. There is a palpable sociality within these children's embodied relations that not only involves them freely determining their own identities through becoming other, but becoming other with, for, and through each other. These are the kinds of identity performances that necessitate "a conception of myself as invariably in community, impressed upon by others and impressing them as well, in ways that are not fully predictable" (202).

Fantasy is a pivotal factor in this play. Although the referent of the fantasy is a traditional fairytale that draws directly upon some of its predictable narrative elements of royal family drama—princess, pony, magical wand, transformations, chase, and heroic capture—there are some significant twists. Apart from one momentary slippage (when Lily declares, "No mans will ride me!") there is no prince. The cross-dressing princess is the "best horse catcher." The pony begs to be chased, but then rears up and defies capture (by a man, or perhaps by humankind?). Magic spells are self-administered. Punishment through restraint can be reversed at will in favor of freedom and reward. Desire is structured around consensual power play. Transformations are multiple, fluid, and self-determined. This is a complex reworking of a heteronormative script that produces an altogether new form of family and community.

By reordering the traditional elements of a heteronormative family script, the children have undone its internal logic and satisfied their otherwise desires. The hegemonic heterosexual family is disrupted because these assumed-to-be-innocent children turn out to be children driven by desires that exceed and challenge the bounds and norms of reality. In fact, the evidence of such desires renders them decidedly uninnocent. They do take up the heteronormative script, but not to rehearse their natural and normal roles within it as coherently gendered boys and girls and in accordance with the conventional wisdom of early childhood orthodoxies. In this case, it is clear that they are not simply engaged in fantasy play as a way of learning how to get heteronormative reality right. Moreover, it is not the real life nonnormative family that has preyed on the vulnerability of innocent children and confused them. The children are the agents here when they embody those desires that are paradoxically triggered by a selective realignment of the fundamentals of supposed-to-be normative fantasy. Without actually setting out so to do, the children in this royal stable have performed the same function as drag in the terms in which Butler explains it: to "allegorize the spectacular and consequential ways in which reality is both reproduced and contested" (2003a, 209).

Although it is only a small window into the world of childhood excess, this freeze frame moment of the royal stable can help us to envisage new kinds of community based on sociality and an ethics of open belonging. In the face of global violence and an adult world of increasingly regulated family norms and national boundaries, this is an encouraging glimpse. It is at least a starting point for thinking about a new kind of inclusive community belonging that "establishes the possible in excess of the real; ... allows us to imagine ourselves and others otherwise; ... points elsewhere" (1993, 208) and offers us insight into the kind of embodied enactments, both queer and postnational, that might enable us to "bring the elsewhere home."

Notes

My thanks go to my research colleague in early childhood studies, Carmel Richardson, for generously allowing me to reuse her sandpit and home corner observations in this essay. Other versions of this research material have been published elsewhere (see Taylor 2005; Taylor and Richardson 2005a, 2005b). Thanks are also due to the University of Canberra for the grant that supported our two-year ethnographic research project, "Early Belongings." Last but not least, thanks to the children, parents, and staff involved in this research who allowed us access to their fascinating and eccentric worlds.

1. Tracts from this essay were also published in revised forms in Butler 2003b; 2004b; and 2004c.
2. In many early childhood centres, "home corner" is a designated space set aside for domestic dramatic play.
3. For some specific case studies of race, racism, and ethnicity issues in early childhood, see the themed collection in *Contemporary Issues in Early Childhood* (2001)
4. The "Tampa Affair" refers to an incident in September 2001, when a Norwegian boat carrying 433 rescued asylum seekers from Afganistan, Iran, and Iraq was intercepted and denied entry into Australia; this act precipitated an international human rights controversy. A month later, Australian Prime Minister John Howard falsely claimed that Iraqi refugees on another intercepted and sinking boat were throwing their children overboard. He made this assertion during an election campaign, in order to convince the Australian public of the threatening and undesirable nature of Middle Eastern asylum seekers. This became known as the "Children Overboard Affair" (see Mares 2002).
5. "Through the Window" is a regular segment of the *Play School* program, which transports the viewer from the *Play School* set out into an external scene of children partaking of their everyday lives. This segment seeks to represent all sectors of Australia's culturally diverse society.

Dressing Up and Growing Up: Rehearsals on the Threshold of Intelligibility: A Response to Affrica Taylor

JONATHAN BOLLEN

Flinders University

It's not my earliest memory. But it's one of the earliest. I was about four years old.

We were living in Eastwood, in suburban Sydney, in the early 1970s. I was in the backyard, playing with my sisters. Today I have five sisters; five sisters and five nieces, no brothers, no nephews. Back then I had three sisters—two older, one younger. I was playing in the backyard with my two older sisters. And I was insistent: "When I grow up, I'm gonna be a girl."

217

Figure 5.1 Eastwood, 1973.

"No, you're not," said the eldest. She thought she knew better. "Boys can't grow up to be girls," she explained.

Like any four-year-old, I was impatient. I was also resourceful.

I didn't wait to grow up.

There's so much pleasure, so much delight in rehearsing accounts of queer childhood play. I was thrilled by the stories of Policeman Thelma and his baby, of Princess Peter and the pony in Affrica Taylor's essay. Even the story of two boys in "home corner" with a campfire in the kitchen to cook chops for breakfast gave me a momentary buzz. And I'm so pleased—proud even—to be able to put on display evidence of gender-dysphoric play from my own time as a child. (This being my first foray into the culture of child's play and performance, and with no data to draw on, I turned on myself.)

I've played at being a girl in more recent times, too.

It was fun. I had a ball. But the performance didn't stick. I couldn't quite get it right. There was pleasure to be had, but not pleasure enough to reward the effort it involved. I found it hard work doing

Figure 5.2   Erskineville, 1995.

drag, which is how I've come to understand what happened: my friend Jim went on to live a viable life of glamour and fame as drag queen Verushka Darling on Sydney's gay scene and Australian MTV, whereas Coco Chenille (that's my drag queen persona) … well, she hasn't been seen for years.

*   *   *

There is much we can learn from the occasions of queer childhood play presented in Taylor's research. As she explains, these occasions of play can show us how children are cultural participants in our world. These children don't play in some garden of innocence, in some state of grace, cordoned off from the social realities of our world. They play with and within our world: with its distinctions of social difference and within its history of social relations. This is so very clear in the story about Hakim, the child from the Middle East whose family migrated to Australia, and whose attempts at playing in the sandpit are refused by two white Australian-born boys who patrol the boundary of their play space with righteous resolve. In analyzing this occasion of children playing at border protection, Taylor writes of how "childhood belongings are 'nested' within the uneven and contested power relations of the nation" and of how this "nesting" invokes a shift in our perspective on the contexts of childhood play. We can no longer imagine that these children are playing in a "parochial protected enclave." As Taylor explains, they are playing upon "extraverted" terrain, exposed to a convergence of transnational flows and embodying the geographic contestations of a racially politicized world.

This shift in perspective on childhood play from introverted and enclosed to extraverted and exposed has far-reaching implications that Taylor indicates here and is developing elsewhere. We can look forward to the elaboration of a postnational pedagogy that Taylor ventures here, a pedagogy that would recast children's struggles over belonging as horizontal rather than hierarchical, as agonistic and open-ended rather than predetermined by prior claims. But the key implication of Taylor's research stems from a question that she asks: What can we learn from these kids and their play? Given the exposure of their play to the politics of our world, given their extravert embodiment of the social struggles of our day, what do these children know—or, more crucially, what do these children know how to do—that we don't know, or don't know *anymore*? It may indeed be the case that in their play these children demonstrate capacities that we, too, as children once embodied and enacted but which, in growing up as adults, we have abandoned and forgotten. Or it may be the case that in their play these children demonstrate capacities for making sense of social differences in our contemporary world that exceed those we ever learned and would therefore be valuable for us to now learn. What is evident from Taylor's research is that these children are theorists—theorists of gender and sexuality, of race and nationality, of the cultural politics of identity—who embody their theories in practice, who enact their theories in play. Taylor writes,

> As I watch the ways in which these children variously "do girl," do boy," or, to be more specific, "do white Australian boy," and so on, and think about Butler's question of "how to acknowledge and 'do' the construction one is invariably in," ... I wonder to what extent children are already doing this. Because of the over-the-top nature of much of children's

endlessly repetitive "doings," I wonder if they see girlness or boyness as constructions even as they "do" them and still recognize that they are "doing" them. Are these "doings" just about trying to get it right, to be acceptable, to belong, or is there another realm of desire operating here?

It is a measure of the reach, the effectiveness, and the sheer sense-making capacity of Judith Butler's ideas about the performativity of gender that we now talk about "doing girl," "doing boy" and so on in this way, that we now recognize the doing of identities in such occasions of everyday practice. It is customary to trace the concept of performativity to the linguistic philosophy of J. L. Austin (see, e.g., Secomb, this volume), but Butler's initial work upon the concept—in *Gender Trouble* (1990a) and early essays (1988, 1990b, 1991)—drew more upon the work of anthropologists and performance theorists like Clifford Geertz (1983), Erving Goffman (1959), Esther Newton (1974), Richard Schechner (1985), and Victor Turner (1974) than it did upon Austin's *How To Do Things With Words* (1975) or on the debate about speech acts between Jacques Derrida (1977a, 1977b) and John Searle (1977).

I came to Butler's writings as a student of performance studies, reading first her 1988 essay "Performative Acts and Gender Constitution," with its extensive recourse to performance theory, and only later reading *Gender Trouble*, where the account of gender performativity is much streamlined and the recourse to performance theory much reduced. In engaging with Butler's concept of performativity, as it was elaborated from that early essay through *Gender Trouble* and on in to *Bodies That Matter* (1993a) and *Excitable Speech* (1997a), I held on to the initial formulation, from that earlier essay, of gender as "an identity instituted through *a stylized repetition of acts*" (1988, 519; emphasis in the original), a formulation that invited us to understand gender as "the mundane way in which bodily gestures, movements, and enactments of various kinds constitute the illusion of an abiding gendered self" (519). In my studies of the dance floor at gay and lesbian dance parties (Bollen 1996, 1997, 2001), I held onto this initial concept of performativity because, in the face of an increasing linguisticism—in the face, that is, of an elaboration of performativity in *Bodies That Matter* and *Excitable Speech* in terms of Austin's speech act theory, Derrida's citationality, Louis Althusser's interpellation, Jacques Lacan's symbolic order, Michel Foucault's discursive regime, and other forms of juridical rhetoric—I wanted to retain something of the ambivalence, with regard to the character of performative acts, that was entailed in Butler's initial proposal of gender as "an identity

instituted through *a stylized repetition of acts*"; for this initial formulation cared little whether such acts were linguistic or somatic, discursive or corporeal, and that seemed useful on the dance floor, where
nothing much is spoken and words have little purchase on what is
going on. What mattered was that such acts were repeated, over time,
as sustained social performances.

"As a corporeal field of cultural play," writes Butler in the conclusion
of that earliest essay, "gender is a basically innovative affair, although
it is quite clear that there are strict punishments for contesting the
script by performing out of turn or through unwarranted improvisations" (1988, 531). Actually, Butler still sees gender as an "innovative
affair," writing recently in *Undoing Gender* that gender is "a practice of improvisation within a scene of constraint" (2004c, 1). As the
distinction between a "practice" and its "scene" would suggest, the
innovative and improvisational aspects of gender are constrained by
its more structural aspects, by those aspects that—like the performative interpellation "It's a girl!"—inaugurate and authorize a process
of gendering understood as the practical instantiation of an abstract
structure or form: the citation of a law, the approximation of an ideal,
the incorporation of a norm, and so on (1993a, 4–12, 230–33).
Butler's work on the performative concept in *Bodies That Matter* and
beyond has emphasized these structural aspects of gender, giving pri-
ority to their discursive and regulatory character to offset voluntarist
misunderstandings that, as Annemarie Jagose has observed, "appropriate Butler's notion of performativity" only to "literalise it as performance" (1996, 86). For Butler, the problem of voluntarism was that
the example of drag performance—or, perhaps, more abstractly, the
idea of dressing up—was taken to be "exemplary of performativity," a
misapprehension compounded by what she saw as "the political needs
of an emergent queer movement in which the publicization of theatrical agency has become quite central" (1993a, 230–31; 1993b, 21).

In my own apprehension of these maneuvers, I wondered at the ease
with which "the publicization of theatrical agency" and "the reduction of performativity to performance" were assimilated to the problem of voluntarism (1993a, 231, 234), for such assimilation could
imply that the willful theatricality of performance—its queerness, if
you like—somehow diverts, if not evades, the everyday operations of a
pervasively mundane performativity. I wondered about this opposition
between the theatrically queer and the performatively banal, about its
function and effects. I questioned the ease with which performance
is set apart from the everyday and imagined to be a queer kind of
playground whose political potential for subversive resignification and

hyperbolic imitation—a potential which is itself reliant upon such framed severing from the everyday—is nevertheless rendered vulnerable to foreclosure in such disarming responses as, "But it's only performance! What difference does it make in the real world?" To the extent that an opposition between queer theatricality and everyday banality structured the performance/performativity relation, it seemed difficult to ask, for example, how occasions of queer performance might exercise a performative force on those who participate or attend, or how the theatricality of queer performance might figure in quite mundane ways in our ongoing engagements with the performative banality of everyday life (Bollen 1997).

On more than one occasion, Taylor draws our attention to the performative labor expended in childhood play, to the "great amount of effort and energy invested by children in 'doing' themselves in the early childhood center." For instance, responding to the "Family Outing" occasion, when the four children go on a camping trip—with Harry driving, Alan reading the map, and the two of them delegating positions and tasks to Ruth and Kathy, who sit in the backseat—Taylor points out how such "hegemonic gender play … is very common and repetitive—to the point of obsession" and how "children engaged in such behavior expend much of their energy regulating the norms of oppositional gender roles.… repeat[ing] their efforts again and again; it can be quite relentless." I am interested in these questions of energy and effort, for what may strike us as relentless, as laborious or tiresome in childhood play, may be that which as adults we have learned to embody with such ease and grace that we have forgotten, in the process, the energy and effort we once invested as children in the labor of learning how through a practice of relentlessly, laboriously repetitive play.

I mentioned at the outset that as an adult I found it hard work doing drag, that the pleasures I derived from dressing up in drag weren't sufficient compensation for the effort it involved. Of course, knowing now what it takes, I'm all the more impressed: "Wow," I'd say to my friend Jim, impressed by his commitment, "you really must love doing drag!" But it's not just the effort of doing drag that I remark upon here, for I may only register drag as effort because I have forgotten, over time, that other effort that is invested, day by day, by others and myself, in sustaining the "illusion" of my own "abiding gendered self" (Butler 1988, 519). In this regard, the effort that registered for me in doing drag is like the effort Taylor sees children investing in normative kinds of play: it may serve as a reminder, in case we have forgotten, of both the effort it has taken in becoming what we are and the effort it would take to overcome what we have been, which is to say it may serve as a reminder of the "social temporality" of the performative (Butler 1988, 520), a reminder of its historicity and futurity within a scene of social practice.

If gender is "a basically innovative affair," a "corporeal field of cultural play," a "practice of improvisation within a scene of constraint," then that which we enact in doing gender—gender as an abstract ideal or norm—must also have a temporal aspect, a history and a future that is made and remade with each enactment. Structuralist tendencies of thought can make it difficult to articulate the temporality of a norm (Derrida 1978) and voluntarist fantasies about proliferating "do-it-yourself" genders may make us reluctant to do so. But, as Butler points out, the distinction between a norm and its incorporations is "an intellectual heuristic, one that helps to guarantee the perpetuation of the norm itself as a timeless and inalterable ideal" (2004c, 48). Indeed, as Butler goes on to propose, "the norm only persists as a norm to the extent that it is acted out in social practice and reidealized and reinstituted in and through the daily social rituals of bodily life" (48).

Taylor's account of the "Family Outing" may illustrate something of the exhausting social labor entailed in enacting and idealizing a norm. By contrast, the stories about Policeman Thelma and the baby and about Princess Peter and the ponies, are much less marked by effort and much less singular in their zeal. In these two stories, the children's play is less predictable and routine, more spontaneous and innovative—at least when compared with the exacting and exhausting demands entailed in more recognizably normative kinds of play. The performances of Lily, Margie, and Peter, in particular, are described as "complete flights of fancy," as "fluid performances unfettered by the constraints of gender or species alignments." Actually, Taylor establishes at the outset the distinction between more innovative and more normative kinds of play, describing how fantasy play "enables all sorts of strange hybridities and transformations," while acknowledging that it is "a key training ground for conformity and compliance." In the terms of this distinction, young children are seen to "pivot between being hyperregulating and exclusionary on the one hand and radically free border crossers on the other." But is this actually the case, is this how they experience their play? Or is this a distinction that only we as adults are capable of making as we register the effort we once made—and have since forgotten—in embodying gender norms, and as we remark upon, in contrast, the queerly innovative agency deployed in children's fantasy play?

The value of distinguishing between performativity and performance—or between the normative and the fantastic, the routine and the innovative, the banal and the queer, and so on—may not be exhausted by using these distinctions to characterize different instances of practice of childhood play, of dance floor choreography, of dressing up, and so on. In fact, we could say that such usage only serves to enhance our comprehension of the distinction. Enhancing our analyses of practice would entail using the distinction to articulate dynamics at work—or play—in each and every instance. In other words, our understanding of any particular instance of practice would only be more sensitive and subtle to the extent that we refuse to apprehend it as really performative or merely performance—and inquire, instead, how its performance lends energy and effort to the performativity it effects.

Taylor's research into the queer and not-so-queer belongings and becomings enacted in children's play invites us to reconsider the performativity of dressing up. We may agree with Butler that putting on clothes is a poor metaphor for performativity (1993a, 230; 1993b, 16). But this doesn't mean that the energies we expend in dressing up are not performative in effect. Whether our dressing up is routinely gender normative in style or occasionally outlandish in its dissonance, responding to the daily provocation of how to dress our bodies (or not) enrolls us inescapably and involuntarily in the performativity of gender. As such, ideas about the presentation or expression of the self inadequately register the sociality of dressing up. But so, too, do ideas of approximating an ideal or instantiating a norm. As structural abstractions, these ideas inadequately comprehend the social temporality of practice and are themselves prone to reductive literalizations—as in those widely circulating concerns about the media and "body image" for girls or the lack of "role models" for boys in schools; for within the occasional kind of dressing up to which I'll now turn, what seems more important than the presentation of the self or the approximation of an ideal is how investing energy in dressing up anticipates, imagines, and invents a social future for itself.

* * *

I would like to propose that dressing up is good for growing up—or, more precisely, that improvisational practices of dressing up in innovative ways are useful for growing up into a social future that is thereby different from the "now." And I would like to propose that this is what connects the dressing up in childhood play that Taylor documents with the dressing up in early adulthood that I shall consider. But it is a tenuous connection, tenuous to the extent that it has been marked by a disruption, interrupted by an incursion, for might not a queer and playful dressing up in early adulthood mark the memory

Figure 5.3 Sleaze Ball, 1991.

Figure 5.4 Macquarie Shopping Centre, 1994.

Figure 5.5   Mardi Gras Party, 1996.

and resumption of an early childhood project that was once forcibly abandoned though not forgotten? As evidence I offer some photos and a story about dressing up and growing up. The photos are of my friends and me when we were in our twenties. They are from a collection that documents the effects of energies we invested in dressing up to go out—an investment that seems indicative of the queer improvisations of our early adulthood only because it no longer so characterizes our socializing now that we are in our thirties.

The story, on the other hand, comes closer to the present day and looks to the future, although like any story it makes appeal to the past. It is not my story—it is from Michael, who wrote this story as an entry in an online journal—though I was a witness to its main event.

Feb. 13th 2005 09:18 PM—Club Arak II: Going Solo

I was apprehensive about going to Club Arak again. I had such an amazing time last time that I didn't want to ruin its novelty. Thankfully I ignored this stupid reasoning and went again last night. And I had an even better time ...

Costume: Silver. White. Lilac.

After having bellydancing lessons last year, I decided to make a proper bellydancing costume this time. It was the most spectacular costume I've made to date! I bought transparent white chiffon and made genie-style pants. I bought coins and beads and made an assortment of jewellery and trimmings. I found a vest and silver coin scarf at C's FlashBack in Surry Hills (a complete bargain!). I had matching silver headpieces and shimmering glitter all over my body. For added effect, I had a lace lilac veil.

("I'll put the pictures up soon!")

Arrival

I felt like a movie star in my shimmering coins and flowing pants and veil. As I slowly glided up the stairs to Manning Bar, I was greeted with a "wow" from the Club Arak organizers.

After stalling near the entrance for a while to wait for friends, I put my things in the cloak room, then prepared for our entrance.

As I walked into Manning Bar, with the lilac veil trailing off my shoulders, I just saw heads turn and light up. People came up to me and commented with excessive flattery that made me feel a little shy. I realized that I would need to match my costume with a confident personality. I took the leap. Tonight I was going to have total faith in myself.

Taking the Plunge

We went straight to the dancefloor. Louisa told me later that as we walked onto the dancefloor, people parted to let us through and a group of guys surrounded us. I didn't really notice; I was too busy negotiating my feet around the lilac veil.

I think we can never really appreciate how other people react to us in such situations. It usually takes friends to tell you "so-and-so-is-looking-at-you" or "he-just-smiled-at-you." I felt so immersed in the spirit of the moment that I was blind to other people's reactions.

Throughout the night, I danced with so many different people. The costume was a definite conversation starter! People would come up and comment on how I looked and by the next sentence we'd be dancing. So many girls and boys came up to say "hi" and shake a hip or two. [...]

I also noticed that the older Arab men were very paternal towards me. When I was dancing they would cheer and clap and make room. It felt like a wedding reception ... and I was the bride! [...]

There were so many highlights to the night that words cannot do the night justice. However, there were some particularly amazing moments.

Stage Appearance

There was a stage at the front of the dancefloor that acted like a podium. When one of the most famous bellydancing songs—"Habibi Ya Ainy" (My Love, My Eyes)—came on, I decided to go up.

While dancing on the stage, the photographer for the Sydney Star Observer asked to take my photo. Who knows, maybe I'll be in the SSO next week!

After the song finished, I came down from the stage and made my way to the outside verandah, passing smiles and compliments along the way.

Verandah

The verandah was one of the best parts of the night. I had room to dance to my heart's content. At first, I was the only one dancing on the verandah. But soon we had a whole heap of people up. By this time, I'd been dancing for about 4 hours but I was so high on adrenalin that I didn't notice my aching muscles.

By 4 am, my friends had decided to call it a night, but I had to wait for my lift home at 4:30 am.

So I decided to go back inside, and I'm so glad I did. What would happen next would be one of the most amazing experiences of my life ...

Premiere

I decided I would get a drink while I waited for 4:30 am to come. I was on the opposite side to the bar, so I began to trek through the dancefloor to get to the other side.

As I began to walk through the crowd and past the stage, I was accosted by a man that hopped off the stage and took my hand. He pulled me up the main staircase of the stage, all the while cheering and yelling. I was flustered and careful to not trip over my veil. I thought I would oblige him to a dance.

What happened next was simply unbelievable.

He put me in the middle of the stage and began to clap around me—an Arabic male move, traditionally used when gathering around bellydancing females. His friends joined him, making a semi-circle around me on the stage. Soon, all the people on stage had surrounded me, clapping and cheering as I bellydanced in the centre.

I did a veil dance, whisking the lace around my body as I moved my hips. Until this point, I had been facing my "accoster." Now, in between lilac swirls, I turned and looked out on the dancefloor.

I couldn't believe it.

People on the dancefloor had stop [*sic*] their dancing. The crowd had pivoted its bodies towards the stage.

I was bellydancing solo.

On stage.

With the dancefloor watching, clapping and cheering.

What an amazing experience! And to think, just moments earlier, I had simply been trying to walk to the bar!

I danced on stage until the drum solo finished and then made my way off. As I walked off the stage, I looked to my left and saw a boy giving me a round of applause. He looked familiar. It was then that I remembered, he was the boy at the last Club Arak who I had complimented on his exquisite dancing. I remember pointing his dancing out to my friend Jon at the time. And here we were, only months later. I had been plucked from the dancefloor and he was giving me a clap for my dancing. It felt like a Hollywood script! If I were to write this experience into a film script, it would read like the Fame movie!

Conclusions

And so I left Club Arak after that experience. After 5 hours of bellydancing I was sore in muscle groups that most people don't even use! But I felt amazing.

As I floated down the stairs, with the sound of Arabic music blasting from Manning, I felt very lucky and very at home. As one girl had earlier said to me: "We are all like family here." How right she was.

I'm gay. I'm Arab. I'm alive. I'm living.

Current Mood: ☺ sore but satisfied
Current Music: Habibi Ya Ainy (My Love, My Eyes)

The author, Michael, is a twenty-year-old arts/law student who lives in Sydney. In 1990, at the age of six, he migrated with his family from Jordan, although he has since learned that his parents are originally from Palestine. Club Arak is an occasional queer dance party featuring "Middle Eastern flavored grooves" and this was the second occasion Michael had gone to Club Arak. I, too, was there that night and I remember Michael's impromptu show. It was a highlight of the night and I remember discussing it afterward with friends—which is how I came across Michael's online journal. What so intrigued and delighted my friends and me was that Michael's approach to dressing up and going out invoked memories of our own, memories of our experiences of having grown up through dressing up. To be honest, we generated a queer kind of parental buzz around Michael—as grown ups in our thirties we were thrilled to see a young queer kid doing something like what we once did—but doing it online in ways that would exceed the post-party gossip and photo swapping that we'd had at our disposal. I've since met Michael on three occasions to talk about his experiences of dressing up and growing up in comparison with mine. What I recognize in his story is the focusing of energies and the "mix-and-match" effect entailed in working out what to wear in advance of an event. And I recognize, thereby, his investment in the social future of the event that generated—indeed, all but guaranteed—the "amazing" time he had. There's little doubting that Michael's dressing up on this occasion transformed the social field of the event. Indeed, as Michael explains, his wearing of that outfit required that he rise to the sociality it inspired by adopting "a confident personality," a new way of being social in the world.

Michael's story makes an appeal to narratives of coming out. The tenor of the title Michael gives to the story and the subheadings he uses to punctuate the narrative make this clear: "Going Solo," "Arrival," "Taking the vPlunge," "Stage Appearance" and "Premiere." But this is *coming out* as social event in a way that restores to that term its original sense: coming out as a debut, as being launched upon a social scene. This is not merely coming out as speech act about the self, although the dissemination of the story to friends and others online ensures that it may be that as well. Michael also reenacted his experience of belly dancing at Club Arak as part of a theatrical performance in which he recognized the cultural politics of his dressing up and coming out by claiming: "In my culture, boys don't make love to boys. In my culture, boys don't bellydance." Although, clearly, they sometimes do!

Butler writes how "fantasy allows us to imagine ourselves and others as otherwise," how "it establishes the possible in excess of the real," and how "when it is embodied, it brings the elsewhere home" (2003, 208). Like Reg's hybrid performance as Policeman Thelma in Taylor's essay, Michael's bellydancing embodiment of the fantasy of being both Arabic and gay first registers as a rendering intelligible of that which was previously unthinkable, incoherent, or aberrant. And yet its intelligibility, its coherence, its sense of "arrival" and "at-home-ness" are not conjured magically from thin air. Nor would Michael's own energies in embodying his fantasy, in creating that bellydancing costume and propelling himself onto the Club Arak scene, have been sufficient in overcoming the resistance of the unthinkable were it not for the socializing responses that his energies and actions anticipated and invoked. And what of the sociality that his performance on this occasion encountered and provoked? Beyond warm feelings of welcome, appreciation, and admiration, one thing surely stands out—and that is Michael's invocation of a traditional, paternal Arabic masculinity. Michael's new way of being social in the world was conditional upon a recontextualizing invocation or citation of that which has been most normative, most traditional, most performatively forceful in his world. "It felt like a wedding reception ... and I was the bride!" he exclaims in describing how his interactions with older Arabic men at Club Arak made him feel.

In one of our discussions Michael commented on how migrants may come to bear the traditionality of their culture more strongly than those who stayed living in the homeland. We were talking about the culture of Middle Eastern dance music and how the Club Arak guest DJ was from a gay club in Beirut. Michael implied that his experience of the incompatibility of being Arabic and gay might be out of step with shifting attitudes in the contemporary Middle East. It made me wonder whether we may sometimes overestimate the performativity of norms in ways that overextend their forceful grip on the real and whether we may thereby underestimate the efficacy of our performances in giving temporal actuality to the reformation of those norms. I sometimes feel that talking in abstract distinctions about the real and the unreal, the possible and the impossible, the intelligible and the unintelligible, as Butler often does, gives our thinking great conceptual reach but can dissociate analyses of practice from contexts of local sense making; for what makes sense and what doesn't, what is normative and what isn't, is not the same across the world or over time. Gender norms have histories, geographies, and futures and these should make a difference to the analyses of gender practice that we write. I've tried to indicate a way of doing this by attending to the "social temporality" of performativity, by enquiring how past practices might persist into the present and by exploring how present energies transform those practices into a future.

Taylor's research encourages us to remember what we have forgotten, to engage and perhaps to reengage with ways of imagining "ourselves and others otherwise" than as we are (Butler 2003, 208). Dressing up is one such practice that can do this imagining for us. But it can only do it because its cessation marks the limits of our becoming at that point when we are reduced to what we are. That point comes in Michael's story when his family moved from Jordan to Australia. Michael has memories as a little boy back in Jordan of dressing up and dancing like bellydancers he saw on TV, but when his family moved to Australia the dressing up and dancing stopped. Although it's not like he's forgotten; in fact, he wasn't allowed to forget. While growing up in Sydney his aunt used to telephone from Jordan and when she spoke to Michael she would ask him, "How's my special child?" and remind him of how he used to dance.

Conversation with Judith Butler V

Judith Butler: It's not easy to think the relation between the dressing up that children do and the dressing up that adults do. I think it's a quite provocative problem. I would start by saying that I agree, Jonathan, with your last claim that gender norms differ over time and space and they have their locations and historical specificities. That's certainly true. I think that's why I understand theoretical work not as establishing universal truths but as developing conceptual schemes that can be taken up and revised in various locations and times. So I appreciate your remarks very much.

I have just a couple of comments about Affrica's quite interesting theorization of the ethnography of childhood. I appreciated very much the fact that you're trying to step away from the idea of early childhood as a site of cultural innocence and I wonder, even in our appreciation of the photos [you showed us][1] and especially in our enjoyment of them, how successful any of us ever are in overcoming that particular temptation to simply enjoy at the visual level. We enjoy what we see from the past, and there is perhaps an arcadian hopefulness that haunts analyses of this kind. There was one point where you talked about approaching the early childhood center as a site which functions to introduce children to the world of human difference. You said you see that center as a conduit between home, where cultural belonging is established, and a broader community, in which struggles over identity and belonging take place as part of

235

the ongoing process of nation building as much as anything else. But should we hold to this distinction? Is it true that home is the place where cultural belonging is established, or is home also the site of precisely such a struggle over questions like nation building or cultural difference? It would depend, in part, on which home we are talking about, and here I worry that perhaps home is being presumed as a site of culturally homogeneity, as a nonporous site that does not sustain strong ties to broader social and cultural institutions. But, depending on which home we are imagining, the home could be a place of blended or extended kinship, for instance, or a home of new immigrants with ties to social services and juridical institutions. So I wonder, then, regarding the childhood center in relation to the home, whether you posit the home over in one place, the childhood center as a site of mediation, and then something called *broader community* over in another place. After all, we could imagine broader communities being *in* the home when the home is regularly visited by social welfare or social service representatives or when the home is also the site of work—both domestic and extradomestic work. Similarly, I wonder whether, in the same way that you wisely caution us against regarding early childhood as a utopic enclave, we have to do that also with notions like *the family* and *the home*. I understand that's not precisely what you're working on, but perhaps these notions are in the background of what you offer here.

I also was very interested in the ways in which you're thinking about cultural belonging here and, in particular, discerning how, in some of these early childhood center scenes, postnational notions of belonging and immigration politics become allegorized in children's play. I use the word *allegorized* because I don't know if they get explicitly thematized: it seems that they are being acted out in inchoate ways. In the sphere of children's play, we can perhaps discern the oblique traces of some of the pressing issues we have already talked about here: internment, admission into the community, asylum seekers. We have many urgent and vexed questions at play in the issue of play, such as, Who's a real Australian? I wonder whether they get played out with more fluidity than they do, say, in national public debate on the same questions. It is probably an error to think that children always evince greater fluidity and versatility than adults. Perhaps already in the scenes of childhood play we can find rigidification, fear, or a structural immobility? In our consideration of early childhood play, do we assume that play is fluid over and against *work*? Is there a parallel with the question of whether children's dressing up is different from adults'? Jonathan was suggesting that children get to do their drag as play, but for drag queens, it is hard work. How do we think about the relation of play and work in both contexts, for children and for adults, and how do we understand adolescence as particularly marked by the demand to negotiate between the two?

Affrica Taylor: If I can just interrupt, I mean, I was actually struck by what a lot of hard work there is involved in a lot of those play performances. I don't know that I'd want to make the distinction between play and work with those things.

Jonathan Bollen: I mean, there are energies being expended in both cases; whether we register it as play or register it as work, it has to do with the degree of habituation and whether it's a kind of laborious task or a new and energizing kind of ...

Affrica Taylor: And as well, whether it's an habituational and energizing task, this is an adult kind of interpretation of childhood innocence that then gives us the word *play* as distinct from work.

Judith Butler: You say, "play as distinct from work." Okay. And so then I have to wonder about the place of childhood cruelty in our efforts to debunk notions of childhood innocence. The photos you have included obviously don't give us that. Even the prison scene seems perfectly delightful: you know, *Intern me, release me* and *I intern you, I release you.* This seems like great play, even though it might well be haunted by social policies that are far from delightful.

Affrica Taylor: That particular one I think I didn't really see as cruel internment ...

Judith Butler: But we smile.

Affrica Taylor: Yeah, the paper's very much a power-desire play.

Judith Butler: Yes. I understood that, but I thought you also might be looking for hopefulness, and I don't want to fault you for that. We need more hopefulness! I guess the realist in me thinks, Okay, fine, we can find some elements of hopefulness there without romanticizing it. At the same time, we do have to come to grips with aggression, something you clearly discern in the narratives. You refer, for instance, to the pain of exclusion, which is obviously extremely cruel. Does the cruelty get worked through? Do people find themselves becoming less cruel and repent for their cruelty? That's perhaps an open question in your research. You know—for Jonathan—I want to know whether you think children have capacities that we've forgotten. Do we romanticize a little bit here?

It also occurred to me that there might be a potential tension between the two of you. Affrica, I think, suggests that children are theorists. It's true, and I enjoyed that remark enormously. [Sigmund] Freud actually says something about this in his *Three Essays on the Theory of Sexuality* (1962). He calls them "little investigators," understanding children as budding theorists. But Jonathan then asks the question of whether we can theorize this from our position as adults, and whether theory is perhaps belated, imposed, and a distinctively adult activity. Maybe Affrica can respond to Jonathan's query because I thought that might be interesting to talk about. And, of course, there's also the question of whether we're interpreting children or whether they're interpreting us, and then a further question: whether interpretations and theories don't sometimes take place precisely as embodiments.

Jonathan Bollen: But that would be an opportunity for adult learning from children, like, it's their reinterpretations about gender performance.

Affrica Taylor: Well I'd say, clearly we're all interpreting each other. I mean they're interpreting us and we're interpreting them.

Judith Butler: So that raises the question of the place of the camera in both of these papers and how the camera plays a role in the scene. I enjoyed Jonathan's discussion of dressing up as anticipatory, as anticipating a certain future, even a future sociality—so that what one is putting on, trying on is the possibility of another future. I really like that idea of a performative opening up of the future through that act of dressing. As much as I enjoyed that, however, I want to ask to what extent the photo is involved in the archiving of the past. We have these gorgeous pictures of you, we have these fabulous children whom we enjoy watching, but are we not archiving, establishing a record of the past, at the same time that we are, as it were, anticipating another possible future? The camera seems to be involved in archiving, preserving the past for the future, but also actively imagining something new. I'm very much interested in dressing up and growing up; it's interesting how dressing up can be understood as aggressive activity, overcoming barriers against gendered dress. It can also be explosive and anticipatory, since children are sometimes *trying on* an older age. When adults dress up, are they reclaiming a playfulness from their youth, and so returning to an earlier age? Is there still something anticipatory going on in that scene? Perhaps the crossing of child desire and adult desire is always at work—at play?—in the moment of dressing, which suggests that dressing up is as much about intergenerationality as it is about gender norms. I also wondered if you had any thoughts on *dressing down*, on children who refuse to dress up for formal occasions or those who go out of their way *not* to have remarkable clothing. How do we understand their desire to appear unremarkable or, in fact, their desire not to appear at all?

Two further remarks and then I would be really glad to hear your response and further thoughts. Interestingly, Michael [the bellydancer in Bollen's essay] poses the question of how he might maintain a tie to a certain traditional ritual, circling the bellydancer, for instance, at the same time that he's performing his transgression and he seems to be asking after the mix of loyalty and transgression at play there. I was wondering, could we see anything similar in the early childhood scene of some of the children as they try to work out (incorporate into their play) immigration politics at the childhood center? To what extent is tradition maintained at the same time that it's somehow displaced?

Affrica Taylor: I think it is in the royal stable, there's so many traditions being enacted there, around the fairy tale, even as they're being transgressed.

Judith Butler: I wonder if the royal stable also could have been a figure for the polity itself, the emerging postnational mode of belonging. I love it!

I wanted to mark, too, the difference between dressing up, drag, transgender, transsexual, and what this says about performance and its relationship to audience. The drag scene, for instance, is extraordinary and it demands its stage and its club, although it may not be okay on the street or at the workplace. And in conjunction with this, does transgender, as a broader category, not ask us to think performance off the proscenium stage, as it were, or beyond the enclosed space of safety and more on the street and in relation to family, friends, workplace environment, airports, immigration authorities and the rest? Of course, the term *transsexuality* has another set of institutional implications, ones that involve questions of legal and medical status as well as how the meaning of *performance* changes when it becomes less based on a theatrical space and more about the vicissitudes of daily life and even psychic survival. I don't know whether it would be useful to understand the early childhood center as a stage—that is, as a theatrical metaphor. I don't know whether it is, in its own terms, extraordinary like the club is—a place where certain kinds of fantasies get played out that are tied to the props, to the restrictive spatiality of the center itself, so that a set of rules or possibilities for play come into being within the confines of that space but would not be transposable outside of it.

Robert Payne: I was thinking that perhaps dressing down is dressing up or is maybe not the same kind of movement, but the same kind of performance. Because, you know, I was going to ask Jonathan whether dressing was the same as dressing up, or dressing up is the same as dressing, and if there are key differences. And I was thinking about the sense in which there is an event, an anticipation, as you say—our future anticipated by dressing up—if not an interest. But the dressing up is creating the image as event in itself in a sense. So maybe dressing down is actually creating the event of the nonevent, marking yourself by not marking yourself, marking yourself as unremarkable and thereby making it uneventful but, in itself, the event is one of uneventfulness?

Bronwyn Davies: Like my granddaughter, who refuses to wear dresses at the age of three and creates an event because there are beautiful dresses to wear that she won't wear so that in the very insistence on dressing down, there's an event they've created.

Cristyn Davies: You can dress up without wearing a dress. There's still a lot of labor put into dressing up without having an *actual* dress involved. I wonder if she does her own kind of production with what *she* desires to wear without frocking up?

Bronwyn Davies: Of being a grub with dirty hair?

Cristyn Davies: Perhaps.

Affrica Taylor: In relation to the children and these kinds of questions about the routineness of it and, you know, whether that changes it and whether the pleasure stays, I mean, I think just as Jim [in Bollen's essay] took a different sort of pathway to you, I think that actually Peter in the early childhood crew there [in Taylor's essay] does it differently, too, to the other kids. Because he doesn't do it in a very specifically located temporal and spatial way; he does it all the time so whilst the other children will only ever dress up when they go into that space of the home corner where the dress up cupboard is, the kind of *closet of gear*, and they do it at the time, you know, when it's the free play time and at the end of free play time, they take the dresses off and they pack them up and they leave them, he doesn't. He's always in the dresses and always—but as far as I can see you know it's a huge pleasure principle for him to be in those dresses.

Susanne Gannon: Can I just say something? Just very quickly, when you described Michael going up onto the stage and the circling, I just had this reaction—[*gasps*]—because there were stories in Cairns, some years ago, there was a rape in a nightclub where a man circled a woman, and I thought of that. It happened in a nightclub full of people that there was a rape and it's happened in other places like that. And also the labeling of the photos of you and your friends in drag for Sleaze Ball. It's one occasion in a park, but yes, in certain spaces, it's safe but it's still not safe in lots of places and that's, you know, still there in the talk of pleasure. I just wanted to just mark that ... danger. Always just a little turn and there it is, still ...

David McInnes: I can hear the *Current Affair* headline now: Rapid Rise in Middle Eastern Drag Amongst Sydney Nightclubs. Two weeks ago I was in the Blue Mountains and it was the first time ever at one of the dances up there that some guys did bellydancing drag and I'd never seen it before and it just strikes me, given the rest of the political landscape, where we see in Australia the impossibilities of doing certain kinds of ethnic, racial identity, that that's really interesting.

Bronwyn Davies: Oh, and that brings together somehow the boy who was excluded because of the color of his skin, standing on the outside of the sandpit [in Taylor's essay] and then these plays of difference inside different spaces.

Jonathan Bollen: Club Arak is quite explicitly articulated to the cultural politics of being Arabic in Australia. The first Club Arak that Michael went to was held on September 11 last year and at this one there was a show—I don't know if you know the movie *Shaft,* and there's a theme song that goes with it, but they restaged it as *Sheik* and kind of terrorist drag, terrorist Middle Eastern drag queens on stage dancing to it; but, yes, Michael's participation is within a broader kind of politics that's being enacted through these events now.

Margaret Somerville: I just wanted to take up a different point and say I actually felt a bit uncomfortable about a performance of an Arabic woman in drag and thinking about an Egyptian Muslim woman that I just read about, the meaning of the veil and the meaning of those clothes for Muslim women and thinking that it would be an interesting line to follow the idea; you used the word *accosted* and …

Jonathan Bollen: Michael used the word.

Margaret Somerville: … where Michael used the word *accosted* and whether there was that experience of being the *other* and some sense of fear and exposure, actual danger in there, because that makes a whole difference to me to the sense of that performance as well, as a woman.

Jonathan Bollen: I think in his talking about that experience in the interview that I did with Michael, he does articulate some kind of anxieties about being positioned in that way by other men and by older men—he kind of marks the age distinction quite clearly. And he reads the age distinction as a kind of gender distinction; that's not evident in that narrative that he published online for his friends to read, and I didn't ask him explicitly to talk about the gender politics, if you like, of that or, for instance, what his mother or his aunt might make of his performance on this night as opposed to, you know, the memory of him performing in front of the TV.

Margaret Somerville: That could be quite productive, to extend that idea further into, you know, Judith's idea, or what it means to become other, or what it means to me to be *you,* taking that idea further, where play becomes the site where the idea of risk and category, real category boundary crossing is enacted.

Jonathan Bollen: Hmm, thanks.

Judith Butler: Maybe I could say one last thing, which is simply to acknowledge that part of what's happening in Affrica's paper is an enactment of how certain gender norms get lived simultaneously, sometimes in a single figure, or concurrently, or with some possibilities of transition. And I think you do go for the more hopeful, fluid moments, for which I'm quite grateful and which makes sense to do, precisely as one is trying to figure out how certain norms do take hold and how that hold can be lessened. Embodying norms happens at a very early age and has to be repeated, and if there is this kind of fluidity or compossibility that exists between competing frameworks of norms, at least in some venues, then it does give us some insight into what finally happens when that domain of fluidity gets foreclosed, if it does. And so, in that way, I think it's extremely interesting to see the child care center as a way of thinking about postnational and queer belonging. It's really fabulous and you have an uncanny ability to think that through—when we start to talk about the unequal geopolitical gender relations in the family car, well, not a lot of people can put those things together. [*Laughter.*] So I want to mark that as a wonderful thing, because it is political theory at the same time that it's a highly specific ethnographic analysis. Part of me is a little bit dystopic, wondering, Oh where's the cruelty and rigidification? What if you start as a cruel and rigid little kid and then end up a more fluid adult—you know, that could happen. But I see that you're marking patterns that give us something to consider and I appreciate the way you link early childhood formation material with the political vision. I think that's really remarkable.

Bronwyn Davies: Okay. Thank you very much—all of you—and I'd like us to join in thanking the people who've given the papers and the respondents and to all of us as discussants.

[*Applause.*]

ENDNOTE

1. Unfortunately, ethics requirements prevent the children's photographs from being reproduced in print (Affrica Taylor).

References

Adler, S. M. (2003). "Racial and Ethnic Identity Formation of Midwestern Asian-American Children." *Contemporary Issues in Early Childhood* 2(3): 265–293.

Adorno, T. (1997). *Problems of Moral Philosophy.* Trans. R. Livingstone. Stanford, CA: Stanford University Press.

Agamben, G. (1995). *Idea of Prose.* Trans. M. Sullivan and S. Whitsitt. Albany: State University of New York Press.

Ahmed, S. (2000). *Strange Encounters: Embodied Others in Post-coloniality.* London: Routledge.

Anderson, K. (2000). "Thinking Post-nationally: Dialogue across Multicultural, Indigenous, and Settler Spaces." *Annals of the Association of American Geographers* 90(2): 381–91.

Anderson, K., and Taylor, A. (2005). "Exclusionary Politics and the Question of National Belonging: Australian Ethnicities in 'Multiscalar' Focus." *Ethnicities* 5(4): 460–485.

Anonymous. (2004). "Cambodia Poem." *Southerly* 64(1): suppl.

Antelme, R. (1998). *The Human Race.* Trans. J. Haight and A. Mahler. Evanston, IL: Marlboro Press/Northwestern University Press.

Arendt, H. (1958). *The Human Condition.* Chicago: University of Chicago Press.

Aries, P. (1962). *Centuries of Childhood.* Trans. R. Balelcik. London: Cape.

Attwood, M., and Beaulieu, V. (1998). *Two Solicitudes: Conversations.* Trans. P. Aronoff and H. Scott. Toronto: McClelland and Stewart.

Austin, J. L. (1975). *How to Do Things with Words.* 2nd ed. Ed. J. O. Urmson and Marina Sbisa. Oxford: Clarendon Press.

Australian Broadcasting Corporation. (2004, May 31). *Play School.* Television broadcast.

Australian Press Council. (2004a, June). Adjudication No. 1242. Retrieved June 2005 from http://www.presscouncil.org.au/pcsite/adj/1242.html.

Australian Press Council. (2004b). Report on Free Speech Issues, 2003–2004. Retrieved June 2005 from http://www.presscouncil.org.au/pcsite/fop/fop_ar/ar04.html.

Australian Press Council. (2004c, June). Reporting Guidelines, Guideline No. 262. Retrieved June 2005 from http://www.presscouncil.org.au/pcsite/activities/guides/guide262.html.

Barns, G. (2005). *Selling the Australian Government: Politics and Propaganda from Whitlam to Howard.* Sydney: University of New South Wales Press.

Barthes, R. (1975). *The Pleasure of the Text.* Trans. R. Muller. New York: Noonday Press.

———. (1989). *The Rustle of language.* Trans. R. Howard. Berkeley and Los Angeles: University of California Press.

Beaumont, G. de, and Tocqueville, A. de. (1964). *On the Penitentiary System in the United States and Its Application in France.* Carbondale: Southern Illinois University Press.

Bernstein, B. (1996). *Pedagogy, Symbolic Control and Identity: Theory, Research, Critique.* London: Taylor and Francis.

Blanchot, M. (1981). "Literature and the Right to Death." In *The Gaze of Orpheus and Other Literary essays.* Trans. L. Davis. Barrytown, NY: Station Hill.

———. (1995). "Literature and the Right to Death." In *The Work of Fire.* Trans. L. Davis. Stanford: Stanford University Press.

Bollen, J. (1996). 'Sexing the Dance at Sleaze Ball 1994." *Drama Review,* 40 (3): 166–91.

———. (1997). "'What a Queen's Gotta Do": Queer Performativity and the Rhetorics of Performance." *Australasian Drama Studies* 31: 106–23.

———. (2001). 'Queer Kinaesthesia: Performativity on the Dance Floor." In *Dancing Desires: Choreographing Sexualities on and off the Stage.* Ed. J. Desmond. Madison: University of Wisconsin Press.

Bonutto, O. (1994). *A Migrant's Story.* St. Lucia, Queensland, Australia: University of Queensland Press.

Bourdieu, P. (1988). *Homo Academicus.* Cambridge: Polity Press.

Bowlby, J. (1960). "Separation anxiety." *International Journal of Psychoanalysis,* 41: 89–113.

Brennan, F. (2003). *Tampering with Asylum: A Universal Humanitarian Problem.* St. Lucia, Queensland, Australia: University of Queensland Press.

Breuer, J., and Freud, S. (1895). "Case 1: Fraulein Anna O (Breuer)." In *The Standard Edition of the Complete Psychological Works of Sigmund Freud.* Vol. 2: *Studies on Hysteria.* London: Hogarth Press/Institute of Psychoanalysis.

Brindle, D. (1999). Media Coverage of Social Policy: A Journalist's Perspective. In *Social Policy, the Media and Misrepresentation.* Ed. B. Franklin. London: Routledge.

Burnside, J., ed. (2003). *From Nothing to Zero: Letters from Refugees in Australia's Detention Centres.* Melbourne: Lonely Planet.

Butler, J. (1988). "Performative Acts and Gender Constitution: An Essay in Feminist Theory and Phenomenology." *Theatre Journal* 40(4): 519–31.

———. (1990a). *Gender Trouble: Feminism and the Subversion of Identity.* New York: Routledge.

———. (1990b). "Gender Trouble, Feminist Theory, and Psychoanalytic Discourse." In *Feminism/Postmodernism.* Ed. L. J. Nicholson. New York: Routledge.

———. (1991). "Imitation and Gender Insubordination." In *Inside/Out: Lesbian Theories, Gay Theories.* Ed. D. Fuss. New York: Routledge.

———. (1993a). *Bodies That Matter: On the Discursive Limits of "Sex."* New York: Routledge.

———. (1993b). "Critically Queer." *GLQ: A Journal of Lesbian and Gay Studies* 1(1): 17–32.

———. (1993c). "Imitation and Gender Insubordination." In *The Lesbian and Gay Studies Reader.* Ed. H. Abelove, M. A. Barale, and D. M. Halperin. New York: Routledge.

———. (1997a). *Excitable Speech: A Politics of the Performative.* New York: Routledge.

———. (1997b). *The Psychic Life of Power.* Stanford, CA: Stanford University Press.

———. (1998). "Afterward." In *Butch/Femme: Inside Lesbian Gender.* Ed. S. Munt. London: Cassell.

———. (1999a). *Gender Trouble: Feminism and the Subversion of Identity.* New York: Routledge.

———. (1999b). *Subjects of Desire: Hegelian Reflections in Twentieth-Century France.* 2d ed. New York: Columbia University Press.

———. (2000). *Antigone's Claim: Kinship between Life and Death.* New York: Columbia University Press.

———. (2001). "Giving an Account of Oneself." *Diacritics* 31(4): 22–40.

———. (2002a). "Human Rights Project: Free Press Interview with Judith Butler, 4/26/02" By K. Chance. Retrieved April 26, 2006 from http://www.bard.edu/hrp/events/spring2002/butler_interview.htm.

———. (2002b). "What is Critique? An Essay on Foucault's Virtue." In *The Political.* Ed. D. Ingram. Malden, MA: Blackwell.

———. (2003a). "Global Violence, Sexual Politics." In *Queer Ideas: The David R. Kessler Lecture Series in Lesbian and Gay Studies.* Ed. Center for Lesbian and Gay Studies, City University of New York. New York: Feminist Press at the City University of New York.

———. (2003b). "Violence, Mourning, Politics." *Studies in Gender and Sexuality,* 4 (1): 7-9.

———. (2004a). "Bracha's Eurydice." *Theory, Culture and Society* 21(1): 95–100.

———. (2004b). *Precarious Life: The Powers of Mourning and Violence.* New York: Routledge.

———. (2004c). *Undoing Gender.* New York: Routledge.

———. (2005). *Giving an Account of Oneself.* New York: Fordham University Press.

Butler, J., and Connolly, W. (2000). "Politics, Power and Ethics: A Discussion between Judith Butler and William Connolly." *Theory and Event*, 4(2). Retrieved April 26, 2006 from http://www.opac.library.usyd.edu.au/search/ttheory+andevent

Carrigan, T., Connell, B., and Lee, J. (1985). "Toward a New Sociology of Masculinity." *Theory and society* 14(5): 551–604.

Case, C., and Dalley, T. (1992). *The Handbook of Art Therapy*. London: Routledge.

Cavarero, A. (2000). *Relating Narratives: Storytelling and Selfhood*. Trans. P. A. Kottman. London: Routledge.

Certeau, M. de. (2002). *The Practice of Everyday Life*. Trans. Steven F. Rendall. Berkeley and Los Angeles: University of California Press.

Colebrook, C. (2001). "Certeau and Foucault: Tactics and Strategic Essentialism." *South Atlantic Quarterly* 100(2): 543–74.

Connell, R. W. (1995). *Masculinities*. Sydney: Allen and Unwin.

———. (2000). *The Men and the Boys*. Sydney: Allen and Unwin.

———. (2003). "Introduction: Australian Masculinities." In *Male Trouble: Looking at Australian Masculinities*. Ed. S. Tomsen and M. Donaldson. Melbourne: Pluto.

Corbett, K. (1999). "Homosexual Boyhood: Notes on Girlyboys." In *Sissies and Tomboys: Gender Nonconformity and Homosexual Childhood*. Ed.: M. Rottnek. New York: New York University Press.

———. (2001). "Faggot = Loser." *Studies in Gender and Sexuality* 2(1): 3-28.

Culler, J. (1997). *Literary Theory: A Very Short Introduction*, Oxford, Oxford University Press.

———. (2000). "Philosophy and Literature: The Fortunes of the Performative." *Poetics Today* 21(3): 503–519.

Cuneen, C. (2001). *Conflict, Politics and Crime: Aboriginal Communities and the Police*. Crows Nest, New South Wales, Australia: Allen and Unwin.

Dahlberg, G., Moss, P., and Pence, A. (1999). *Beyond Quality in Early Childhood Education and Care: Postmodern Perspectives*. London: Falmer.

Davies, B. (1989). *Frogs and Snails and Feminist Tales*. Sydney: Allen and Unwin.

———. (1993). *Shards of Glass: Children Reading and Writing beyond Gendered Identities*. Sydney: Allen and Unwin.

———. (2000). *A Body of Writing 1990–1999*. Walnut Creek, CA: Alta Mira.

———. (2003). *Frogs and Snails and Feminist Tales*. 2nd Edition 2003, NJ: Cresskill: Hampton Press.

———. (2004). "Identity, Abjection and Otherness: Creating the Self, Creating Difference." *International Journal in Equity and Innovation in Early Childhood Education* 2(1): 58–80.

Davies, B., Dormer, S., Honan, E., McAllister, N., O'Reilly, R., Rocco, S., and Walker, A. (1997). "Ruptures in the Skin of Silence: A Collective Biography." *Hecate—A Women's Studies Interdisciplinary Journal* 23(1): 62–79.

Davies, B., Dormer, S., Gannon. S., Laws, S., Rocco. S., Lenz Taguchi, H., and McCann, H. (2001). "Becoming Schoolgirls: The Ambivalent Processes of Subjectification." *Gender and Education* 13(2): 167–82.

Davies, B., Flemmen, A., Gannon, S., Laws, C., and Watson, B. (2002). "Working on the Ground: A Collective Biography of Feminine Subjectivities: Mapping the Traces of Power and Knowledge." *Social Semiotics* 12(3): 291–313.

Davies, B., and Harré, R. (2000). "Positioning: The Discursive Production of Selves." In B. Davies, *A Body of Writing 1990–1999*. Walnut Creek, CA: Alta Mira.

Davies, C., (2005a). "Encountering Identity: Affect, Writing and the Feminist Scholar." *MP* 1(2). Retrieved November 11, 2006 from http://www.academinist.org/mp/archive/march05/amp022.html.

———. (2005b, April 18). "Role of Respondent at Butler Symposium." E-mail.

Davis, A. (1998). "Race and Criminalization: Black Americans and the Punishment Industry. " In *The Angela Davis Reader*. Ed. J. James. Oxford: Blackwell.

Davis, K. (1997). "Was Will der Mann? Some Reflections on Theorizing Masculinity." *Theory and Psychology* 7(4): 555–64.

Department of Immigration and Multicultural and Indigenous Affairs (2004, June 28). Correspondence to Australian Press Council. Belconnen, Australian Capital Territory: Department of Immigration and Multicultural and Indigenous Affairs.

Deleuze, G. and Guattari, F. (1994), *What is Philosophy?*, Trans. Graham Burchell and Hugh Tomlinson. London: Verso.

Derrida, J. (1977a). "Signature Event Context." *Glyph* 1: 172–97.

———. (1977b). "Limited Inc ABC . . ." *Glyph* 2: 162–54.

———. (1978). "Structure, Sign and Play in the Discourse of the Human Sciences." In *Writing and Difference*. Trans. A. Bass. London: Routledge and Kegan Paul.

———. (1986). "Declarations of Independence." *New Political Science* 15: 7–15.

Douglas, M. (1966). *Purity and Danger*. London: Routledge.

Düttmann, A. G. (1995). "Integral Actuality." Introduction to G. Agamben, *Idea of Prose*. Trans. M. Sullivan and S. Whitsitt. Albany: State University of New York Press.

———. (2000). *The Gift of Language: Memory and Promise in Adorno, Benjamin, Heidegger, and Rosenzweig*. London: Athlone.

Ellison, C. (2003). "Transcript of Doorstop." Retrieved from http://www.ag.gov.au/www/justiceministerHome.nsf/0/D4B58AD856A12475C A256DD70010B3AB?OpenDocument.

Ettinger, B. L. (2004). "Weaving a Woman Artist within the Matrixial Encounter-Event." *Theory, Culture and Society* 21(1): 69–93.

Fanon, F. (1967), *Black Skin White Mask*, Trans. Charles Lam Markmann. New York: Grove Books.

Felman, S. (2002). *The Scandal of the Speaking Body,* Stanford, CA: Stanford University Press.

Foucault, M. (1977). *Discipline and Punish: The Birth of the Prison.* Trans. A. Sheridan. New York: Cassell.

———. (1978). *The History of Sexuality.* Vol. 1: *An Introduction.* Trans. R. Hurley. New York: Random House.

———. (1980). *Power/Knowledge: Selected Interviews and Other Writings 1972–1977.* Ed. C. Gordon. New York: Pantheon.

———. (1982). "The Subject and Power." In *Michel Foucault: Beyond Structuralism and Hermeneutics.* Ed. H. L. Dreyfuss and P. Rabinow. Chicago: University of Chicago Press.

———. (1985). *The History of Sexuality.* Vol. 2: *The Use of Pleasure.* Trans. R. Hurley. New York: Random House.

———. (1988). *Politics, Philosophy, Culture: Interviews and Other Writings 1977–1984.* Ed. L. D. Kritzman. New York: Routledge.

———. (1991a). "Politics and the Study of Discourse." In *The Foucault Effect: Studies in Governmentality.* Ed. G. Burchell, C. Gordon, and P. Miller. Chicago: University of Chicago Press.

———. (1991b). "Questions of Method." In *The Foucault Effect: Studies in Governmentality.* Ed. G. Burchell, C. Gordon, and P. Miller. Chicago: University of Chicago Press.

———. (1991c). "What is Critique?" In *The Political.* Ed. D. Ingram. Malden, MA: Blackwell.

———. (1994). "Polemics, Politics and Problematizations: An Interview with Michel Foucault," by P. Rabinow. In *Essential Works of Foucault 1954–1984.* Vol. 1: *Ethics: Subjectivity and Truth.* Ed. P. Rabinow. New York: New Press.

———. (2000). "Technologies of the Self." In *Essential Works of Foucault 1954–1984.* Vol. 1: *Ethics: Subjectivity and Truth.* Ed. P. Rabinow. New York: New Press.

———. (2002). "Truth and Juridical Forms." In *Essential Works of Foucault 1954–1984.* Vol. 3: *Power.* Ed. J. Faubion. London: Sage.

———. (2003). *Abnormal: Lectures at the College de France 1974–75.* Trans. G. Burchell. Ed. V. Marchetti and A. Salomoni. London: Verso.

Freud, S. (1917). "Mourning and Melancholia." In *The Standard Edition of the Complete Psychological Works of Sigmund Freud.* Vol. 14: *On the History of the Psychoanalytic Movement, Papers on Metapsychology and Other Works.* London: Hogarth/Institute of Psychoanalysis, 245–258.

———. (1926). "Inhibitions, Symptoms and Anxiety." In *The Standard Edition of the Complete Psychological Works of Sigmund Freud.* Vol. 20. London: Hogarth/Institute of Psychoanalysis, 77–174.

———. (1995). "Anxiety and Instinctual Life" (1932). In *The Freud Reader.* Ed. P. Gay. London: Vintage.

———. (1962). *Three Essays on the Theory of Sexuality.* Trans. James Strachey. New York: Basic Books.

Gannon, S. (2006). "The (Im)possibilities of Writing the Self Writing: French Poststructural Theory and Autoethnography." *Cultural studies >> Critical Methodologies* 6(4): 475–95.

"Gay Play School Backlash." (2004, June 3). *Sydney Morning Herald*. Retrieved April 26, 2006 from http://smh.com.au/articles/2004/06/03/1086203545100.html.

Geertz, C. (1983). *Local Knowledge: Further Essays in Interpretive Anthropology*. New York: Basic.

Giannacopoulos, M. (2005). 'Tampa: violence at the border', *Social Semiotics* 15 (1): 29-42.

Gilbert, O. (1991), *Narrative of Sojourner*. Oxford: Oxford University Press.

Gilroy, A. (1997). "In Search of an Australian Art Therapy." Paper presented at the Eighth Annual Conference of the Australian National Art Therapy Association, University of Western Sydney.

Gittins, D. (1998). *The Child in Question*. London: Macmillan.

Goffman, E. (1959). *The Presentation of the Self in Everyday Life*. Garden City, NY: Doubleday.

Gramsci, A. (1992). *Prison Notebooks*. Trans. J. Buttigieg and A. Callari. New York: Columbia University Press.

Grosz, E. (1989). *Sexual Subversions: Three French Feminists*. Sydney: Allen and Unwin.

Halberstam, J. (1998). *Female Masculinity*. Durham, NC: Duke University Press.

Hage, G. (1998). *White Nation: Fantasies of White Supremacy in a Multicultural Society*. Sydney: Pluto.

———. (2003). *Against Paranoid Nationalism: Searching for Hope in a Shrinking Society*. Annandale, New South Wales, Australia: Pluto Press.

Harris, J. (2005, April 13). "Telling His Story." *Central Western Gazette* (Orange, New South Wales, Australia). Retrieved from http://orange.yourguide.com.au/detail.asp?class=news&subclass=local&category=general%20news&story_id=385394&y=2005&m=4

Hasse, U. and Large, W. (2001). *Maurice Blanchot*. London: Routledge.

Heidegger, M. (1982). *On the Way to Language*. Trans. P. D Hertz. San Fransisco: Harper.

Hirschfeld, L. A. (1996). *Race in the Making: Cognition, Culture and the Child's Construction of Humankind*. Cambridge, MA: MIT Press.

Holmes, R. M. (1995). *How Young Children Perceive Race*. Thousand Oaks, CA: Sage.

Horin, R. (2004). *Through the Wire*. Unpublished play manuscript.

Howard, J. (2001). "Prime Minister of Australia, John Howard, Newsroom." Retrieved April 26, 2006 from http://www.pm.gov.au/news/interviews/2001/ interview1434.htm.

Human Rights and Equal Opportunity Commission. (1996). *Indigenous Deaths in Custody, 1989–1996*. Canberra, Australian Capital Territory: Human Rights and Equal Opportunity Commission.

————. (1997). *Bringing Them Home: Report of the National Inquiry into the Separation of Aboriginal and Torres Strait Islander Children from Their Families.* Canberra, Australian Capital Territory: Human Rights and Equal Opportunity Commission. Retrieved June 2005 from http://www.austlii.edu.au/au/special/rsjproject/rsjlibrary/hreoc/stolen/.

Jagose, A. (1996). *Queer Theory.* Melbourne: University of Melbourne Press.

Jenkins, F. (2002). "Plurality, Dialogue and Response: Addressing Vulnerability." *Contretemps* 3(July). Retrieved February 2, 2006 from http://www.usyd.edu.au/contretemps/contretemps3.html.

————. (2005, June). "Response to Catherine Mills: Towards a Non-violent Ethics." Paper presented at "A Lived History of the Thought of Judith Butler" symposium, University of Western Sydney. In *Differences*, Summer 2007.

Jones, N. (2001). *The Control Freaks: How New Labour Gets Its Own Way.* London: Politicos.

Keddie, A. (2003). "Little Boys: Tomorrow's Macho Lads." *Discourse: Studies in the Cultural Politics of Education* 24(3): 289–306.

Kenway, J. (1996). "Reasserting Masculinity in Australian Schools." *Women's Studies International Forum* 19(4): 447–66.

Klein, M. (1935). "A Contribution to the Psychogenesis of Manic-Depressive States." *International Journal of Psychoanalysis* 16: 145–74.

————. (1940). "Mourning and Its Relation to Manic-Depressive States." *International Journal of Psychoanalysis* 21: 125–53.

Kline, S. (1995). *Out of the Garden: Toys, TV, and Children's Culture in the Age of Marketing.* London: Verso.

Kofman, S. (1998), *Smothered Words,* (trans Madeleine Dobie), Evanston, Illinois, Northwestern University Press.

Laclau, E., and Mouffe, C. (1985). *Hegemony and Socialist Strategy: Towards a Radical Democratic Politics.* London: Verso.

Lather, P. (2000). "Against Empathy, Voice, and Authenticity." *Kvinder, Køn und Forskning* [Women, Gender and Research] 9(4): 16–26.

Levinas, E. (1997). *Otherwise than Being, or Beyond Essence.* Trans. A. Lingis. Boston: Kluwer.

Lingis, A. (2000). *Dangerous Emotions.* Berkeley and Los Angeles: University of California Press.

Linnell, S. (2004). "Towards a 'Poethics' of Therapeutic Practice: Extending the Relationship of Ethics and Aesthetics in Narrative Therapies through a Consideration of the Late Work of Michel Foucault." *International Journal of Narrative Therapy and Community Work* 4: 42–54.

McFayden, A. (2004). "Rapprochement in sight? Postmodern family therapy and psychoanalysis." *Journal of Family Therapy* 19(3): 241–62.

McInnes, D. (1997). "Into the Queerzone: Iterative Potential and Semiotic Tensions." In J. Hobson, D. McInnes, L. Secomb, and K. Schumack, *Queerzone.* Working Papers in Women's Studies, Feminist Cultural Studies Series No. 4. Sydney: University of Western Sydney–Nepean.

McInnes, D. (2002). "Thighs and Sighs: A Sissy Boy's Take on Rugby League's Gay Hero." *Word is Out e-journal* no. 4. Retrieved February 19, 2005 from http:/www.arts.usyd.au/publications/wordisout/front.htm.

———. (2004). "Melancholy and the Productive Negotiation of Power in Sissy Boy Experience." In *Youth and Sexualities: Pleasure, Subversion, and Insubordination In and Out of Schools.* Ed. M. Rasmussen, E. Rofes, and S. Talburt. New York: Palgrave.

———. (2005, June). "'When All the World Is a Hopeless Jumble': Sissy Boy Melancholy and the Educational Possibilities of Melancholy." Paper presented at "A Lived History of the Thought of Judith Butler" symposium, University of Western Sydney.

McInnes, D., and Couch, M. (2004). "Quiet Please! There's a Lady on the Stage: Boys, Gender and Sexuality Non-conformity and Class." *Discourse: Studies in the Cultural Politics of Education,* 24(4): 431–443.

McInnes, D. and Davies, C. (2007). "Articulating Sissy Boy Queerness within and against Discourses of Tolerance and Pride." In *Queer Youth Cultures.* Ed. S. Driver. Albany: State University of New York Press.

McLean, C. (1995). "What about 'What about the Boys?'" *South Australian Education of Girls and Female Students' Association Journal* 4(3): 15–25.

McMaster, D. (2001). *Asylum Seekers.* Melbourne: Melbourne University Press.

McMullen, J., (1997, March 23). "Pride and Prejudice." *Sixty Minutes* (Channel 9, Australia). Television broadcast.

MacNaughton, G. (2000). *Rethinking Gender in Early Childhood.* Sydney: Allen and Unwin.

Madigan, S., and Epston, D. (1995). "From 'Psychiatric Gaze' to Communities of Concern." In *The Reflecting Team in Action: Collaborative Practice in Family Therapy.* Ed. S. Friedman. New York: Guildford.

Mares, P. (2002). *Borderline: Australia's Response to Refugees and Asylum Seekers in the Wake of the Tampa.* Sydney: University of New South Wales Press.

Marr, D., and Wilkinson, M. (2003). *Dark Victory.* Sydney: Allen and Unwin.

Martino, W. (1997). "'A Bunch of Arseholes': Exploring the Politics of Masculinity for Adolescent Boys in Schools." *Social Alternatives* 16(3): 39–43.

———. (1998). "'Dickheads,' 'Poofs,' 'Try Hards,' and 'Losers': Critical Literacy for Boys in the English Classroom." *Aotearoa* (New Zealand Journal for Teachers of English) 35: 31–57.

———. (1999). "'Cool boys.' 'Party Animals,' 'Squids,' and 'Poofters': Interrogating the Dynamics and Politics of Adolescent Masculinities in School." *British Journal of Sociology of Education* 20(2): 239–64.

———. (2000). "Mucking Around in Class, Giving Crap, and Acting Cool: Adolescent Boys Enacting Masculinities at School." *Canadian Journal of Education* 25(2): 102–12.

Martino, W., Lingard, B., and Mills, M. (2004). "Issues in Boys' Education: A Question of Teacher Threshold Knowledges?" *Gender and Education* 16(4): 435–54.

Martino, W., and Pallotta-Chiarolli, M. (2001). *Boys Stuff: Boys Talk about What Really Matters*. Sydney: Allen and Unwin.

———. (2003). *So What's a Boy? Addressing Issues of Masculinity and Schooling*. Maidenhead, England: Open University Press.

Massey, D. (1993). "Power-Geometry and a Progressive Sense of Place." In *Mapping the Future: Local Cultures, Global Change*. Ed. J. Bird, B. Curtis, T. Putnam, G. Robertson, and L. Tickner. New York: Routledge.

Merleau-Ponty, M. (1995). *The Visible and the Invisible*. Trans. Alphonso Lingis. Evanston, IL: Northwestern University Press.

Ministerial Council on Education, Employment, Training and Youth Affairs, Tasmanian Department of Education. (1996). *Gender Equity: A Framework for Australian Schools*. Retrieved February 24, 2005 from http://www.education.tas.gov.au/equitystandards/gender/framewrk/default.htm.

Mitscherlich, A., and Mitscherlich, B. (1984). *The Inability to Mourn: Principles of Collective Behavior*. New York: Grove.

Morgan, J. (2004, January 5). "A Playwright behind the Wire." *Sydney Morning Herald*.

"MPs Stunned by Play School Gay Mums." (2004, June 3). *Sydney Morning Herald*. Retrieved April 26, 2006 from http://smh.com.au/articles/2004/06/ 03/1086203554478.html.

Newton, E. (1974). *Mother Camp: Female Impersonators in America*. Englewood Cliffs, NJ: Prentice-Hall.

Nietzsche, F. (1969). *On the Genealogy of Morals*. Trans. W. Kaufmann. New York: Random House.

Palmer, M. (2005, July). *Report of the Inquiry into the Circumstances of the Immigration Detention of Cornelia Rau*. Retrieved June 2005 from http://www.minister.immi.gov.au/media_releases/media05/palmer-report.pdf.

Perera, S. (2002). "A Line in the Sea: The Tampa, Boat Stories and the Border." *Cultural Studies Review* 8(1): 11–27.

Perera, S., and Pugliese, J. (1997). "'Racial Suicide': The Re-licensing of Racism in Australia." *Race and Class* 39(2): 1–19.

Peters, N. (2003, 25 March). "From Aliens to Austr(aliens): A Look at Immigration and Internment Policies. Paper presented at "From Curtin to Coombs: War and Peace in Australia" seminar, Curtin University of Technology, Perth, Western Australia. Retrieved June 20005 from http://john.curtin.edu.au/events/seminar2003_peters.html.

Peterson, A. (2003). "Research on Men and Masculinities: Some Implications of Recent Theory for Future Work." *Men and Masculinities* 6(1): 54–69.

Petersen, E. B. (1999). *Køn, Virksomhed und Kompetence—En destabiliserende Diskursanalyse af Videnskabssamfundets kønnede Konstruktioner* [Gender, Activity and Competence—A Destabilizing Discourse Analysis of the Academy's Gendered Constructions]. Ed. Inge Henningsen. Arbejdspapir nr. 6. Copenhagen: Køn i den Akademiske Organisation.

———. (2004). "Academic Boundary Work: The Discursive Constitution of 'Scientificity' Amongst Researchers within the Social Sciences and Humanities. Ph.D. diss., University of Copenhagen.

———. (2007). "The Conduct of Concern: Exclusionary Discursive Practices and Subject Positions in Academia." *Educational Theory and Philosophy* (in press).

Phillips, A. (1997). 'Keeping It Moving: Commentary on Judith Butler's "Melancholy Gender/Refused Identification.'" In J. Butler, *The Psychic Life of Power.* Stanford, CA: Stanford University Press.

Ramsey, P. G. (1995). "Growing Up with the Contradictions of Race and Class." *Young Children* 50(6): 18–22.

Rural Australians for Refugees. Detainee Letters. Retrieved May 2005 from http://www.ruralaustraliansforrefugees.org.

Rasmussen, M. L. (2004). "Safety and Subversion: The Production of Sexualities and Genders in School Spaces." In *Youth and Sexualities: Pleasure, Subversion, and Insubordination In and Out of Schools.* Ed. M. L. Rasmussen, E. Rofes, and S. Talburt. New York: Palgrave.

Robinson, K. H. (2002). "Making the Invisible Visible: Gay and Lesbian Issues in Early Childhood Education." *Contemporary Issues in Early Childhood* 3(3): 415–34.

———. (2005). "Reinforcing Hegemonic Masculinities through Sexual Harassment: Issues of Identity, Power and Popularity in Secondary Schools." *Gender and Education* 17(1): 19–37.

Rofes, E. (1995). "Making Our Schools Safe for Sissies." In *The Gay Teen: Educational Practice and Theory for Lesbian, Gay, and Bisexual Adolescents.* Ed. G. Unks. New York: Routledge.

Rose, N. (1998). *Inventing Ourselves: Psychology, Power and Personhood,* Cambridge: Cambridge University Press.

———. (1999). *Powers of Freedom: Reframing Political Thought.* Cambridge: Cambridge University Press.

Ryan, L. (1996). *The Aboriginal Tasmanians.* St. Leonards, New South Wales, Australia: Allen and Unwin.

Said, E. (2004). *Humanism and Democratic Criticism.* Hampshire, England: Palgrave Macmillan.

Salih, S. (2002). *Judith Butler.* London: Routledge.

Schechner, R. (1985). *Between Theater and Anthropology.* Philadelphia: University of Pennsylvania Press.

Searle, J. R. (1977). "Reiterating the Differences: A Reply to Derrida." *Glyph* 1: 198–208.

Sedgwick, E. K. (1990). *Epistemology of the Closet*. London: Penguin, 1990.
———. (2003). *Touching Feeling: Affect, Pedagogy, Performativity*. Durham, NC: Duke University Press.
Sedgwick, E. K., and Frank, A., eds. (1995). *Shame and Its Sisters: A Silvan Tomkins Reader*. Durham, NC: Duke University Press.
Shafaei, S. (2004). "Refugitive: A One-Man Theatre Work." *Southerly* 61(1): 11–18.
———. (2005, March 21). Interview with Gabby Schultz. *Enough Rope with Andrew Denton*. Australian Broadcasting Corporation. Television broadcast.
Skattebol, J. (2003). "Dark, Dark and Darker: Negotiations of Identity in an Early Childhood Setting." *Contemporary Issues in Early Childhood* 4(2): 149–165.
Søndergaard, D. M. (1994). "Køn som Metaprincip" [Gender as Meta-principle]. *Kvinder, Køn and Forskning* [Women, Gender and Research] 3(3): 40–62.
———. (2002). "III. Theorising Subjectivity: Contesting the Monopoly of Psychoanalysis." *Feminism and Psychology* 12(4): 445–54.
———. (2005a). "Academic Desire Trajectories: Re-tooling the Concepts of Subject, Desire and Biography." *European Journal of Women's Studies* 12(3): 297–314.
———. (2005b). "Making Sense of Gender, Age, Power and Disciplinary Position: Intersecting Discourses in the Academy." *Feminism and Psychology* 15(2): 191–210.
Supriya, K. (1999). "White Difference: Cultural Constructions of White Identity." In *Whiteness: The Communication of Social Identity*. Ed. J. K. Nakayama and J. N. Martin. Thousand Oaks, CA: Sage.
Targowska, A. U. (2001). "Exploring Young Children's 'Racial' Attitudes in the Australian Context: The Link between Research and Practice. Paper presented at the Australian Association for Research in Education 2001 Conference, Freemantle, Western Australia. Retrieved April 26, 2006 from http://www.aare.edu.au/01pap/tar01193.htm.
Talburt, S. (2004). "Intelligibility and Narrating Queer Youth." In *Youth and Sexualities: Pleasure, Subversion, and Insubordination In and Out of Schools*. Ed. M. L. Rasmussen, E. Rofes, and S. Talburt. New York: Palgrave.
Taylor, A. (2005). "Situating Whiteness Critique in Early Childhood: The Cultural Politics of the Sandpit." *International Journal of Equity and Innovation in Early Childhood* 3(1): 5–17. Retrieved April 26, 2006 from http://www.edfac.unimelb.edu.au/eesc/ceiec/members/IJEIEC/nonmembers/IJEIECNonVol3No1.html.
Taylor, A., and Richardson, C. (2005a). "Home Renovations, Border Protection and the Hard Work of Belonging." *Australian Research in Early Childhood Education* 12(1): 93–100.

————. (2005b). "Queering Home Corner." *Contemporary Issues in Early Childhood* 6(2): 163–174. Retrieved April 26, 2006 from http://www.wwwords.co.uk/ciec/content/pdfs/6/issue6_2.asp.

Traweek, S. (1988). *Beamtimes and Lifetimes: The World of High Energy Physicists.* Cambridge, MA: Harvard University Press.

Turner, G. (2002). "Public Relations." In *The Media and Communications in Australia.* Ed. S. Cunningham and G. Turner. St. Leonard's: Allen and Unwin.

Turner, V. (1974), *Drama, Fields and Metaphors: Symbolic Action in Human Society.* Ithaca, NY: Cornell University Press.

Vanstone, A. (2003). "Border Protection." Retrieved April 26, 2006 from http://www.minister.immi.gov.au/borders/index.htm.

Walkerdine, V. (1999). "Violent Boys and Precocious Girls: Regulating Childhood at the End of the Millennium." *Contemporary Issues in Early Childhood* 1(1): 3–22.

Wenger, E. (1998). *Communities of Practice: Learning, Meaning and Identity.* Cambridge: Cambridge University Press.

White, M. (1992). "Deconstruction and Therapy." In *Experience, Contradiction, Narrative and Imagination: Selected Papers of David Epston and Michael White 1989–1991*, Ed. D. Epston and M. White. Adelaide, South Australia: Dulwich Centre Publications.

————. (1995). "Reflecting Teamwork as Definitional Ceremony." In *Re-authoring lives: Interviews and Essays.* Adelaide, South Australia: Dulwich Centre Publications.

————. (1997). *Narratives of Therapists' Lives.* Adelaide, South Australia: Dulwich Centre Publications.

————. (2000a). "On Ethics and the Spiritualities of the Surface." In *Reflections on Narrative Practice: Essays and Interviews.* Adelaide, South Australia: Dulwich Centre Publications.

————. (2000b). "Reflecting Teamwork as Definitional Ceremony Revisited." In *Reflections on Narrative Practice: Essays and Interviews.* Adelaide, South Australia: Dulwich Centre Publications.

————. (2002). "Addressing Personal Failure." *International Journal of Narrative Therapy and Community Work* 2002(3): 33–76.

————. (2004). "Working with People Who Are Suffering the Consequences of Multiple Trauma, Part 3: Memory Systems and the Consequences of Trauma." *International Journal of Narrative Therapy and Community Work* 2004(1): 67–73.

White, M., and Epston, D. (1990). *Narrative Means to Therapeutic Ends.* New York: W. W. Norton.

Williams, C. and Linnell, S. (2007). "When the Doctors Consulted the Narrative Therapist …: An Experiment in Questioning Dominant Stories of Ph.D. pedagogy." *The International Journal of Critical Psychology* 18: 56–80.

Wittig, M. (1993). "One Is Not Born a Woman." In *The Lesbian and Gay Studies Reader*. Ed. H. Abelove, M. A. Barale, and D. M. Halperin. New York: Routledge.

Wyschogrod, E. (1985). *Spirit in Ashes: Hegel, Heidegger, and Man-Made Mass Death*. New Haven. CT: Yale University Press.

Young, I. M. (2005). *On Female Body Experience: "Throwing Like a Girl" and Other Essays*. London: Oxford University Press.

Index

I

J

S